THE IMPACT OF RESEARCH IN EDUCATION

An international perspective

Edited by Ben Levin, Jie Qi, Hilary Edelstein and
Jacqueline Sohn

First published in Great Britain in 2013 by

The Policy Press
University of Bristol
Fourth Floor
Beacon House
Queen's Road
Bristol BS8 1QU
UK
Tel +44 (0)117 331 4054
Fax +44 (0)117 331 4093
e-mail tpp-info@bristol.ac.uk
www.policypress.co.uk

North American office:
The Policy Press
c/o The University of Chicago Press
1427 East 60th Street
Chicago, IL 60637, USA
t: +1 773 702 7700
f: +1 773-702-9756
e:sales@press.uchicago.edu
www.press.uchicago.edu

British Library Cataloguing in Publication Data
A catalogue record for this book is available from the British Library.

Library of Congress Cataloging-in-Publication Data
A catalog record for this book has been requested.

ISBN 978 1 44730 620 7 hardcover

Cover design by Policy Press.
Front cover: image kindly supplied by istock
Printed and bound in Great Britain by TJ International, Padstow
The Policy Press uses environmentally responsible print partners.

Contents

List of figures and tables

Figures

Tables

Notes on contributors

Amanda Cooper, PhD, is an Assistant Professor in Educational Policy and Leadership at Queen's University, Kingston, Ontario. Her interests professionally and academically revolve around improving research use in public services. She is the former program manager of Ontario's Knowledge Network for Applied Education Research (KNAER), an effort to improve KM in education across Ontario.

Clive Dimmock, PhD, is currently Visiting Professor at the National Institute of Education, Nanyang Technological University, Singapore. He is also Professor Emeritus at the University of Leicester, UK, where he directed the Centre for Educational Leadership and Management. Recently, he was invited to lead a major government-funded research project mapping leadership practices across the whole Singapore school system.

Hilary Edelstein is a PhD candidate at the Ontario Institute for Studies in Education. Her research explores how university researchers collaborate with non-university based partners to do knowledge mobilisation.

David Gough, PhD, is Professor of Evidence Informed Policy and Practice, and Director of the EPPI-Centre at the Institute of Education at the University of London. He is a Managing Editor of the Journal of Evidence and Policy, and his research focuses on child welfare, education, and other areas of social policy.

Ursula Hoadley, PhD, is a Professor at the University of Cape Town, focusing on the sociology of education in curriculum, pedagogy and teachers' work. Her recent work includes comparative studies of primary curricula across different countries, considerations of standards, and the context of their implementation. She is currently involved in the review and revision of the South African national curriculum.

David Hogan, PhD, is Professor and Principal Research Scientist at the Office of Education Research at the National Institute of Education (NIE), Nanyang Technological University, Singapore. Previously, he was the Dean at the Office of Education Research and the Centre for Research in Pedagogy and Practice. He has won a series of awards for his work, including the American Educational Research Association

Outstanding Book Award (1986), and a National Endowment of the Humanities Fellowship.

Claus Holm, PhD, is the editor in chief and executive director of the International Alliance of Leading Education Institutes (IALEI). He is also a Professor in the Department of Education, Aarhus Faulty of Arts at Aarhus University, Denmark.

Chengwen Hong, PhD, is Professor and Deputy Director at the Institute of Higher Education Studies, Beijing Normal University. He is also the executive vice director of the National Educational Testing & Evaluation Institution. Previously, he was Advisor to the Minister of the Macau Department of Education and Youth Affairs, Macau Special Administration.

David Hough, PhD, is the Principal Research Scientist at Singapore's National Institute of Education (NIE), and former Dean of the Office of Education Research and the Centre for Research on Pedagogy and Practice – NIE. Prior to his appointments at the NIE, he was a Professor at the University of Tasmania in Australia, and the University of Pennsylvania.

Lynn Ilon, PhD, is a Professor at Seoul National University (SNU), and co-founder of SNU's programme in Global Cooperation Education. She is an education economist specialising in the effects of globalisation on education, most recently heading a large-scale project to build the strategic systems undergirding the Ministry of Education in Zambia.

Ben Levin, PhD, is a Professor and Canada Research Chair in Education Leadership and Policy at the Ontario Institute for Studies in Education, University of Toronto. Previously he served as Deputy Minister of Education for the Provinces of Ontario and Manitoba. His current interests are in large-scale change, poverty and inequity, and finding better ways to connect research to policy and practice in education.

Sarah Mason is a researcher specialising in public policy analysis and education research and evaluation at the Wisconsin Center for Education Research, School of Education, at UW-Madison. She research interests include: how educators can make effective use of data by transforming it into information and knowledge for improvement of practice, as well as the challenges, mechanisms and bridges for transferring education research into effective policy and useful application by practitioners.

Joe Muller, PhD, is Professor Emeritus at the School of Education, University of Cape Town. His research focuses on curriculum and qualifications policy, including qualification frameworks, standard-setting, and curriculum statements. He has been part of large-scale national research initiatives for the National Education Policy Investigation and the National Commission on Higher Education, as well as nationally commissioned reviews for the Review Committee on Curriculum and the External Review of the Higher Education Quality Committee.

Sandra Nutley, PhD, is Professor of Public Policy and Management at the University of St. Andrews and an Associate of the University of Edinburgh Business School. She also serves as Director of the Research Unit for Research Utilisation (RURU). Her research interests include: the use of research, evidence-based policy and practice, public service audit and inspection, public management reform, managing change and human resource management. She is known internationally for her work on research use and evidence-based policy and practice.

John Polesel, PhD, is a Principal Research Fellow at the University of Melbourne and has won numerous national Australian Research Council Grants. Currently, he coordinates the graduate coursework programmes in the Melbourne Graduate School of Education, as well as the Master of Education Policy International, focusing on education and training systems in Australia and Europe.

Jie Qi is a doctoral graduate of the University of Toronto's Ontario Institute for Studies in Education, who is now living and working in Beijing. Her doctoral work focused on professional learning of teachers in China.

Robyn Read is a PhD student at the University of Toronto's Ontario Institute for Studies in Education. Her research interests are in education policy in the developing world, including the role of the World Bank and other supranational organisations, and how research influences policy in education and development.

Jacqueline Sohn is a PhD candidate at the University of Toronto's Ontario Institute for Studies in Education, in the Educational Policy program. Her research interests include: how multi/interdisciplinary research informs social and educational policy for children and youth.

Laikwoon Teh, PhD, is a Senior Fellow at Singapore's Office of Education Research National Institute of Education, and Principal Research Specialist for the Ministry of Education. His research interest is in the application of statistical and measurement models in policy analysis and programme evaluation. Findings from his studies have contributed to establishing and developiong educational policies and programmes in Singapore.

Foreword

Much has been written about educational research and knowledge production in universities. Much has also been said about the lack of rigour or theoretical incoherence of educational research, or its failure to produce cumulative findings. What makes this book unique is the emphasis it places on the relationship between knowledge production and knowledge utilisation. This book is not about improving the educational research enterprise itself, but about mobilising its findings to improve educational practice.

That emphasis is much needed. Of course, the limited scope of educational research is in itself striking – on average, the industrialised world devotes roughly 15 times more of public budgets to health research than to educational research, even if both sectors use similar shares of public spending. But even more striking is the limited impact that the existing educational research has on professional practice – with research funding still heavily weighted towards doing rather than sharing and using research.

There is no question that education is a knowledge industry in that it is concerned with the transmission of knowledge; but it is still far from a knowledge industry in terms of its own practices being systematically transformed by knowledge about their efficacy. In many other fields, people enter their professional lives expecting their practice to be changed by research, but this is still less the case in education. There is, of course, a large body of research about learning but much of it is unrelated to the kind of real-life learning that is the focus of formal education. Even then, it has an insufficient impact when education continues as a cottage industry, with practitioners working in isolation and building their practice on folk wisdom. Central prescription of what teachers should do, which still dominates today's education systems, will not transform teachers' practices in the way that professional engagement in the search for evidence of what makes a difference can.

While a knowledge-based teaching profession might have been a 'nice to have' in the past, it is a 'must have' now. When one could still assume that what students learn in school will last for their lifetime, the focus of practitioners could be on educational content and routine cognitive skills that are packaged in curriculum departments. Central prescription could short-circuit professional practice, with governments telling their teachers exactly what to do and exactly how they want it done, using an industrial organisation of work to get the results they want. Today, where individuals can access content on Google, where routine cognitive skills are being digitised or outsourced, and where jobs are changing rapidly, schooling needs to be much more about ways of thinking, such as creativity, critical thinking, problem-solving and decision making; about ways of working – including communication and collaboration; about tools for working such as the capacity to exploit the potential of new technologies; and, last but not least, about the capacity to live in a multifaceted world as active and responsible citizens. The trouble is that this challenge requires a very different calibre of teaching and a commitment to professionalised teaching, such that teachers are on a par with other professions in terms of diagnosis, the application of evidence-based practices and professional pride. The image here is of teachers who use data to evaluate the learning needs of their students, and who are consistently expanding their repertoire of pedagogic strategies to address the diversity in students' interests and abilities. In the past, different students were taught in similar ways, today the challenge is to embrace diversity with differentiated pedagogical practices. The goal of the past was standardisation and conformity, now it's about being ingenious, about personalising educational experiences. The past was curriculum centred, the future is learner centred. In the past, the policy focus was on the provision of education, today it's on outcomes, shifting from looking upwards in the bureaucracy towards looking outwards to the next teacher, the next school. In short, while the past of education was about delivered wisdom, education now is about user-generated wisdom.

An education system conducive to research, innovation and constant improvement must be based on the attitudes and prevailing culture of the various players in the sector, the development and transmission of knowledge, and initiative and calculated risk taking. It needs to draw on innovation and knowledge inspired by science, on innovation inspired by entrepreneurial development of new products and services, on innovation and knowledge inspired by practitioners, and on innovation inspired by users including students, parents and communities. As many of the chapters note, this is not a one-way route of disseminating knowledge from universities to practitioners, but of mobilising knowledge throughout the system and of developing more and better ways of acting regarding appropriate research mobilisation channels for various purposes. As the book also notes, this requires a shift in the locus of knowledge production from universities to classrooms and networks of schools, and it will require teachers to abandon privatised forms of professional practice in favour of strategically focused, evidence-based, collaborative partnerships with fellow practitioners and researchers.

These are daunting challenges. As the chapter on Singapore shows (Chapter Three), even in the institutional contexts most favourable to close linkages between research, policy and practice, issues around relevance, accessibility and involvement of teachers still linger. But this book makes a start. It makes clear that knowledge mobilisation must go well beyond writing up results and hoping people read them, to comprise a sophisticated set of actions and processes to connect research to a range of users in a variety of ways, recognising that the use of evidence is primarily a social process that is deeply affected by organisational practices as well as by individual knowledge or inclination. The bottom line is that making effective use of research must involve research producers, research consumers, and the various intermediaries that link them at all levels of an education system, including individuals, institutions and national governance systems.

Andreas Schleicher
Deputy Director for Education and Skills and
Special Advisor on Education Policy to the OECD's Secretary-General

ONE

Introduction and overview

Jie Qi and Ben Levin, Ontario Institute for Studies in Education, University of Toronto

Introduction

This book is an examination of the role of universities around the world in mobilising research knowledge in education. The idea of 'mobilising' research knowledge is explained more fully in the next chapter, but essentially is about building stronger connections between research, policy and practice so that, to the extent possible, education practice can be based on reliable evidence rather than belief, ideology or whim.

The ability of universities to be effective mobilisers of research knowledge depends on several factors. One is the overall organisation of research in a country – how much is done, how it is funded, and so on. Another is the organisation of the higher education system, the roles of various institutions, and the relationship between universities and government. And the final and most important is the way universities think about and undertake the work of making their research more accessible and useful to policy and practice. These issues provide the frame for this chapter.

The main content of the book is chapters from scholars at universities in Australia, Canada, China, Denmark, England, Korea, Singapore, South Africa, and the United States. Each of those chapters looks at the way education research done by universities is organised and shared in that country. This first chapter provides an overview of the book drawing out themes, commonalities and differences in relation to its central organising questions.

This work grows out of the International Alliance of Leading Educational Institutions, a network of research-focused faculties of education in 10 countries (www.intlalliance.org). Each year, the Alliance organises an international conference based on national reports from the member countries on a theme of common interest. At its 2011 meeting, held in Toronto, the theme was 'research knowledge mobilisation', and the papers generated at that meeting, subsequently revised, form much of the content of this book. That meeting, and the creation of this book, were both facilitated by the Research Supporting Practice in Education (RSPE) research team at the Ontario Institute for Studies in Education (OISE) at the University of Toronto (www.oise.utoronto.ca/rspe), a group of researchers and graduate students who are conducting various studies and projects on this theme.

Why knowledge mobilisation matters

Education is increasingly recognised as essential to human and national development. Various rationales have been advanced for the importance of education, such as economic competitiveness, social cohesion, individual freedom, inculcation of democratic values, or promotion of social mobility. Considerable bodies of evidence support the relationship between higher levels of education and all these outcomes. For all these reasons, education policy has become a matter of increasing interest all around the world.

As part of the growing interest in providing effective education, there is also growing interest in the role that research can play in supporting more effective policy and practice. As societies are more educated, and as the research enterprise itself develops more fully, it is natural for various parties to consider how that increasing knowledge can be applied to education policy and practice.

This interest manifests itself in various ways. For example, The World Bank devoted its 1998-99 World Development Report to examining 'the role of knowledge in advancing and developing economic and social well-being' (World Bank, 1999, v), and has restyled itself as 'the knowledge bank' with a huge focus on sharing research knowledge. UNESCO devoted its 2005 World Report (Binde, 2005) to building knowledge societies in developing countries and the following year published a book looking at the role of higher education in building the knowledge society (Neave, 2006). *Tertiary Education for the Knowledge Society*, a report done by the OECD (2008), highlights the importance of higher education in this field today. National governments, too, have recognised, if sometimes more in rhetoric than practice, the importance of sound knowledge bases to better inform educational policy and practice (Nutley et al, 2007, Levin, 2010).

Around the world there continue to be concerns about the degree to which education research contributes effectively to education policy and practice. Many of the chapters in this book (for example those relating to the UK, the US, Canada, South Africa and Denmark) point out the criticisms made of education research over the past few decades. Yet, while there has been much dispute about the quality and value of research in education, there are also growing efforts around the world to connect research to policy and practice, not only in education but in other fields of public policy (Nutley et al, 2007; Tetroe et al, 2007; Cooper, Levin et al, 2009; Levin, 2011). As the chapters reveal, many governments are increasingly interested in the role that research evidence can play in making their education systems more efficient and effective.

Since universities are, virtually everywhere in the world, the largest single providers of education research, their work in this field is vitally important. Yet there is little empirical work on the way that universities approach their responsibility as research knowledge mobilisers, and even less that looks at this work in an international comparative perspective – hence the value of this collection.

Focus of the chapters

A challenge in any edited book, and especially one looking at a single issue across multiple countries, is to create enough commonality in the chapters so that the reader can make some reasonable comparisons or conclusions about developments across countries.

To this end, in preparing the initial papers for the conference and then revising them for publication in this book, all the authors were asked to address a common set of elements:

1. provide background on the country, its education system, its research and post-secondary education systems;
2. analyse the current state of university-based research in education, including amounts, funding sources, research structures, dominant methods, capacity and any indicators of quality;
3. examine strategies and mechanisms currently used by universities, faculties of education, and various researchers and research centres to share their research and to increase its impact;
4. report major policies, data or research that have been influential in forming the current arrangements;
5. provide suggestions as to how major research universities could do better in promoting research information to the wider public.

Relatively short chapters cannot do full justice to all of these points; even a reasonably clear exposition of the relevant context in each country would take more space than is available for entire chapters. Necessarily, some elements in this outline are treated briefly, including the descriptions of national contexts. In other areas, for example funding levels, good national data are not available for all countries. The authors also had to consider how to create a picture of the real situation around research mobilisation in education in their country. And as researchers themselves, authors had particular ideas and orientations that informed their approach. Each chapter therefore has a somewhat different core message, even though all chapters do try to address all the five points.

The importance of context

Caution is always necessary in making comparisons of policies and practices across contexts. The nine countries represented in this project vary greatly in many respects, including their histories, political systems, the nature and structure of the university system, the way in which research is organised and supported, and the links between universities and the larger education system.

These differences in context are apparent if one compares the country chapters. Some differences are obvious, such as size – from Singapore or Denmark, with a few million people and a few universities, to the US or China, with hundreds of millions of people and thousands of higher education institutions. But the differences are also political – in the relationships between universities and governments – and cultural – in the place of the university as social critic, for example. One should therefore be cautious in drawing conclusions about what universities, taken generically, can or should do; strategy will always require contextual understanding as well.

Organisation of higher education

The larger policy context and funding channels for research influence the research enterprise and the mobilisation of research knowledge. The size and scope of the systems varies – from essentially one major institution in Singapore, to a small number in some of the other countries, to more than 1,100 institutions offering graduate studies in education in the US. Of course, China dwarfs all the other countries in population and therefore in the scope of its institutions, although it is still early in the process of developing a truly large number of research universities.

In almost all countries the higher education sector is also diversified to some extent, with differing roles and relationships for various kinds of institutions. Some countries, such as England, have clear hierarchies of institutions based on perceived quality and exclusiveness.

In some countries, such as Canada, there is much less variance among universities in these areas. In other cases universities may be assigned specific roles; for example Chinese universities are organised to have a national, regional, provincial or local role. However, in other countries universities are able, to the extent resources permit, to define their own roles. In most settings universities are independent organisations with their own governing bodies and enjoy a considerable degree of autonomy even though most of their financing comes from the state; however, in some cases the links between the government or political apparatus and the universities are very close, while in others they are much more distant.

Federal systems also shape the university world. As in all areas of education in Canada, the primary responsibility for higher education lies with provinces, although the federal government is a main funder of research. In Australia, higher education is funded and administered by the Commonwealth Government, in spite of the fact that the states have the constitutional responsibility for education. In the US, which has large public and private sectors in higher education, an enormous variety of institutions of all sizes, with many different missions, are increasingly reliant on non-government funding, although both state and national governments do provide some financial support and various degrees of regulation or policy direction. In many federal systems, operating costs of higher education are paid from provincial funds while research is often supported mainly at the national level.

Then there are differences in national wealth, support for universities and the ability of universities to serve even basic requirements for higher education. South Africa is an example of a country in which the higher education system is under enormous stress simply trying to serve the needs of a rapidly increasing student body with the additional complication of coping with all the post-apartheid challenges. China is dramatically expanding its higher education sector, with consequent pressures on quality, as it seeks to provide advanced education for many more of its people.

In almost all settings there is at least some degree of competition among universities, for students and funding. The degree to which universities have to compete for resources may affect their willingness to collaborate with others in the area of research.

Yet despite these differences there are also important similarities among universities in all countries. All of them see engagement in research as a fundamental part of what they do. All recognise the need for individual scholars to have considerable discretion in their research work, and all embody relatively loose forms of organisation, in which the institution has only limited tools to influence the work that faculty members do. In all cases, faculties of education see themselves as having a role in the application of knowledge as well as its generation.

Relations with government

In every case in this book, relations between universities and governments are vital in shaping the research environment and framing the research agenda in universities. The South African chapter emphasises that the relation of research-producing agencies to the state is determinative in creating conditions for something as innocuous seeming as 'mobilisation', 'utilisation' or 'engagement'. As the US chapter points out, 'current national policies and priorities for education research set a new course by prescribing what is to be researched and how that research is to be designed, conducted, and disseminated to education policy makers and practitioners'. In the last 10 years, US government policy has deeply affected the education research agenda including promoting 'scientifically based research' – although, as the chapter notes, there is much debate over what that phrase means. As another example, policies in Korea set up three overriding values for Korea's education research agenda: (1) equity of educational opportunity, (2) a society which can and does learn continuously, and (3) economic growth through investment in education. These have shaped important government research commitments as well as university projects.

In all systems the state plays a significant role in assessing the use of public resources, setting strategic goals, and shaping the autonomy of the university. Varying arrangements for higher education reflect different dynamics between universities and the government. In some cases, such as South Africa, research relationships reflect how much trust has been built up (or not) between these two parties. The state primarily determines the degree to which institutions are competitive with each other, which can also act to reduce trust levels.

An important feature of some national research systems, such as China, Korea, or Singapore, is that the linkage between researchers, ministry officials and the universities is very tight. For example, many professors in these systems have held positions within the ministry of education as well as in top universities or national research institutes. The same close connection is not evident in most of the other countries, although there are cases of people moving back and forth between the university and government.

In this regard, one issue that emerges from the national chapters is the degree to which research in universities, and even more the funding of research, should be focused on what might be seen as practical problems or issues in schools and school systems. While in many systems governments are trying to be more directive about ensuring that research addresses policy priorities, researchers may fear that funding oriented primarily to immediate priorities will drive research in narrow directions, to the detriment of the long-term interests of advancing knowledge. The Australian chapter notes that

> ... the difficulty in translating research into practice had its origins in the structure of the funding opportunities themselves, with difficulties arising from the fact that so much research is commissioned and narrowly conceptualised ... which suggest that a significant proportion of educational research funded in Australia is commissioned research rather than research that has been conceptualised and submitted for funding by educational researchers themselves.

While acknowledging the important influence of policy priorities on the direction of research, education researchers also believe that there is a need for interest-driven research, and for research that is not addressing immediate policy priorities. Moreover, universities do have an important role as places where critiques can be made, even, or perhaps especially, of official policies. Indeed, one tension between universities and governments is that researchers may see themselves as a main source of opposition to government policies. In some cases, such as England and South Africa, researchers may see themselves as a kind of unofficial opposition to government policy.

On the other hand, as stated in the Canadian chapter, there is often public scepticism about public spending on research. In education, research programmes are under pressure to demonstrate value for money. It is relatively easy for the public to criticise research results as vacuous or obvious, as has been the case in the US and England. So continued government and public support for education research must also depend on some demonstration of relevance and application.

The system of education research

Although in every country the education sector is one of the largest areas of government spending, the education research enterprise is much smaller in proportion.

It is difficult in most settings to determine how many active researchers there actually are in education, but in virtually every case the research community is small compared with the larger educational enterprise. For example, the Canadian chapter suggests that there might be 300–400 active researchers (meaning people with externally funded research) in faculties of education across the entire country compared with some 500,000 teachers and 12,000 schools. Denmark has a roughly similar number of researchers, either full or part time, for about 2,000 schools. In England, as in other countries, many members of university staff are part time or contractual, and so are less likely to have active research programmes. The imbalance between the education sector and the research community is even greater when one takes into account the multiple areas of interest and research within education – for example, curriculum areas, psychology, special education, leadership, community relationships, pedagogy, and so on. It is likely, in most cases, that there are only a few researchers in each country working in any given area of education, which works against substantial research programmes or the accumulation of results over time. One common suggestion for a solution to the research–practice gap is having researchers work much more closely with schools. However, that is not an approach that can ever reach most schools, given the numbers.

Another important aspect of research in education is that typically a few institutions dominate the research landscape. In some cases, such as England or China, this disproportion is actually created through policy, which is designed to focus funding for research on a few institutions. However, the hierarchy of institutions in terms of research exists in virtually every country (except Singapore, which essentially has only one institution in this field). In Australia major research projects actually are conducted by a relatively small number of researchers in a relatively small number of institutions, but an interesting feature in Australia is that the universities that receive the most funding for applied research are not always the same as those receiving the most funding for interest-driven research. South Africa has 23 institutions in the public higher education sector but more than 75% of expenditure on research is allocated to six of them, and 'the nature and extent of education research in South African universities is uneven … the highest publishers are formerly white institutions … the majority of former black institutions produce less than 10 articles in education per year and in some cases none'.

Funding for research

All the chapters pay attention to funding of research, but in few countries was it possible to quantify expenditures on education research, either generally or in universities. This is an area calling out for further empirical work.

The cases in this book indicate that funding allocated for education research is increasing over the years, at least in several countries. National governments have invested in education research in various ways. Singapore invested a substantial amount to establish the Centre for Research in Pedagogy and Practice (CRPP) in the National Institute of Education (NIE). The investment in education and scientific research in China continues to grow quite rapidly, and Korea has also increased research funding. In other cases, because funding comes from multiple sources, it is very difficult to compare levels across time.

Still, what can be said, consistent with earlier evidence from the OECD (2008), is that education research funding remains very small as a share of total education spending. In very few cases would research funding in education reach even 1% of expenditure on schooling. More recently, the OECD has estimated that research in health receives about 15 times more funding across member countries than does research in education, even though in fiscal terms health is not even twice as large as education (OECD, 2012).

Of course the amount of funding for research is important, but one should be cautious about assuming that more funding necessarily leads to better research performance, and even less so to better mobilisation of research knowledge. There is very little research concerning the different ways in which research funding programmes are monitored and evaluated, and hardly any evidence on the connection between funding and research capacity, so the material in this book provides some very helpful data on these questions. Liefner (2003) compared six well-acknowledged universities in four countries and found that the connection between funding and research productivity is weak. Payne and Siow (1999) found in the US that when the federal funding increased, 'as a first approximation, universities buy more federal research funding and produce more but not necessarily higher quality research output' (p 3). As in education generally, money is a necessary condition for a strong research enterprise, but not in itself enough, especially when, as described later, one considers the mobilisation of research knowledge as opposed to the conducting of research studies.

In all countries, government is the largest provider of research funding. For example, in Korea the government funds 28% of all research studies in education, but provides 66% of the research funding. However, governments do not necessarily fund education research directly. In most countries (for example Canada, the US, Australia,

South Africa, England) governments operate some kind of granting council to allocate public funding for research.

Canada has three major research funding agencies including the Natural Science and Engineering Research Council (NSERC), the Social Sciences and Humanities Research Council (SSHRC), and the Canadian Institutes for Health Research (CIHR). In Australia, the Australian Research Council (ARC) is a main funder with some other organisations also contributing. In other cases (US, Korea, Singapore), government funds research institutes of various kinds, which in turn may contract with universities to conduct research. In Korea, primary research is funded by government-sponsored research foundations such as the Korean Research Foundation.

In a few countries, other organisations are also important funders of research. In the US, philanthropic foundations play that role, while in South Africa, and presumably in much of the developing world, most of the research is undertaken with external donor funding. A central administrator of funding in South Africa for research in higher education is the National Research Foundation (NRF).

A key point to be made in relation to funding is that very little of the money goes towards mobilising research knowledge as compared with conducting the research in the first place. However, this situation is slowly changing, as in some countries the research funding agencies place increasing emphasis on what happens after the research is completed. In England, the ESRC is asking researchers to give more attention to mobilising their knowledge, and the research rankings of universities will in future place much more emphasis on the impact of research, not only on its publication in academic journals. However, for the most part the funding system is still heavily weighted towards doing, as opposed to sharing, research, which is one reason for the relatively weak efforts on sharing research reported in this book.

Concerns about university-based research in education

While not all education research is produced in universities, they are still very much central institutions in that world; in most countries they are the single largest producers of education research, and often by a very large margin.

There is plenty of criticism about the current approach to education research in universities. We have already noted, however, the important issues of a relatively weak funding base and a relatively small number of researchers. But those are by no means the only concerns. Whitty

(2006, p 161), in the UK, noted some of the main criticisms made, including lack of rigour, failure to produce cumulative findings, theoretical incoherence, ideological bias, irrelevance to schools, lack of involvement of teachers, inaccessibility and poor dissemination.

Nor are these new criticisms, having been made many times before and in many countries: a large literature documents the purported problems and limitations of research in education (Biddle and Saha, 2002; Cordingley, 2008; Levin, 2008). However, the focus of this book is not on how to improve the research enterprise itself, but more on how to do a better job of communicating the research we do have.

Capacity for research knowledge mobilisation

Effective research mobilisation requires not just a dialogue on research, but also institutional, national and local capacity to do the necessary work – that is, to find, assess, share and use research well. As we learn more about effective practice in these areas – as outlined in the next chapter – it is increasingly evident that the knowledge mobilisation work of universities goes well beyond writing up the results and hoping people read them, and requires a sophisticated set of actions and processes to connect research to a range of users in a variety of ways. In particular, effective work in this area has to recognise that the use of evidence is primarily a social process that is deeply affected by organisational practices as well as by individual knowledge or inclination.

Building the capacity for effective research knowledge mobilisation is a concern increasingly highlighted in the literature (Nutley et al, 2007; Levin, 2011). Attention and funding are being devoted to this task in many countries through new structures and relationships, some of which are described in later chapters.

The examples provided in this book show that the process of strengthening a nation's capacity in this area has challenges, in part because there is no agreed definition in the education sector about what is meant by research mobilisation capacity. In other words, to seek ways to strengthen something that itself is hard to define is an extremely complex undertaking. The capacity to make effective use of research involves all levels of an education system including individuals, institutions, and national governance systems. It also involves research producers, research consumers, and the various intermediaries that link them. No single step will be sufficient, and no country, despite the various efforts described in this book, has yet fully built a capacity to use research effectively.

As the next chapter indicates, the effective use of research knowledge is a social process involving many players. Based on that model, and considering the situations described in the country chapters, effective research mobilisation seems to require leadership, appropriate infrastructure, sufficient funding, effective communication systems, and strong networks among researchers, policy makers and other research users. Importantly, Munn (2008) notes that strengthening mobilisation is not only about altering the supply of research (quantity, quality and forms of distribution), but it is also closely related to the demand side's ability to select and apply available research evidence; what Schuller (2007) called the ability to formulate effective demand for further research. The cases in this book verify these points by introducing the range and purposes of improvement made by policy makers and other stakeholder groups. They also point to the importance of seeing universities and their efforts as part of a larger system of knowledge mobilisation.

Among the cases in this book some of the most coordinated efforts are in Singapore and Korea, consistent with a generally stronger connection between government and higher education in these countries. Korea, in order to address structural problems in coordinating national research and development, formed a Ministry of Education, Science and Technology and a Ministry of Knowledge Economy (Park and Leydesdorff, 2010). Moreover, the Korean chapter emphasises improving the public capacity to understand and use research over the years. Since 2008, the government has funded the 'World Class University Program' to attract top scholars worldwide to conduct research and share research knowledge in Korea.

Singapore terms the knowledge mobilisation effort 'strengthening the theory–practice nexus'. Major strategies identified in the Singaporean chapter include investment in databases to support informed dialogue among researchers, practitioners and policy makers; design research as intervention work in schools; and mediating knowledge application in a sustained manner. Moreover, in 2008, an Office of Education Research was set up to strengthen the connection between NIE researchers, school practitioners and government policy makers. In addition, over the past decade, the Ministry of Education has introduced an alternative career track for a key group of 200 education officers to build their research knowledge and skills by spending about 20% of their time carrying out research and development work. It is expected that they will play the role of knowledge brokers to bring advanced research to impact on policy and practice.

A rather different approach has been taken in England, where the Labour government after 1997 introduced a variety of mechanisms to strengthen the role of research and evidence across government, including education. As noted in Chapter Four, England has increased its emphasis on social research and has established various structures for that purpose, including several new applied research centres as well as various efforts to coordinate the sharing of research in education. There has also been increased attention to training and improving the impact of social research (Coffey, 2010). As the chapter reports, this has led to a wide range of initiatives, though not necessarily with sufficient coherence or sustainability.

In many settings, major research centres are especially important in sharing the results of research. Every country has research centres of one kind or another, often located in or operated by universities. This model is perhaps most developed in the US, where such institutions as the National Center for Education Research (NCER), the National Center for Education Statistics (NCES), the National Center for Education Evaluation and Regional Assistance (NCEE), and the National Center for Special Education Research (NCSER) all play a role, along with a large array of other centres all involved in some way with research dissemination and application.

In Canada, national organisations are relatively weak because of its large territory, sparse population and the lack of national government input to education. Canadian education research is also heavily influenced by US academic work. The province of Ontario has just launched an initiative named the 'Knowledge Network for Applied Education Research' (www.knaer-recrae.ca), which is funded by the Ministry of Education and led by two universities and is an attempt to bring together researchers and practitioners in Ontario to strengthen research–practice connections.

Education policy makers in China are especially concerned with the use of research results. Many education experts are invited to take part in major education policy developments. Chinese governments have made substantial efforts to develop science and technology and to emphasise the quality and comprehensiveness of basic research, including changes in the allocation of research resources to universities. In addition, Chinese governments work closely with major research institutes and universities to conduct education research and promote the use of the research results. For example, led by the national Ministry of Education, Beijing Normal University and the China National Institute for Educational Research worked together to conduct a comprehensive analysis of the equity situation in urban and rural, regional, and local levels. The results were part of a major change in education policy in the most recent national plan in China.

The US American Recovery and Reinvestment Act of 2009 (ARRA) provided a large amount of one-time funding to education. The aims of this large but short-term investment were to improve schools, raise achievement, drive reform and produce better results. A small part of this funding has been focused on strengthening research capacity. The Institute of Education Sciences (IES), the research arm of the US Department of Education, has worked to strengthen capacity for education research rigour but has also become more serious about improving research relevance. In 2010, five 'big ideas' for IES were set out to support education research that matters to schools and improves educational outcomes for children including:

1. making research more useful and relevant;
2. shifting from a model of dissemination to a model of facilitation;
3. creating stronger links between research development and innovation;
4. building state and district capacity to use longitudinal data systems for research and evaluation;
5. developing an understanding of schools as learning organisations (Easton, 2010).

While good intentions are evident in these efforts, actual implementation can be much more difficult. Institutional jealousies and self-interest can derail many initiatives, as can simple lack of real support. Many aspects of research impact also require collaborative work of researchers and institutions engaged in various research initiatives. The chapter from Denmark shows well how relationships among and between universities can complicate this work and interfere with policy intentions, while the South African chapter clearly describes the impact of limited resources and a history of bad relationships on research capacity.

University efforts to mobilise research

Although universities are central in producing research knowledge, the extent to which they take strong measures to share and mobilise this knowledge is less evident. Since the whole enterprise of active efforts to share or communicate research is relatively recent, it would be surprising if these were already well integrated in the structures and systems of universities, which are, after all, conservative institutions.

The base of evidence on how universities are trying to address these issues is rather limited. The country chapters in this book focus more on system-level issues, although in some of them (for example those from Singapore and China) there is discussion of the work of particular universities. In reviewing literature, our team found much anecdotal comment on the problems of universities and research knowledge mobilisation, but few empirical studies, especially at the institutional level. Some of our own work is reported in the next chapter.

Overall, the reports in this book indicate that the mobilisation of research knowledge remains a relatively low priority in most universities in most countries. Some steps have been taken in some places, and there is growing awareness of the importance of this work, but there are few instances of really substantial efforts by particular universities to make the mobilisation of research knowledge a priority area of activity, or to develop a range of actions that are well grounded in analysis and evidence.

For example:

- In most universities, it is hard to find out what research is being done or has been done, let alone its implications for policy and practice.
- Much more priority goes to getting research grants and publishing for academic audiences than to sharing research with other users.
- The supports that are available in universities for technology transfer in the sciences or medicine are usually not present in social sciences, including education.
- Neither undergraduate nor graduate programmes in most universities have a strong connection to mobilising research knowledge.

In addition to being shaped by external factors already discussed, these limitations are deeply engrained in various aspects of the way universities function – for example their highly decentralised nature, or the 'pecking order' of disciplines within universities, which typically rank education fairly low in internal prestige. So changing them requires sustained effort on several fronts. As can be seen in later chapters, although various steps have been taken in various places, very few countries can claim to have anything like a reasonably comprehensive strategy.

On the other hand, a comparison of the knowledge mobilisation work of universities in comparison with other kinds of organisations (Cooper, 2012), shows that, cautious as they are, university knowledge mobilisation practices are ahead of those of user organisations such as school districts and ministries of education, and comparable to those of intermediary organisations. So the real issue is that the entire sector has not developed this work very fully yet.

A fundamental change in the research world, and one that deeply affects universities, has been the astonishing impact of new information technologies on the ways that people find and share information, including research information. The US chapter notes the increasing role of the internet as a vehicle for sharing research:

> Innovations in technology have changed the patterns of communication as well as the quality and quantity of research dissemination. Online resources and universal access to the Internet have contributed to the growth of traditional scholarly education research outlets.... Innovations have also led to an explosion of online dissemination tools and networks: online publishers, digital libraries, blogs, websites, professional networks, specialised information clearing houses, newsletters, and online versions of traditional print media such as newspapers and magazines.

In addition, new communication tools are being used in utilising research results such as online search options, feedback messaging, and social media.

However this new capacity is not necessarily well used. It is not clear that the education research world has caught up to these avenues for sharing or mobilising knowledge. Of course, all universities have websites, and all make attempts to share findings from research on those sites. However, that remains a limited view of what is possible. Indeed, on the websites of many universities, including some of those participating in this volume, it is very difficult to find out what research is being done, let alone what its implications might be for policy or practice. Growing knowledge about the importance of interpersonal connections in creating research take-up (Levin, 2011) is not generally reflected in the work of universities, which still tend to value products such as reports. Social media, becoming a major means of dissemination of ideas in the broader society, are still infrequently used as mechanisms to share university research.

The authors of the chapters from Australia and South Africa also looked at mobilisation practices on institutional websites and found a similar low level of effort reflected. Two of the universities represented in this volume – London and Melbourne – were found to have more extensive approaches to sharing research, including building them into university reward systems. Systems such as those that are in place in the natural sciences or engineering to support commercialisation of research are notably absent in education, although the US chapter reports extensive commercialisation of education research in that country.

Examples of efforts to improve

The NIE in Singapore has taken concrete measures to involve practitioners during the conduct of the research studies, to make sure 'that teachers and students are not merely research subjects, but research is also honed and informed by classroom practice'. Also, the NIE has a dedicated publication unit in the Office of Education Research to translate and disseminate its research findings through regular print and online media.

An important element in mobilising research knowledge is the extent to which it is integrated into the teaching programmes of the university. Several national chapters discuss this connection in the training of teachers. For example, in Singapore there is a strong and explicit emphasis on connecting research work to the education of new teachers, which is easier given that most of the country's teachers are trained in a single institution. However, the relationship between research and teaching in universities has long been a subject of debate, and one cannot assume that all or even most teacher training gives adequate attention to locating, understanding and applying research. The Danish chapter notes the degree to which the continuing education of teachers is seen as a key field for sharing research, but many chapters do not take up this issue. In the US, initial teacher training is still a subject of great contention, while in China, universities are not very involved in the continuing education of teachers (Qi, 2011).

Similarly, graduate studies is a major activity for all universities, but is not always well connected to the mobilisation of research knowledge, even though many graduate students are practitioners who are also learning about research. The Canadian chapter points out that graduate programmes currently lack connections between students' experiences as practitioners and their graduate research. It seems that more efforts could be made in using graduate students as mediators between research and school systems.

Barriers and facilitators to effective research knowledge mobilisation are well known and identified in several of the national reports. They include accessibility of academic material to non-academic audiences, lack of support for researchers around dissemination to practitioners, and absence of time and support to help practitioners to access research and current promotion structures for academics in universities. In general, tenure and promotion policies in universities do not recognise research mobilisation work.

Although this situation appears to be improving gradually, there is still heavy weighting in the academic world towards academic rather than professional or lay publications. An exception for the University of Melbourne is reported in the Australian chapter, in which knowledge transfer is viewed 'as a key indicator in staff performance development frameworks ... counting towards an individual staff member's overall workload, along with teaching and research. It is also one of the four criteria to be used by academic staff in preparing applications for promotion.' On the other hand, recent work by the OISE team in Toronto has found that the scholars who are most productive in traditional academic forums are also most likely to be active in other forms of knowledge mobilisation, such as working with practitioner groups (Cooper et al, 2011).

A further important issue for universities is the role of research syntheses. The importance of cumulative knowledge is widely recognised, and almost all research begins with a literature review, but research communication still rests heavily on reporting the results of individual studies rather than the kinds of careful syntheses being done by, for example, the EPPI-Centre in England (see Chapter Four).

Several country chapters note the existence of incentives such as awards or small grants to support better research dissemination by faculty. However, for the most part these remain rather marginal and the work of research mobilisation is borne primarily by individual researchers.

> In terms of costs associated with the research sharing and the strategies suggested, the higher the dissemination efforts of the research results, the more important the adaptations of the research products, the higher the transaction costs supported by the researchers. This interpretation suggests that knowledge utilization of the social science research results could be increased by creating incentives targeting dissemination. It could be achieved by compensating and even rewarding the researchers for the transaction costs incurred by their dissemination activities. (Lomas, 2000, p 238).

All of this analysis points out that a major difficulty for universities is to develop a clear sense of what should be counted as research dissemination effort and how to match individual efforts with institutional supports and commitments at the faculty and the university level. Further development of this effort in research universities is largely constrained by the norms and culture of scholarship. Effective use of academic research in education is 'more likely to occur when university researchers work in collaboration with teachers in professional learning communities, and in carefully designed, evidence-backed, strategically focused projects' (see the Australian chapter). The Consortium on Chicago School Research (CCSR) identified four traditional roles university education researchers have pursued in the past to influence practice with their research. And the reports reveal that what lack are 'sustained connections between education researchers and local policy makers and practitioners' (see the US chapter). However, as noted earlier, the number of researchers is entirely insufficient to make such relationships practical in many schools. It is also true that universities can put in place structures and incentives, even outside the tenure and promotion process, that would support more knowledge mobilisation.

Conclusions: towards a future for research capacity

In fields such as health, agriculture, transportation and technology, advanced research has progressively and systematically contributed to the development of our economy and society; indeed it is taken for granted as a key part of these fields. Despite education research being largely accepted as having the potential to contribute to educational policy and practice in a profound way (Shavelson and Towne, 2002), knowledge mobilisation in the field of education is still a relatively new area. Although many efforts are being made, we are at the early stages of knowing about how best to identify, target and affect the many factors that are key for effective and efficient research use.

The right options for research mobilisation will vary from country to country and even between institutions within a country. However, given the current patterns and infrastructure, those who are heavily involved or interested in improving the quality of education worldwide first need to pay more attention to this issue overall. If we want educational research truly to contribute to the improvement of national education systems, and ultimately to be integrated into the overall knowledge economy, then it is key to develop more and better ways of acting regarding appropriate research mobilisation channels for various purposes.

The chapters in this book make many useful suggestions and give many examples both of problems and of approaches with potential. Thus this volume can be used by many who are interested in education research to identify both challenges and solutions that will lead to a stronger role for universities as mobilisers of research knowledge in education.

References

Biddle, B. and Saha, L. (2002) *The untested accusation: principals, research knowledge, and policy making in schools*, Westport, CT: Ablex.

Binde, J. (2005) *Toward knowledge societies – first UNESCO world report*, Geneva: UNESCO.

Cordingley, P. (2008) 'Research and evidence-informed practice: focusing on practice and practitioners', *Cambridge Journal of Education*, vol 38, no 1, pp 37-52.

Coffey, A (2010) 'Methodological development and enhancing research capacity', *British Journal of Society of Education*, vol 31, no 3, pp 367-73.

Cooper, A. (2012) *Knowledge mobilization intermediaries in education: a cross-case analysis of 44 Canadian organizations*, unpublished doctoral thesis, University of Toronto.

Cooper, A., Levin, B. and Campbell, C. (2009) 'The growing (but still limited) importance of evidence in education policy and practice', *Journal of Educational Change*, vol 10, pp 159-71.

Cooper, A., Rodway Macri, J. and Read, R. (2011) *Knowledge mobilization practices of educational researchers in Canada*, paper presented to the 35th American Educational Research Association Conference, New Orleans, MS.

Easton, J. (2010) *Five big ideas for IES*, speech presented at the American Association of Colleges for Teacher Education (AACTE) Conference, Atlanta, GA (available at http://ies.ed.gov/director/pdf/easton022010.pdf).

Levin, B. (2008) *Thinking about knowledge mobilization*, paper prepared for an invitational symposium sponsored by the Canadian Council on Learning and the Social Sciences and Humanities Research Council of Canada, May, Vancouver.

Levin, B. (2010) 'Leadership for evidence-informed education', *School Leadership and Management*, vol 30, no 4, pp 303-15.

Levin, B. (2011) 'Theory, research and practice in mobilising research knowledge in education', *London Review of Education*, vol 9, no 1, pp 15-26.

Liefner, I. (2003) 'Funding, resource allocation, and performance in higher education system', *Higher Education*, vol 46, pp 469-89.

Lomas, J. (2000) 'Using linkage and exchange to move research into policy at a Canadian Foundation', *Health Affairs*, vol 19, no 3, pp 236-40.

Munn, P. (2008) 'Building research capacity collaboratively: can we take ownership of our future?' *British Educational Research Journal*, vol 34, no 4, pp 413-30.

Neave, G. (ed) (2006) *Knowledge, power and dissent: critical perspective on higher education and research in knowledge society*, Geneva: UNESCO.

Nutley, S., Walter, I. and Davies, H. T. O. (2007) *Using evidence: how research can inform public services*, Bristol: The Policy Press.

OECD (Organization for Economic Cooperation and Development) (2000a) *Knowledge management in the learning society*, Paris: OECD.

OECD (Organization for Economic Cooperation and Development) (2008) *Tertiary education for a knowledge society*, Paris: OECD.

OECD (Organization for Economic Cooperation and Development) (2012) *Education at a glance 2012: highlights*, Paris: OECD.

Park, H. W. and Leydesdorff, L. (2010) 'Longitudinal trends in networks of university–industry–government relations in South Korea: the role of programmatic incentives', *Research Policy*, vol 39, pp 640-49.

Payne, A. A. and Siow, A. (1999) 'Does federal research funding increase university research output?', IGPA Working Paper 74.

Qi, J. (2011) 'The role of Chinese normal universities in the professional development of teachers', unpublished doctoral dissertation, University of Toronto.

Schuller, T. (2007) 'Capacity building in educational research: sketching an international picture', *Scottish Educational Review*, vol 39, no 1, pp 84–91.

Shavelson, R. J. and Towne, L. (eds) (2002) *Scientific research in education*, Washington, DC: National Academy Press.

Tetroe, J. M., Graham, I. D., Foy, R., Robinson, N., Eccles, M. P., Wensing, M., Durieux, P., Legare, F., Nielson, C. P., Adily, A., Ward, J., Porter, C., Shea, B. and Grimshaw, J. M. (2007) 'Health research funding agencies' support and promotion of knowledge translation: an international study', *The Milbank Quarterly*, vol 86, no 1, pp 125-55.

Whitty, G. (2006) 'Educational research and education policy: is conflict inevitable?', *British Educational Research Journal*, vol 32, no 2, pp 159-76.

World Bank (1999) *World development report: knowledge for development*, New York: Oxford University Press.

TWO

Knowledge mobilisation and utilisation

Robyn Read, Amanda Cooper, Hilary Edelstein, Jacqueline Sohn and Ben Levin, Ontario Institute for Studies in Education, University of Toronto

This chapter aims to provide insight into what is meant by 'knowledge mobilisation' (KM) in the field of research and how we might think about the work and role of universities in sharing research knowledge. To this end, we discuss ideas about mobilising research knowledge generally, and then report on a study that explored the KM efforts of faculties of education, showing how the findings illuminate the way that universities approach this work.

What do we mean by KM?

Studies on the links between research, policy and practice are by no means new to the academic community, and in fact can be traced back to the days of Plato and Aristotle (Estabrooks et al, 2008; Levin, 2008). In recent years, the scope and scale of this field has increased dramatically across disciplines. As in many areas of academia, there is a lack of consistency in terminology being used to address this topic. This is easily demonstrated by the various terms being used throughout this book. For example, John Polesel, in the chapter on the state of KM in Australia, refers to how the term 'engaged scholarship' is used to denote the transfer of research from theory to practice involving collaboration (see also Qi and Levin, Chapter One, and Polesel, Chapter Five). Similarly, in Denmark terms such as the 'transfer of knowledge', 'communication', and 'knowledge sharing' are more often used (see Holm, Chapter Seven). In the chapter on the US, Sarah Mason also uses knowledge transfer and dissemination to refer to the activity of moving research to practice (see Chapter Eleven). Muller and Hoadley, in the chapter on South Africa, argue that although the term KM is used, it 'suffers from ... conceptual disorientation' and needs clarification (see Chapter Nine and also Chapter One). Meanwhile, the Asian countries (China, Korea and Singapore) have taken on the term 'KM and utilisation', drawing heavily on the UK and Canadian models (see Chapters Four and Eight in this book; see also Davies et al, 2000; Levin, 2008).

Frequently used terms for the process of linking research to policy and practice include KM in education (Levin, 2004; Davies et al, 2005; Cooper et al, 2009); knowledge sharing and knowledge management in development (Court and Young, 2003; Hovland, 2003); knowledge transfer and knowledge management in business (Inkpen and Dinur, 1998; Argote and Ingram, 2000); as well as knowledge transfer, knowledge translation and knowledge exchange in health (Lavis et al, 2003; Mitton et al, 2007). The Research Supporting Practice in Education (RSPE) team at the Ontario Institute for Studies in Education (OISE) has created a synthesised list of the various terms and definitions currently being used (www.oise.utoronto.ca/rspe). This list demonstrates the considerable overlap in the definitions; however, it is important to recognise that these subtle differences between various terminologies affect our understanding of the topic. For example, the term 'knowledge transfer' implies that knowledge is like an object that can be transferred in a linear fashion by simply handing from one person to another. Alternatively, terms such as 'knowledge exchange' or 'knowledge mobilisation' imply that knowledge moves in a non-linear fashion and can be altered or shaped into different forms as it passes from person to person.

KM is complex and involves 'more than simply getting the right information into the hands of the right people at the right time; (Dobbins et al, 2007, p 9). The process is interactive and non-linear in that research does not move directly between research producers and users. We use the term 'knowledge mobilisation' as the term preferred by the Social Sciences and Humanities Research Council (SSHRC), the major national funder of social science research in Canada, and because it conveys the active and social element that is so key to this work. SSHRC defines KM as:

> … moving knowledge into active service for the broadest possible common good. Here **knowledge** is understood to mean any or all of (1) findings from specific social sciences and humanities research, (2) the accumulated knowledge and experience of social sciences and humanities researchers, and (3) the accumulated knowledge and experience of stakeholders concerned with social, cultural, economic and related issues. (SSHRC, 2008, para 5, original emphasis).

SSHRC's definition is broad and includes many types of knowledge. This reflects literature that identifies two types of knowledge: explicit and tacit. Tacit knowledge is thought to be gained through personal experience, and is therefore difficult to codify and transfer; whereas explicit knowledge is often instrumental and therefore can be more easily shared through various mediums (Cummings, 2003; Milton, 2006; Bennet and Bennet, 2007; Nutley and Davies, 2007; Cordingley 2009; Jones et al, 2009). There is much evidence that experience is one of the strongest influences on the beliefs and practices of people in all fields, including professionals (Nutley et al, 2007; Titler, 2008; Levin and Edelstein, 2010; Levin, 2011). However, our concern here is with explicit knowledge, and in particular knowledge derived from formal research.

Our conception of KM has several dimensions. First, we focus specifically on knowledge from formal research rather than other types of knowledge. Nutley and Davies (2010) define research as evidence gained through '... any systematic process of critical investigation and evaluation, theory building, data collection, analysis and codification' (p 4). We are also concerned with mobilising knowledge from widely accepted bodies of empirical work as opposed to single studies, since it is only when the results of many studies are in agreement that we can have enough confidence in the findings to apply them broadly. We take the view that KM happens between diverse people or organisations, so researchers presenting to other researchers at an academic conference does not fit our definition of KM. Rather, research knowledge is mobilised effectively when organisational leaders, practitioners, policy makers, and researchers from different institutions and contexts learn together using research to inform thinking and professional practice. Ultimately, we define KM as the movement of research from production to its ultimate impact on policy and practice.

This definition draws attention particularly to the social nature of knowledge use. While much of the empirical work on research knowledge mobilisation focuses on individual knowledge and dispositions, in our view KM is even more about social arrangements and organisational policies and practices. People's behaviour and professional practice are largely shaped by the way organisations work; too much emphasis on individuals draws attention away from these latter factors.

Ideas of 'research' and 'use'

Although the raison d'être for KM may be palpable, it is not without controversy. Just as there is disagreement when it comes to what terminology we should use to describe efforts to connect research to policy and practice, there is controversy over both what counts as research and what counts as use of research.

The debates as to what counts as research reflect the greater trend across the literature that addresses two types of knowledge, explicit and tacit, as outlined above. Although less formal ways of knowing, such as experience, are undeniably important when considering the realities of practice and policy contexts (Jones et al, 2009; Levin, 2011), there is no doubt that research can help improve the quality of education. As Stiglitz (1999) reminds us, 'knowledge … goes beyond the collection of best practices and the accumulation of successful anecdotes … [and] thus research is a central element of knowledge' (p 319). In part, the assessment of what counts as research is a technical question calling for careful methodological judgements. Researchers do not agree among themselves as to which methods yield reliable findings, or on the criteria by which one should evaluate the quality of research. These debates over research methods and findings can be very frustrating to lay people, who may conclude that research does not or cannot yield clear results.

At the same time, the labelling of particular types of knowledge as 'research' is not only a matter of technical expertise but also of politics. Which research will be seen as legitimate or important gets worked out through political processes (Nutley and Davies, 2010). Given limited resources, there are no value-free ways to define what counts as research. The 'attaching of labels such as *evidence* or *research* to particular types of knowledge are political acts' (Davies and Nutley, 2008, p 3, original emphasis). It is for this reason that some of the major criticisms of ideas such as knowledge mobilisation focus on suspicions regarding: whose voices are most prominent; sources of information; power imbalances; political agendas; and the challenges to meaningful collaboration between policy makers, researchers, and practitioners (Clarence, 2002; Cooper et al, 2009). Critics are concerned that the language of research use may be a disguise for less desirable motives, and can be used as a political ploy rather than as a real interest in evidence. Critics also argue that all research derives from values and that no research can be considered value free or context free. Moreover, the lack of evidence showing that using evidence produces better results is pointed out by critics as being a serious flaw in the evidence-based approach (Lemiux-Charles and Champagne, 2004).

While acknowledging the gaps and potential challenges, proponents recognise that the reservations and criticisms are, in essence, about *how* research evidence might be applied, rather than *whether* it should be used (Cooper et al, 2009). Consistent bodies of evidence are more powerful and effective over time than single studies, and the cumulative weight of a strong body of evidence built over time tends to have the greatest impact (Levin, 2008, p 5). Furthermore, high-quality research evidence can (and should) be representative of diverse views, sources and types of information. It is beyond the scope of this chapter to make a full argument for the value of using research evidence, but disseminating research clearly has the potential to have widespread influence.

Although KM as a field of inquiry can be dated back to Weiss's (1979) seven models of research use, the literature tends to address ways in which research can be better disseminated rather than how it is actually being used (Cooper et al, 2009). This may be because, despite the significance of the concept of research impact, there is little empirical work on the impact of educational research on policy and practice (Levin, 2008).

Nutley et al (2007) suggest that research use be placed on a continuum from conceptual forms of use, like awareness raising, to more influential forms of use by being adapted into policy and practice. Amara et al (2004), borrowing from Weiss (1979), discuss research use in terms of instrumental use, where research results are applied in specific and direct ways: conceptual use where research results are used for general enlightenment, and symbolic use where research is used to support predetermined positions or beliefs. Through the analyses of empirical studies, Walter et al (2003) identified multiple forms of impact, including: 'changes in access to research, changes in the extent to which research is considered, referred to or read, citation in documents, changes in knowledge and understanding, changes in attitudes and beliefs, and changes in behaviour' (p 11).

Alternatively, many have outlined the importance of organisational structures, rules and norms in research utilisation (Yin and Moore, 1988; Rich, 1991; Rich and Oh, 1993; Landry et al, 2001). Where research use is embedded in organisational work (for example a culture that encourages evidence-based practice, policies that require supporting empirical evidence accompany strategic plans, database systems to find and share research), higher levels of research use have been noted (Levin, 2011).

There have been some attempts to develop frameworks to measure research impact in the health sector (Kitson et al, 1998; Lavis et al, 2003; Kuruvilla et al, 2006), but few exist in the education sector. Kuruvilla et al (2006) provide a catalogue of potential impacts from research in the health sector that could also be applied to education. These are grouped in four categories:

1. **Research-related impacts**: type of problem/knowledge; research methods; publications and papers; products, patents and translatability potential; research networks; leadership and awards; research management; communication;
2. **Policy impacts**: level of policy making; type of policy; nature of policy impact; policy networks; political capital;
3. **Service impacts:** type of services – health/intersectoral; evidence-based practice; patient outcomes; information systems; services management; cost-containment and cost-effectiveness;
4. **Societal impacts:** knowledge, attitudes and behaviour; literacy; health status; equity and human rights; macroeconomic/related to the economy; social capital and empowerment; culture and art; sustainable development outcomes. (Summarised from Kuruvilla et al, 2006, p 137)

These different notions of research use/impact, as already outlined, could have enormous implications for public policy and practice – in all realms of public service. However, the literature provides us with limited evidence to inform our understanding of what KM strategies work in what contexts, especially in education.

KM and faculties of education

Although, as has been clearly demonstrated, we have many gaps in our knowledge on KM, there is much that we have already learned about the nature of this work. Programmes of research (such as the work done by the Lavis and Landry teams in Canada – see Cooper and Levin, 2010), have increased potential for impact due to sustained efforts towards influencing policy and practice through a variety of activities over time, such as combining empirical work with network building, KM events, and so on. The RSPE research programme at OISE – in which the authors of this chapter are involved – aspires to do such work in education.

Since 2007, the RSPE team has undertaken a combination of conceptual work, empirical studies, network building, partnership creation, and KM projects. In the rest of this chapter we share some of our findings that are pertinent to faculties of education, with the hope that some of our results will support others involved in this important work. In particular, this section will focus on the findings of our recently completed study of KM practices in faculties of education. This three-phase study, funded by the Social Sciences and Humanities Research Council of Canada (SSHRC), aimed to increase our knowledge about the steps being taken by faculties of education to increase the profile and potential value of their work, the challenges in doing so, and the value and merits of different strategies.

Phase one explored the strategies put in place by selected faculties of education in order to facilitate knowledge mobilisation to various audiences. Our sample for this phase focused on research-intensive faculties of education including five from Canada (University of Alberta, Memorial University of Newfoundland, OISE, University of Saskatchewan, and York University), five from the US (Harvard University, University of Michigan, Pennsylvania State University, Stanford University, and University of Washington), and three from other countries (University of Melbourne, University of London, and Nanyang Technological University, Singapore). Although this sample does cross borders, it was not intended to be representative of the various countries involved, and much more is said about faculties of education elsewhere in the rest of this book.

A total of 17 senior administrators representing the various faculties were interviewed by telephone between January and April 2009. Participants were asked questions about the KM strategies employed within their institution based in five areas:

- incentives such as tenure and promotion, or awards for KM work;
- institutional supports such as administrative support, or dedicated offices for KM, and so on;
- programme changes including new courses, changes in course content or cooperative and joint programmes;
- changes in social norms through leadership or recognition;
- building connections between researchers and their potential partners through events, research programmes, and so on. (For a detailed description of this study see Sà et al, 2011.)

Interviewees were asked to discuss how effective their strategies were, and also about any evidence available to demonstrate effectiveness. All interviews were recorded and detailed summaries were produced for analysis.

Analysis of this first phase revealed four main trends:

- KM in these faculties of education is under-institutionalised and conducted in an ad-hoc fashion. None of the faculties had an overarching knowledge mobilisation strategy, while only two faculties of education had incorporated KM at the organisational level: one with funding directly linked to partnership building and KM efforts and the other with a half-time faculty member assigned with an explicit role to support faculty members' KM efforts (Sà et al, 2011).
- Institutional infrastructure in support of KM is dependent on the institution's scale of resources, and uptake tends to be dependent on jurisdiction; in particular whether KM work is encouraged by government policy or funding schemes and by research funding agencies.
- A number of barriers to KM were cited by the institutions, listed here in order of salience: financial constraints, divergent views among faculty members regarding the importance of KM, limited timelines, establishing measurable targets and outcomes for KM, communicating scholarly research to the wider public, navigating through the multitude of competing information sources, coordinating KM at the institutional level, tenure/promotion criteria, lack of history of KM in social sciences, and the need for sustained leadership committed to KM.
- When some strategies *were* put into effect (such as sharing research results on websites), they were not based on the literature. For instance, although empirical evidence shows that face-to-face interaction and network building is most effective in KM efforts, faculties emphasised insufficient spending on academic journal publication efforts as a major barrier to KM (Cooper and Levin, 2010).

We chose to focus on deans and high-level administrators for the first phase of this study, as we believed that if there were an institutional KM strategy, they would be able to speak to its application across departments. Upon completion of the interviews, however, we realised that one of the major limitations of the first phase was the assumption that deans would be aware of all the KM efforts happening in their organisations. In universities, KM tends to be done by individual faculty members in an ad-hoc fashion, and this work might not be known to deans. Universities tend to be decentralised organisations, and we recognised that by focusing at the faculty level we might be missing out on much of the KM work. We therefore designed a second phase of the study around surveying faculty members directly about their

KM practices. For this second phase, we wanted to continue to explore what supports are available at the organisational level, and also see if researchers utilised these supports when they were available.

The second phase of this study involved a survey of Canadian researchers who had been awarded a standard research grant in education by the SSHRC – the main funding source in Canada for basic research in education – between 2000 and 2005. Just as phase one of this study focused on research-intensive faculties of education, the second phase focused on the most productive education researchers in Canada, based on the assumption that these researchers would also be the most actively involved in KM work. Through a strategic search of the SSHRC website we identified a list of 520 grant recipients. Duplicate names for those researchers who had received more than one grant during this time period were removed from the list and email addresses were sourced for the remaining researchers. This resulted in a survey sample of 278 researchers. A total of 111 responded to our survey, a response rate of approximately 40%. The survey was divided into five sections including: Institutional Supports Available to Assist Researchers with KM Efforts; Project Information; Audience Information; Academic versus Non-academic Outreach; and Dissemination Mechanisms.

Overall, our survey found that generally researchers do not have (or are not aware of) institutional administrative supports and communication resources to support research sharing practices. Of the 94 researchers who responded, 37 (39%) reported no supports available at their institution and 57 reported the availability of at least one kind of administrative support available for KM efforts. However, even when these resources were available, we found they were accessed less than 50% of the time. This could be because, as the empirical evidence suggests, KM is not well aligned with the priorities of academia, which focus on generating publications within academic communities rather than making research accessible and useful to practitioners and policy makers (Hargreaves, 1999; Willinsky, 2000; Lavis, 2006). Literature on the pressure put on faculty members to produce peer-reviewed journal articles abounds (McGrail et al, 2006). Incentive structures throughout academia, including tenure and promotion, heavily favour academic production over non-academic outreach (Sà et al, 2011).

Our study found that researchers tended to give more weight to academic events and publications over non-academic events and publications. Researchers were asked to identify how many publications were produced from their studies. Publications were classified into different types based on whether the intended audience was primarily academic or non-academic. Overall, many more academic publications were reported than non-academic publications, with a total of 607 academic publications (39 books, 166 book chapters, 217 refereed journal articles and 144 reports) versus 260 non-academic publications produced across the sample (99 plain language summaries, 68 recommendations, and 93 alternative formats tailored for audiences such as brochures and newsletters). This is especially off balance considering non-academic publications are much shorter and take less time to produce. It is important to note that a significant number of respondents did not answer this question. We assume that those who did respond were more likely to have produced publications, which would suggest that the numbers reported are higher than would be revealed in an accurate census. We also asked researchers about the proportion of their time they spent on various KM activities. Researchers reported spending the majority of their time conducting research followed by academic publishing and attending academic events. Very little of researchers' time was spent in non-academic pursuits such as publications (M = 8%), events (M = 7%) and networks (M = 4%). It is clear from these data that academic mobilisation work received significantly more attention than did non-academic mobilisation work. It is also interesting to note that both academic and non-academic networks received less than 4% of researchers' time.

The most prolific academic researchers (researchers with four or more referred articles from their most recently completed SSHRC project) also produce more non-academic publications than researchers who have three or fewer referred articles. However, one significant finding was that those who did more academic dissemination also tended to do more non-academic dissemination, which indicates that despite the pressure put on faculty members to publish in peer-reviewed journals (McGrail et al, 2006), academic efforts do not seem to detract from non-academic endeavours. This data contradicts the interview data from phase one, where deans cited the time spent on academic publications as a major barrier to KM work.

The other dissemination mechanisms investigated in this study included online strategies, communication through the media and work with intermediary organisations. Use of web-based dissemination was low: only 42 researchers reported using websites to communicate their research findings (38%). Fifteen used listservs (14%), three used blogs (3%) and two used social networking tools (2%). This is surprising, given that the original purpose of the internet was to enable researchers to share critical information with each other (Spar, 1999). However, while the internet has great potential as a vehicle for mobilising knowledge, web strategies also need to take into account how people and organisations really work. The reality is that most web pages get very few visitors, most documents on the web are rarely viewed or downloaded, and most discussion boards do not generate much discussion (Edelstein et al, 2012). Much of the effort to share research knowledge through the internet is wasted because it is passive. A third of the researchers reported having their findings communicated through the media, but only five researchers reported contacting the media themselves. In most reported cases (61%), the media picked up the story without contact from the institution or researcher. The use of intermediaries for dissemination by Canadian researchers is also low. Only 16% reported working with intermediaries to share their findings, although the literature suggests that intermediaries are integral to translating research into policy and practice (Nutley et al, 2007; Cooper and Levin, 2010; Cooper, 2012). Dissemination mechanisms could be improved in all three areas: online strategies, use of intermediaries, and increasing the use of the media. These low levels of use represent areas in which improvements could be made, probably, in all three areas, with small investments of time and resources. After all, online dissemination channels are free, the media is always looking for a story, and intermediaries are often open to partnerships with researchers and the media.

Suggestions for improvement

Taken as a whole, these data suggest that levels of KM in Canadian education research are quite modest. Although researchers recognise the importance of their work to external audiences, they invest relatively little time and effort in building connections with those audiences. These results seem problematic from several standpoints. First, researchers themselves report that their work has implications that presumably are not being exploited. Second, governments and research funders are increasingly concerned about the impact of research, so more efforts to mobilise research knowledge would seem to be important to maintain public support for research. And most importantly, the education of young people could presumably be improved if there were strong and more consistent connections of high-quality research to policy and practice (Levin, 2011). For all these reasons, the present situation cannot be regarded as desirable.

At the same time, our data provide some positive indicators. Clearly many researchers see educators as a key audience and are interested in sharing their work more effectively. Many already make efforts to do so, including, we suggest, many highly productive researchers. We also find that doing more non-academic KM is not associated with less academic dissemination; in fact, those who report more of the former also report more of the latter. There is a good base on which faculties of education could build more effective sharing of research knowledge, with consequent benefits to the education system generally. Based on our work, we make the following recommendations for universities and individual researchers to improve the impact of research:

- Recognise that the impact of research is a diffuse process that depends largely on interpersonal connections, relationships and persistence. Studies maintain that research utilisation is increased when research products are tailored to particular audiences (Lavis et al, 2003; Nutley et al, 2007). A body of empirical work emphasises that, in addition to audience focus, involving stakeholders throughout the research process increases subsequent use of the findings (Garner et al, 1998; Sheldon et al 1998; Jacobson et al, 2005). Publishing one's results in academic journals, while necessary, is not sufficient as a way of mobilising knowledge. In many fields, potential users of research have little capacity to find, share and use research, so even the most valid and vital knowledge will not get the take-up it deserves. Universities and researchers can improve this situation by building ongoing relationships with key service providers, so that over time these organisations become more adept at understanding and using research to guide their work.
- Recognise that knowledge mobilisation, like any other activity, takes time, energy and organisation. While many researchers do put effort into sharing research findings in various ways, it is not reasonable to expect individual researchers to do all the work of knowledge mobilisation. Researchers may need support in articulating implications of their work for practitioners (Cordingley, 2008), as researchers from specialist areas are not necessarily adept at articulating the implications of their findings to practitioners or policy makers. Universities need to build systems to support various aspects of this work, such as alternative forms of communication, working with the media, working with third parties to share research findings, supporting plain language writing, and so on.
- Organisational structures to support KM efforts are not widely available in faculties of education. Even where they do exist, they are not heavily accessed. It cannot be assumed that just because administrative and communication supports are created for dissemination at the organisational level that researchers will use them. Although much of the literature on KM in universities focuses

on tenure and promotion, a large number of the most productive researchers are, in fact, tenured and senior, so one has to look at a broader set of factors. In our view, increasing the mobilisation of research knowledge needs to be seen as requiring action on a number of fronts – providing resources, changing incentive systems, building relationships that would support networking, providing social media platforms, and so on. These structures need to be accompanied with a variety of other factors – such as providing training to develop the skills necessary to do this work, creating more time for researchers to spend on KM efforts, building ongoing partnerships with school systems and third parties that would support both more research access and better mobilisation of results, and integrating an acknowledgement of these efforts in institutional reward systems in order to cultivate an academic culture in which outreach to non-academic groups is valued and recognised.

- Graduate students can act as bridges. In many fields, notably the professions, graduate students are also experienced practitioners who have the potential to connect research to practice in effective ways. Yet universities often ignore students' practical experience, while their work settings denigrate the value of research. If graduate students were trained explicitly in how to act as knowledge brokers, they could make a huge contribution.

Later chapters in this book show that several of these ideas are already being acted on in some places, but not systematically or consistently. The possibilities for improvement are considerable and we hope that another edition of this book in a decade or so would show a very different and much stronger picture.

References

Amara, N., Ouimet, M. and Landry, R. (2004) 'New evidence on instrumental, conceptual, and symbolic utilization of university research in government agencies', *Science Communication*, vol 26, no 1, pp 75-106.

Argote, L. and Ingram, P. (2000) 'Knowledge transfer: a basis for competitive advantage in firms', *Organizational Behavior and Human Decision Processes*, vol 82, no 1, pp 150-69.

Bennet, A. and Bennet, D. (2007) *Knowledge mobilization in the social sciences and humanities: moving from research to action,* Frost, VA: MQI Press.

Clarence, E. (2002) 'Technocracy reinvented: the new evidence-based policy movement', *Public Policy and Administration,* vol 17, no 3, pp 1-11.

Cooper, A. (2012) *Knowledge mobilization intermediaries in education: a cross-case analysis of 44 Canadian organizations,* unpublished doctoral thesis, University of Toronto.

Cooper, A. and Levin, B. (2010) 'Some Canadian contributions to understanding knowledge mobilisation', *Evidence and Policy,* vol 6, no 3, pp 351-69.

Cooper, A., Levin, B. and Campbell, C. (2009) 'The growing (but still limited) importance of evidence in education policy and practice', *Journal of Educational Change,* vol 10, pp 159-71.

Cordingley, P. (2008) 'Research and evidence-informed practice focusing on practice and practitioners', *Cambridge Journal of Education,* vol 38, no 1, pp 37-52.

Cordingley, P. (2009) *Using research and evidence as a lever for change at classroom level,* paper presented to the American Educational Research Association Annual Meeting, Denver, CO.

Court, J. and Young, J. (2003) *Bridging research and policy: insights from 50 case studies* (retrieved October 2009 from Overseas Development Institute: available at http://www.odi.org.uk/resources/details. asp?id=148andtitle=bridging-research-policy-insights-50-case-studies).

Cummings, J. (2003) *Knowledge sharing: a review of the literature.* Washington DC: World Bank.

Davies, H.T.O. and Nutley, S. (2008) *Learning more about how research-based knowledge gets used: guidance in the development of new empirical research,* New York, NY: William T. Grant Foundation.

Davies, H.T.O., Nutley, S. and Smith, P. (2000) *What works: evidence-based policy and practice in public services.* Bristol: The Policy Press.

Davies, H.T.O., Nutley, S. and Walter, I. (2005) 'Approaches to assessing research impact: report of the ESRC symposium on assessing the non-academic impact of research' (available at http://www. esrcsocietytoday.ac.uk/ESRCInfoCentre/Forums/attach.aspx?a=64)

Dobbins, M., Rosenbaum, P., Plews, N., Law, M. and Fysh, A. (2007) 'Information transfer: what do decision makers want and need from researchers?', *Implementation Science,* vol 2, no 20, pp 1-12.

Edelstein, H., Shah, S. and Levin, B. (2012) 'Mining for data: assessing the use of online research', *International Journal of Humanities and Social Sciences,* vol 2, no 9, pp 1-12.

Estabrooks, C.A., Derksen, L., Winther, C., Lavis, J.N., Scott, S.D., Wallin, L. and Profetto-McGrath, J. (2008) 'The intellectual structure and substance of the knowledge utilization field: a longitudinal author co-citation analysis, 1945 to 2004', *Implementation Science*, vol 3, no 49, pp 1-22.

Garner, P., Kale, R., Dickson, R., Dans, T. and Salinas, R. (1998) 'Implementing research findings in developing countries', *BMJ*, vol 317, pp 5315.

Hargreaves, D. (1999) 'The knowledge-creating school', *British Journal of Educational Studies*, vol 47, no 2, pp 122-44.

Hovland, I. (2003) *Knowledge management and organizational learning: an international development perspective* (retrieved 2010 from Overseas Development Institute: available at http://www.odi.org.uk/resources/download/143.pdf).

Inkpen, A.C. and Dinur, A. (1998) 'Knowledge management processes and international joint ventures', *Organization Science*, vol 9, no 4, pp 454-68.

Jacobson, N., Butterill, D. and Goering, P. (2005) 'Consulting as a strategy for knowledge transfer', *The Milbank Quarterly*, vol 83, no 2, pp 299-321.

Jones, N., Datta, A. and Jones, H. (2009) *Knowledge, policy and power: six dimensions of the knowledge–development policy interface*, London: Overseas Development Institute.

Kitson, A., Harvey, G. and McCormack, B. (1998) 'Enabling the implementation of evidence based practice: a conceputal framework', *Quality in Health Care*, vol 7, pp 149-58.

Kuruvilla, S., Mays, N., Pleasant, A. and Walt, G. (2006) 'Describing the impact of health research: a research impact framework', *BMC Health Services Research*, vol 6, pp 1-18.

Landry, R., Amara, N. and Lamari, M. (2001) 'Climbing the ladder of research utilization: evidence from social science research', *Science Communication*, vol 22, no 4, pp 396-422.

Lavis, J. (2006) 'Research, public policymaking, and knowledge-translation processes: Canadian efforts to build bridges', *The Journal of Continuing Education in the Health Professions*, vol 26, no 1, pp 37-45.

Lavis, J., Robertson, D., Woodside, J., McLeod, C. and Abelson, J. (2003) 'How can research organizations more effectively transfer research knowledge to decision makers', *The Milbank Quarterly*, vol 81, no 2, pp 221-48.

Lemieux-Charles, L. and Champagne, F. (2004) *Using knowledge and evidence in health care: multidisciplinary perspectives.* Toronto: University of Toronto Press.

Levin, B. (2004) 'Making research matter more', *Education Policy Analysis Archives*, vol 12, no 56, pp 1-20.

Levin, B. (2008) *Thinking about knowledge mobilization*, paper prepared for an invitational symposium sponsored by the Canadian Council on Learning and the Social Sciences and Humanities research Council of Canada.

Levin, B. (2011) 'Mobilising research knowledge in education', *London Review of Education*, vol 9, no 1, pp 15-26.

Levin, B. and Edelstein, H. (2010) 'Research, policy and practice in education', *Education Canada*, vol 50, no 2, pp 29-30.

Levin, B., Cooper, A., Arjomand, S. and Thompson, K. (2010) *Research use and its impact in secondary schools: exploring knowledge mobilization in education*, CEA/OISE Collaborative Mixed Methods Research Project Final Report (available at http://www.cea-ace.ca/sites/default/files/cea-2011-research-use.pdf).

McGrail, M.R., Rickard, C.M. and Jones, R. (2006) 'Publish or perish: a systematic review of interventions to increase academic publication rates', *Higher Education Research and Development,* vol 25, no 1, pp 19-35.

Milton, P. (2006) 'Opening minds to change the role of research in education', *Education Canada*, vol 47, no 1, pp 39-42.

Mitton, C., Adair, C., McKenzie, E., Patten, S. and Perry, B. (2007) 'Knowledge transfer and exchange: review and synthesis of the literature', *The Milbank Quarterly*, vol 85, no 4, pp 729-68.

Nutley, S. and Davies, H. (2010) *Using research to provide stronger services and programs for youth: a discussion paper*, New York, NY: William T Grant Foundation (available at http://www.nekia.org/files/DP1_Promoting_research_use_v2_6.doc),

Nutley, S., Walter, I. and Davies, H. T. O. (2007) *Using evidence: how research can inform public services*, Bristol: The Policy Press.

Rich, R. (1991) 'Knowledge creation, dissemination, and utilization: knowledge', *The International Journal of Knowledge Transfer and Utilization*, vol 12, no 3, pp 319-37.

Rich, R. and Oh, C. (1993) 'Utilization of policy research', in S. Nagel (ed) *Encyclopedia of policy studies* (2nd edn), New York, NY: Marcel Dekker, pp 69-84.

Sá, C., Li, S. and Faubert, B. (2011) 'Faculties of education and institutional strategies for knowledge mobilization: an exploratory study', *Higher Education*, vol 61, no 4, pp 501-12.

Sheldon, T., Guyatt, G. and Haines, A. (1998) 'Getting research findings into practice: when to act on evidence', *BMJ*, vol, 317, pp 139-49.

Spar, D.L. (1999) 'The public face of cyberspace', in I. Kaul, I. Grunberg and M.A. Stern (eds) *Global public goods: international cooperation in the 21st century*, New York, NY: Oxford University Press (published for the United Nations Development Programme), pp 344–362.

SSHRC (Social Sciences and Humanities Research Council) (2008) *SSHRC's knowledge mobilization strategy*, Ottawa: SSHRC.

Stiglitz, J. (1999) 'Knowledge as a global public good', in I. Kaul, I. Grunberg, and M. Stern (eds), *Global public goods: international cooperation in the 21st century*, New York, NY: Oxford University Press (published for United Nations Development Programme), pp 308–25.

Titler, M. (2008) 'The evidence for evidence-based practice implementation', in R.G. Hughes (ed) *Patient safety and quality: an evidence-based handbook for nurses*, Rockville, MD: Agency for Healthcare Research and Quality (available at: http://www.ncbi.nlm. nih.gov/books/NBK2659).

Walter, I., Nutley, S. and Davies, H. (2003) *Research impact: a cross sector review*, St Andrews: Research Unit for Research Utilisation, University of St Andrews.

Weiss, C. H. (1979) 'The many meanings of research utilization', *Public Administration Review*, vol 39, no 5, pp 426–31.

Willinsky, J. (2000) *If only we knew: increasing the public value of social science research*, New York, NY: Routledge.

Yin, R.K. and Moore, G.B. (1988) 'Lessons on the utilization of research from nine case experiences in the natural hazards field', *Knowledge in Society: the International Journal of Knowledge Transfer*, vol 1, no 3, pp 25–44.

THREE

Knowledge mobilisation and utilisation in the Singapore education system: the nexus between researchers, policy makers and practitioners

Laikwoon Teh, David Hogan and Clive Dimmock, National Institute of Education, Nanyang Technological University, Singapore

Introduction

This chapter outlines how knowledge is mobilised – produced, mediated and applied – to improve education practice and policy in Singapore. It pays specific attention to the distinctive institutional relationships that link the National Institute of Education (NIE), the Ministry of Education (MOE) and Singapore's school system and their respective roles in the development of a unique nexus between research, policy and practice in Singapore's education system.

The chapter begins with an introduction to Singapore and Singapore's education system, highlighting the constraints faced by Singapore as a small economy with limited human capital, research expertise and research funding. It then describes how we have framed the problem of knowledge mobilisation theoretically, its key differences with traditional knowledge utilisation frameworks, and how and why Singaporean researchers, policy makers and practitioners have attempted to mobilise knowledge through development of a strategically focused national Research, Development and Innovation (RD&I) Programme. This framework is carefully calibrated to heighten the likelihood that education research will produce knowledge that is both rigorous and relevant to policy and practice (*production*), that knowledge will be shared in a timely and appropriate manner (*mediation*) among all stakeholders, and that it will be adopted, internalised and socialised by users in ways that impact policies and school practices (*application*). The chapter then ends with a discussion of how the Singapore experience, notwithstanding its unique context, may contribute to the international education research community's drive to increase its impact on policy and practice.

The organisation of education in Singapore

Singapore is a small and highly urbanised city state. It has a total population of 4.987 million with a population density of 7,022 per sq km in 2009 (Department of Statistics Singapore, 2011). Its per capita gross domestic product (GDP) of S$53,143 (or US$36,537) is one of the highest in Asia. Today, based on the latest official estimates, Chinese, Malays and Indians make up 74%, 13% and 9% of the Singapore resident population, respectively. The remainder are classified as 'Others', including 'Eurasians' (those from European and Asian descent). In 2009, the non-resident population of Singapore was estimated to be about 25% of the total population.

The diversity and size of the Singapore population are mirrored in its education system. Singapore has a small education system with a relatively short history, and an ethnically diverse school population. There are about 180 primary schools (grades 1–6), 170 secondary schools (grades 7–10) and about 20 junior colleges, centralised institutes and specialised schools that offer academic pre-university curriculum (grades 11–12). All these publicly funded schools employ English language as the medium of instruction and cater to almost all Singaporean students of school-going age. Prior to 1978, besides English medium schools, there were vernacular schools where lessons were taught primarily in Chinese, Malay and Tamil. All the publicly funded schools are organised into 28 school clusters, each with 12–14 schools. Each cluster is headed by a cluster superintendent who supervises and advises the school principals. Currently, principals have substantial autonomy in managing the learning programme of the schools within MOE guidelines.

The typical size of each primary 1 cohort is about 40,000, and the enrolment of a typical Singapore school is approximately 1,300 and 1,500 for secondary and primary schools, respectively. Schools are relatively well resourced. The pupil to teacher ratio is 19.6 in primary schools and 16.4 in secondary schools (MOE, 2010). The Singapore government's total expenditure (both recurrent and development) on primary, secondary and pre-university education in the financial year 2009/10 was S$4,924 million or about 2% of Singapore's annual GDP. This compares with the typical OECD figures of 5.5% of GDP in Nordic countries and approximately 3% in Japan, Luxembourg and the Slovak Republic (OECD, 2010).

The Singaporean educational system remains highly centralised and regulated following three decades of reorganisation, rationalisation, consolidation and reformation (Gopinathan, 1985; Hogan and Gopinathan, 2008). Over the last four or five years, however, there has been a significant decentralisation of administrative and pedagogical authority to individual schools. Virtually all Singaporean students study in one of the publicly funded schools, and virtually all the school leaders and teachers in these schools (except a small number of independent schools and specialised schools) are recruited, paid and managed (in terms of appointment and promotion) by the Ministry of Education. The highly centralised school system allows it to leverage substantial economies of scale, which may partly explain the lower education expenditure as a percentage of GDP relative to other OECD countries.

Almost all Singaporean school teachers receive their pre-service teacher training from the NIE within an agreed policy framework decided by NIE and MOE. Approximately 94% of Singaporean secondary school and junior college teachers and 62% of Singaporean primary school teachers are college graduates, while the remainder have acquired a two-year Diploma in Education training after completing high school. NIE is also the only institution in Singapore that has a research focus on education, although it also supports research in most major disciplines (Gopinathan and Hung, 2010). As at February 2011, NIE had a total of 255 professorial staff members on the tenure track, 81 lecturers (non-tenurable) and seven research scientists. The great majority of NIE professorial track staff members are research active and are involved in one or more of the funded education research projects.

Internationally, Singapore is a top academic achiever based on student performance in international studies such as the Progress in International Reading Literacy Study (PIRLS), the Trends in International Mathematics and Science Study (TIMSS) and the Programme for International Student Assessment (PISA). In 2007, the McKinsey Report identified Singapore's educational system as one of the top 10 in the world, noting in particular its strategic approach to educational reform and the provision of a support system to sustain reforms. A second McKinsey Report (Mourshed et al, 2010) further identified Singapore as one of the top five systems and sustained improvers that had moved from 'good to great'. Yet despite – or perhaps because of – these successes and its international profile, Singapore has not been willing to rest idly on its laurels. As early as 1997, at the height of the Asian financial crisis, the then Prime Minister, Goh Chok Tong, announced that while Singaporeans should celebrate their educational accomplishments, the world had changed dramatically since 1979, when the then government established the basic architecture of the contemporary educational system in Singapore. It was timely, therefore, to adjust its educational system accordingly:

> We cannot assume that what has worked well in the past will work for the future. The old formulae for success are unlikely to prepare our young for the new circumstances and new problems they will face. We do not even know what these problems will be, let alone be able to provide the answers and solutions to them. But we must ensure that our young can think for themselves, so that the next generation can find their own solutions to whatever new problems they may face. (Goh, 1997)

For the past decade or so, since the launch of *Thinking Schools, Learning Nation (TSLN)* in 1997, educational policy in Singapore has been dominated at the broadest level by a vision of 'a nation of thinking and committed citizens capable of meeting the challenges of the future, and an education system geared to the needs of the 21st century' (Dimmock and Goh, 2011; Dimmock, 2012). Not the least of the consequences of this fundamental resetting of policy priorities has been a very substantial commitment to developing a wholly new system of knowledge production and utilisation in Singapore to support the efforts of the government to improve the quality of teaching and learning in ways consistent with its long-term policy priorities and the changing character of 21st-century institutional arrangements (Dimmock and Goh, 2011; Dimmock, 2012).

The organisation of education research in Singapore

Apart from being the main provider of school education, the Singapore government (through the MOE) is also the main sponsor and funder of educational research in Singapore. Almost all education research in Singapore is conducted by NIE academics. NIE has well over 300 academics, most of them engaged in both teacher education and research. In addition, it customarily has a significant number of seconded MOE staff, currently standing at 68, many of whom are also involved in both teacher education and research. This brings the total number of teacher educators at any one time close to 400.

In addition, over the past decade, the MOE, keen to keep Singapore at the leading edge of the international education landscape, has introduced a separate career track for a core group of around 200 education officers to build knowledge and skills in specific areas of education, while working within MOE headquarters. These officers are expected to spend about 20% of their time carrying out research and development work in their respective areas and playing the role of knowledge brokers to bring cutting-edge research to impact on policy and practice. In addition, in each publicly funded school, the MOE has taken steps to train teacher researchers to undertake practice-oriented action research. Since 2006, MOE has put in place the Research Activist (RA) scheme to provide additional professional training to selected teachers beyond their pre-service training. These teachers are expected to conduct action research and to scrutinise how the prototypes they introduce to their schools contribute meaningfully to teaching and learning. The objective of the RA scheme is to build capacity, heighten appreciation of research in all Singapore schools, and support development of the schools as professional learning communities (PLCs).

While NIE (and its predecessors) have conducted education and pedagogical research for decades (Koay, 2010), dedicated and regular funding for education research was only made available by MOE to NIE in 1999 in the form of the Education Research Fund (EdRF), with an annual budget of S$1 million. This initiative was in response to the *Thinking Schools, Learning Nation* policy of 1997 (Gopinathan and Hung, 2010). However, following an MOE decision to establish NIE as a research-intensive institute focused on generating primary research findings from the local context to inform education policy and practice in Singapore, the MOE announced, in January 2003, the award of S$47.29 million to NIE to establish the Centre for Research in Pedagogy and Practice (CRPP).

From its opening in March 2003 until the time of writing (2011) CRPP has pursued five key objectives (Luke et al, 2004; Luke et al, 2005; Luke and Hogan, 2006; Hogan, 2011):

1. describe and measure patterns of classroom pedagogy in Singaporean schools;
2. measure the impact of pedagogical practices on student outcomes controlling for student characteristics;
3. design technologically enriched learning environments and support their integration into classroom pedagogy;

4. identify opportunities for the improvement of pedagogical practice through a carefully designed and evidence-based intervention strategy;
5. support evidence-based policy formulation and instructional practice to meet the challenges of 21st-century institutional environments.

Another NIE research centre, the Learning Sciences Laboratory (LSL), was set up in 2005 with the aim of integrating ICT more effectively into existing pedagogies on the assumption that doing so would better engage students and improve learning outcomes. LSL also advocated the transformation of existing pedagogies into inquiry-based learning activities and student–centred interactions through the innovative use of ICT. LSL's efforts have resulted in more than 70 projects including knowledge-building communities, new media and new literacies, mathematics and problem solving, science inquiry, and productive failure.

NIE's track record in both building up research and mobilising the knowledge generated to enrich policy deliberation and to suggest new possibilities to improve classroom practice created the opportunity for CRPP to apply for a second five-year grant in 2007/08. This was based on a strategically focused RD&I proposal that built upon the findings of the first five years and took into account MOE policy priorities, international research findings and the changing institutional landscape of education in Singapore (Hogan, 2007). The RD&I Framework set out the following priorities:

1. developing a comprehensive baseline database on teaching and learning in Singapore classrooms in order to evaluate the impact of policy initiatives and to support evidence-based interventions and policy development;
2. deepening understanding of the logic of teaching, classroom interaction and student learning in Singapore classrooms;
3. identifying and mapping the nature of the skills, understandings, dispositions and values that young people are likely to need to effectively negotiate 21st-century institutional environments, and identifying and developing curricular frameworks and pedagogies that are likely to cultivate them;
4. strengthening the intellectual quality of knowledge work in classrooms by improving the quality of the enacted curriculum and organising classrooms as epistemic communities of learning with a clear focus on participating in high–quality knowledge work and the development of appropriate skills, understandings and dispositions;

5. supporting the development of schools as professional learning communities that support strategically focused professional development and strong knowledge management and instructional systems;
6. expanding the use of formative assessment and summative school-based assessment to improve the quality of teaching and learning;
7. developing pedagogical resources, including technologically enriched learning environments, to enhance the quality of teaching and learning.

The MOE responded with a substantial grant of S$96.6 million. To expand education research within NIE beyond CRPP and LSL, a new Office of Education Research (OER) was set up in April 2008 to chart directions for NIE education research, to manage and ensure the qualities of education research projects, and to enhance the linkage between NIE researchers, school practitioners and MOE policy makers. To date, five calls for proposals have been issued to NIE staff. These proposals direct, encourage and support submissions in key areas and on topics that are directly relevant to issues faced by the Singapore education system and which are likely to result in improvements in teaching and learning. Among these is leadership and organisational change. Since the beginning of the second grant cycle (April 2008) up to the time of writing (December 2011) more than 130 ERFP projects have been approved at a grant value in excess of S$29 million. Almost 200 NIE faculty members have been involved in these projects.

Theoretical context: knowledge production, mediation and utilisation

For the past 40 years, the dominant framework used to understand how knowledge utilisation can improve policy and practice in education has been known, reasonably enough, as the Knowledge Utilisation (KU) framework, dating back to the seminal work of Eidell and Kitcher (1968) and Short (1973). Since then, a voluminous literature has accumulated. A keyword search of 'knowledge utilisation' in ERIC yielded 2,663 results. These studies are embedded in an even larger literature of work done in other disciplines that span engineering, information technology, health sciences, management, marketing, sociology and psychology. In the early 1990s, Backer (1991) reported that there were more than 10,000 citations of knowledge utilisation in all fields, although related terms are often used – dissemination, diffusion, technology transfer and others – with a similar meaning (see Levin, 2004). Comprehensive reviews of the literature in KU in education more than two decades ago can be found in Short (1973) and Love (1985). Key recent studies were reviewed by Hood (2002), Hemsley-Brown and Sharp (2003) and Levin (2008). The literature is also referred to extensively in two CERI/OECD publications, namely, *Knowledge Management in the Learning Society* (OECD, 2000) and *Evidence in Education: Linking Research and Policy* (OECD, 2007).

The problem of knowledge utilisation in education is often framed in terms of an entrenched hiatus between research and practice. This hiatus in turn is typically traced to a well-established institutional division of labour that splits research and practice into independent social practices: academics research and teachers teach. The former specialise in knowledge production, the latter in knowledge transmission. Universities focus on theoretical problematics and research methodology, schools on practical problems and practical solutions. The resulting institutional hiatus between knowledge production and knowledge application means that research has limited relevance and limited impact on policy and practice, to the detriment of both.

Not everyone, however, is convinced that this is the complete story. David Hargreaves (2000), for example, writes in an important OECD publication that this account ignores the fact that there is substantial knowledge production in schools that takes at least three forms: lots of informal 'tinkering', 'chatting' and action research; some development of professional learning communities focused on solving local practical problems within schools; and the rapid expansion of networks of teachers and schools in distributed professional learning communities. In this revisionist account, knowledge production in education is multi-modal rather than uni-modal (**Figure 3.1**).

We think this revisionist account is substantially more accurate than the conventional wisdom and at least partially explains the persistent evidence of what we might term 'vernacular innovation' in schools in highly localised contexts, particularly at the individual classroom level by committed teachers, sometimes at the behest of energetic (and/ or ambitious) principals. Overwhelmingly though, the great bulk of knowledge production is formalised and conducted by university researchers – often exclusively for their own benefit – with very little transfer to policy and practice. The impact of research on the scalability and sustainability of innovative practices is even rarer. Yet, as David Hargreaves (2000) pointed out more than a decade ago, despite this considerable investment in supply-side research, educational researchers have failed to provide a strongly validated social scientific foundation for professional practice in schools in comparison with their counterpart researchers in medicine and engineering. Moreover, educational systems have not been especially good at codifying and disseminating the tacit knowledge that expert teachers develop in the course of their professional practice (Hargreaves, 2000; Fullan et al, 2006). This raises a host of challenges to educational systems, but two are particularly important: 'they need to learn how to become more effective at learning and innovating than they have been in the past', and they need to integrate R&D and knowledge management (OECD, 2000, p 98).

Figure 3.1: Modes of educational knowledge production (EKP)

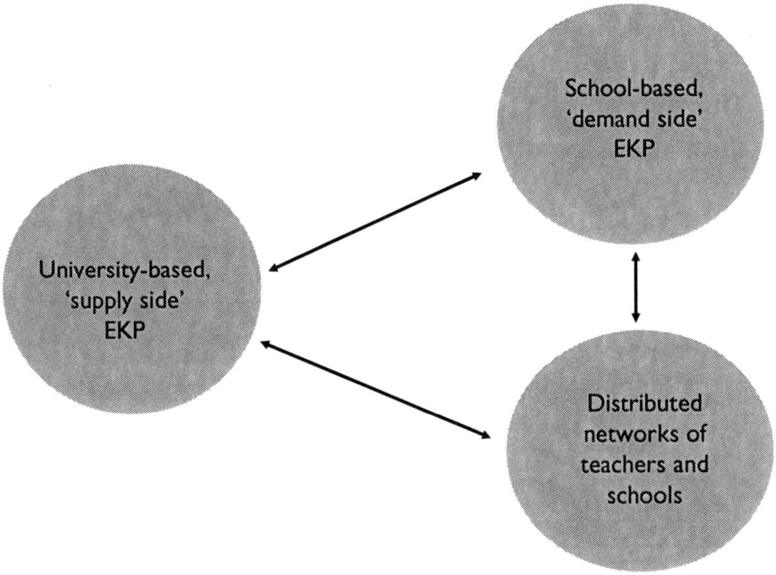

We agree with this judgement, but we believe that achieving these outcomes will require a radical rethink of the relationship between knowledge production and knowledge utilisation. In particular, it will require a dramatic shift in the locus of knowledge production from universities to schools (specifically to classrooms) and networks of schools, and it will require teachers to abandon privatised forms of professional practice in favour of strategically focused, evidence-based, collaborative partnerships with fellow practitioners and researchers. This in turn will require abandonment of conventional linear models of offline, supply-side, knowledge production and codification and utilisation and their replacement with newer models that balance supply-side and demand-side (online) knowledge production, codification, dissemination and application of the tacit knowledge of expert teachers (OECD, 2000, p 74).

This is, however, a lot easier said than done. Furthermore, ideally it will need to be implemented in a way that reconciles rigour, relevance, strategic focus, sustainability and scalability. Drawing upon a framework developed by Donald Stokes (1997) for use in a very different context, we might describe the range of university educational research as encompassing the following: rigorous but not relevant, neither relevant nor rigorous, relevant but not rigorous, and both rigorous and relevant. Unfortunately, school-based knowledge production (for example, by teachers utilising action research frameworks) is generally relevant but rarely rigorous, not always useful, effective or consequential, rarely strategically focused, seldom codified, validated or disseminated, and hardly ever sustained or sustainable. We can formalise this taxonomy in 2 × 2 matrix borrowed from Tushman and O'Reilly (2007) and reported in **Table 3.1**.

Table 3.1: Relevance and rigour in educational knowledge production

Rigour	Relevance/utility	
	No	Yes
Yes	Bohr's Quadrant *High-quality 'basic' disciplinary research (for example cognition and learning)*	Pasteur's Quadrant *High-quality 'basic' research (for example cognition and learning); high-quality policy-related research; high-quality 'partnership' innovations; high-quality school-based action research*
No	Merlin's Quadrant *Small, non-representative, under-theorised, methodologically sloppy 'Mickey Mouse' research studies*	Edison's Quadrant *Informal, practical 'tinkering' by classroom practitioners; semi-formalised action research by classroom teachers; some university research*

Clearly, in order to tighten the nexus between research and practice, educational knowledge production needs to take place in Pasteur's quadrant – the quadrant that captures knowledge production that is both rigorous and relevant. But while these are desirable criteria, rigorous and relevant research is not always strategically focused, nor capable of meeting both sustainability and scalability requirements. All of these criteria need to be satisfied. Critically, while we believe that some very carefully specified research might satisfy these desiderata, we also believe that it is more likely to occur when the following three elements, which we believe can foster effective knowledge mobilisation, are present.

First, prior to knowledge production, all stakeholders including researchers, practitioners, policy makers, parents and students should be engaged in informed dialogue (Reimers and McGinns, 1997) to co-construct the evidence in situ, that is, in the light of local beliefs, knowledge, values and problems (Spillane and Miele, 2007). Part of this entails engaging in collective deliberation to establish precisely the problems that knowledge users face and to identity what knowledge innovations are congruent with the practitioner's practical theory/knowledge, beliefs, values and norms (Dewey, 1904; Hirst, 1966; Sternberg, 2006). Second, university researchers must work in collaboration with teachers, for example in professional learning communities, and in carefully designed, evidence-backed, strategically focused projects so that both explicit and tacit knowledge (Polanyi, 1967; Nonaka and Takeuchi, 1995; Sternberg and Horvath, 1995) can be mobilised and transformed into knowledge innovations to improve the quality of instruction and learning in situ. Third, we believe that teacher professional learning is central to improving the quality of instruction and learning and to bringing knowledge innovations to fruition in classrooms and schools. Instead of the traditional knowledge dissemination through one-off workshops, seminars or discussions, knowledge mediation and knowledge application should be in line with the new accounts of professional learning that treat teachers as active learners and allow them to engage in concrete tasks of teaching, assessment, observation and reflection in situ (Lewis, 1997; Ball and Cohen, 1999; Wilson and Berne, 1999; Elmore, 2004; Bransford et al, 2005; Fullan 2007; Timperley et al, 2007; Hogan and Gopinathan, 2008; Timperley and Alton-Lee, 2008). Such learning is grounded in participants' questions, inquiry and experimentation as well as research on effective practice, and is focused on very specific and contextualised aspects of instruction. It should be iterative and extended over time, supported by follow-up activities, properly scaffolded by expert teachers, and embedded in schools functioning as collections of communities of learning and inquiry. It should also be focused systematically on instructional innovation and cultural change at the school level to address the implicit (often uncontested) conceptions of, or *beliefs* about, teaching, learning, knowledge, assessment and epistemic authority that teachers hold. Finally, we also believe that such research is more likely to be focused and effective when it is embedded in a national (or at least jurisdictional) strategic research, development and innovation programme. But while a knowledge mobilisation programme of this kind will help, it is by no means a sufficient condition to close the gap between research, on the one hand, and policy and practice, on the other (Hogan, 2011).

NIE's strategies to tighten the theory–practice nexus to actualise iterative knowledge mobilisation

We have highlighted three key elements of an iterative knowledge mobilisation effort that we believe will increase the likelihood of producing useful knowledge and its meaningful use by practitioners and policy makers. NIE has made some attempts to actualise an iterative knowledge mobilisation process between researchers, practitioners and policy makers, termed by NIE as 'Strengthening the Theory–Practice Nexus', which is the overarching idea behind NIE's Teacher Education 21 – TE21 – (NIE, 2010) framework and also its Strategic Research, Development and Innovation framework (Hogan, 2007; 2011). In this section, we will describe three NIE strategies that are cornerstones of the NIE–MOE–school partnership.

Substantial investment in the development of baseline databases to support informed dialogue among researchers, practitioners and policy makers

As argued above, informed dialogue of an extended and iterative nature between researchers, practitioners and policy makers increases the likelihood of reaching a consensus about the key problems encountered by the education system and the knowledge that the system needs to address these problems. Having a consensus helps mobilise the necessary resources needed to produce the knowledge, and heightens the likelihood of the knowledge, once produced, being adopted and implemented by practitioners and policy makers. This makes the knowledge production process significantly closer to Mode 2 (demand-driven) than Mode 1 (supply-driven) (see Figure 3.1).

A necessary component of this informed dialogue is the construction of a rich and robust database that comprehensively describes the status of teaching and learning in Singapore classrooms, and leadership and organisation practices in Singapore schools. The substantial investment on CRPP's Core 1 and Core 2 baseline studies demonstrates NIE and MOE's commitment to build this database. In addition, NIE and MOE have also approved a million dollar project to collect baseline data on school leadership and organisational change. This school leadership baseline research is still in its early phase and more information will be shared with the international research community once completed.

The breadth and the depth of these baseline research studies illustrate the amount of tangible resources which NIE and MOE have made available to the Core research teams. Almost 25% of all Singapore primary and secondary schools, and 10% of the teachers were involved in the Core 1 and Core 2 projects. The leadership baseline study has an even wider reach, covering all the Singaporean principals and vice-principals, and approximately one third of the middle management and classroom teachers, respectively. Perhaps more importantly, through being involved in the baseline data collection exercise as 'research subjects', these school practitioners gain considerable knowledge of both research methods and the substantive content of the knowledge areas being investigated. The CRPP research teams have invested substantial time and effort in sharing the research findings with school practitioners in multi-modal platforms such as teacher forums and sharing sessions at the national and school cluster level. Besides the involvement of teachers in such research endeavours, the purpose of these sessions is to engender a level of consensus among a large number of Singaporean teachers and school leaders with regard to what is happening in Singapore schools and classrooms, and to signal possible directions for further improvement of classroom practices.

Extensive dialogue – based on the baseline findings – between NIE researchers and MOE senior and middle-level policy makers are also initiated by NIE's Office of Educational Research (OER) and MOE's Planning Division. Through such dialogues, NIE researchers and MOE policy makers share their views based not just on baseline Singapore data, but also on cutting-edge research conducted worldwide and on policy imperatives grounded in the Singapore context. This information has formed the evidence base from which NIE's educational research agenda and MOE's innovation programmes have been developed. It has created a research and policy culture and enabled different stakeholders to enter into a partnership to co-develop shared research and policy frameworks.

Besides dialogue between NIE, MOE and schools, the Core research teams regularly convey to NIE those key research findings that have implications for the design and delivery of the pre-service programme and in-service teacher professional development. NIE staff members in turn review, scrutinise and interrogate the Core findings during annual NIE-wide platforms and deliberate on the refinements needed to ensure that NIE's pre-service and in-service programmes can better serve the needs of Singapore school practitioners.

In short: the rigour of the Core research programmes, the extensive involvements of school practitioners and the in-depth discussions among the various stakeholders on the Core findings strengthen the relationship between research, policy, programme design and delivery, and practice, within the educational community in Singapore.

Design research as a research approach to incorporate rich contextual information and practitioner knowledge

Besides involving practitioners and policy makers in the development of the NIE research agenda and the planning of research projects, the NIE has also taken concrete steps to support development of close partnerships between researchers and practitioners before, during and after the research process. These steps ensure that teachers and students are not merely research subjects, but that the research itself is honed and informed by classroom practice and that classroom practice is informed by research findings to the point where, optimally, classroom practice becomes a form of research practice (Wagner, 1997).

One step towards this end is that in some 'intervention' projects, principal investigators employ a design research approach to intervention work in schools. At its best, design research is iterative, collaborative and reflective in ways that test and refine instructional innovation and learning environments with due attention to developing and testing principles of learning (Brown, 1992; Collins, 1992; Cobb et al, 2003; Design-based Research Collective, 2003). Critically, design-based research is iterative and collaborative since both researchers and practitioners collaborate to engage in the design and implementation of the interventions in classroom settings. This process ensures research takes place in context, that theories of learning are developed and refined, and that researchers and teachers engage in re-design and continue the cycle of design and implementation. Design research is therefore often characterised as interventionist, iterative, process oriented, utility oriented and theory oriented (Van den Akker et al, 2006). The close collaboration of researchers and practitioners throughout the course of the research enhances and facilitates the incorporation of the tacit dimension of practitioner knowledge in the systematic explication of the research process.

While design research is still considered an emerging research method, NIE's (particularly LSL's) experience over the past five years suggests that it is an approach that meets the needs of the practitioners because it supports co-design, learning design, curriculum development, technology development and professional development – thereby actualising the iterative knowledge mobilisation cycle. Many of the LSL interventions have reported success in terms of positive changes in student outcomes and teacher competency and satisfaction (see Kapur, 2009; Looi et al, 2011; Pathak, 2011; Wong, et al, 2011). Given that design research studies are highly labour intensive, executed in situ and typically involve a small number of teachers and classrooms, it is premature to judge whether the success or otherwise of design research-based interventions is as much a result of the pedagogical innovation per se or the intensive and prolonged interactions between researchers and practitioners, or both.

Professional learning as a strategy to ensure knowledge mediation and application

A third NIE strategy to mediate knowledge, support its application and increase the impact on practice in a sustained manner is to leverage on NIE's pre-service and in-service programmes, which have been increasingly modelled after the professional learning framework, described in an earlier section.

Like many other university departments, NIE has a dedicated publication unit (housed in the OER) to translate and disseminate its research findings through regular print and online media. NIE also organises regular international academic conferences that include special sessions that are designed to reach out to school practitioners. The conferences are always exceptionally well attended by local teachers (with support from the MOE). Our experience, however, has been that while these efforts may generally be effective in raising awareness among practitioners about the new knowledge produced by NIE researchers, there is little assurance that the knowledge will be retained, adopted and implemented in practice.

As NIE is the single source of initial teacher education and provides 70-80% of professional development courses for Singapore teachers, pre-service teacher education and in-service professional development programmes are effective avenues to ensure that research findings are disseminated widely and adopted on a sustainable basis. NIE has taken two particular steps to enhance this outcome. One, mentioned earlier, is to strengthen the theory–practice nexus between teacher education and education research. In NIE, this is made easier because between 80% and 90% of NIE faculty members are active researchers as well as teacher educators. NIE has also created additional institution-wide platforms (for example colloquiums and sharing sessions) to disseminate research findings from the Core research programme and intervention projects so that these form the knowledge base of NIE teacher education programmes.

In addition, NIE has also attempted to strengthen the theory–practice nexus with the adoption of TE21, a new NIE teacher education model (NIE, 2010). Within TE21, both the Initial Teacher Preparation programme and in-service Teacher Professional Development programmes have adopted a structured mentorship model to increase the likelihood of teachers adopting new practices based on explicit knowledge received from the programme and feedback from their mentors. The model also advocates and supports the development of the tacit dimension of knowledge through the NIE Reflective Teaching Model and involvement in PLCs. As TE21 incorporates many of the features which are in line with the new theory of professional learning described earlier, we believe that it will be a more effective way to ensure that practitioners learn the relevant knowledge and its application to improve practice in a sustained manner. However, as this new model is in its early stage of implementation, we do not have empirical evidence of its impact to report.

Discussion

Singapore is a highly urbanised city state that remains a 'tightly coupled' system of instructional governance despite recent efforts to promote school-based curriculum development and instructional innovation (Hogan and Gopinathan, 2008; Hogan 2011, Hogan, 2012; Dimmock and Tan, in press). Since Singapore gained its independence in 1965, the government has exercised continual and substantial political, bureaucratic and professional authority over the organisation, funding and administration, and distribution of instructional practices within schools (Gopinathan, 1985, 2007; Hogan and Gopinathan, 2008; Hogan 2011). Also, given the small size of the Singapore education system and the fact that NIE is the only teacher training and education research institution in Singapore, it is also not uncommon for NIE researchers, MOE policy makers and administrators, and school practitioners to play more than one role in the iterative knowledge mobilisation process. For example, the most senior MOE official, the Permanent Secretary, also chairs the NIE Governing Council. The Director of NIE attends regular policy meetings with senior MOE policy makers and officials. NIE researchers and faculty members are routinely seconded to MOE to take on senior administrative positions. School practitioners (at all levels of seniority) also spend two to four years in MOE Headquarters as MOE officials, and both school practitioners and MOE officials are also posted to NIE to become involved in teacher education, education research and research management. And perhaps most important in relation to a strong theory–practice nexus, as stated earlier, at least 80-90% of all NIE faculty members partake in both educational research and pre-service or in-service teacher training.

While this duplication of roles can have its drawbacks, it generates substantial positives, not the least of them being that key actors, particularly those in senior leadership roles, develop an understanding of the process of knowledge production, mediation and application from more than one perspective. This opportunity to develop a broad understanding of the institutional perspectives and interests of multiple stakeholder groups has very substantial benefits for the system as a whole, in terms of the systemic alignment of institutional goals and practices, but also for the policy and funding environment in which research, policy and practice take place. In turn, this facilitates the alignment of the institutional goals of NIE, MOE and schools, and gives all stakeholders the confidence that, while everyone is working to secure their respective institutional interests, the wider mission – to improve learning and teaching in Singapore schools to meet the challenge of the 21st century – is not ignored. This is perhaps a key contributing factor behind the stable and substantial source of MOE research funding to NIE over the last decade, and the willingness of key NIE researchers to dedicate much of their research effort to strategic, policy-directed research (rather than individual researcher initiatives) and the increasing impact of NIE research on teacher classroom practices.

Our argument is not suggesting that the duplication (or confusion) of roles among knowledge producers, mediators and users, is *necessary* to facilitate a close theory–practice nexus. However, we do believe that high levels of articulation at a policy and planning level across institutions are necessary to the design of a national knowledge mobilisation strategy that is strategically focused, sustainable and scalable as well as rigorous and relevant. Rather, what we are highlighting is the value of researchers, practitioners and policy makers recognising their specific (often conflicting) institutional interests and working out a national (or jurisdictional) knowledge mobilisation strategy that simultaneously supports high-quality knowledge production in the form of research publications and also *usable knowledge* that is relevant to policy makers and that is owned by teachers seeking to improve the quality of teaching and learning in their classrooms. It is important, however, not to understate the difficulties of pursuing such a strategy successfully. Our sense is that in Singapore, where circumstances are especially favourable to a high level of policy, research and practice articulation and alignment, we have to date been a lot more successful in conceptualising what we think it would be good to do than we have been in putting in place a system that institutionalises what should be done. This is not to say that we have not had some successes: in particular, we have developed a number of strategically focused research programmes (particularly the Core research programmes) that have had substantial impacts on policy and programme development at the national level and will increasingly impact practice at the school and classroom level. Moreover, we have been able to support a number of projects that range from fairly conventional experimental design projects to design research projects that have had a considerable impact on a small number of schools. Less success has been experienced in demonstrating (let alone securing) the sustainability of these projects or taking them to scale in partnership with the MOE and schools. More broadly, we have not been especially successful in institutionalising a model of knowledge production, mediation and utilisation that is strategically focused, responsive to local school priorities and needs, and which supports development of collaborative partnerships between academic researchers and classroom teachers across the system. And we have made no progress at all in setting up procedures that would support the codification, verification and dissemination of expert teacher knowledge. There are many reasons for our lack of success in these important areas, but that is a matter for another time and place. Meanwhile, it remains our goal that knowledge mobilisation efforts – such as they are – will be located in Pasteur's Quadrant.

References

Backer, T. (1991) 'Knowledge utilization: the third wave', *Knowledge, Creation, Diffusion, Utilization*, vol 12, no 3, pp 225-40.

Ball, D.L. and Cohen, D.K. (1999) 'Developing practice, developing practitioners: toward a practice-based theory of professional education', in L. Darling-Hammond and G. Sykes (eds) *Teaching as the learning profession: handbook of policy and practice*, San Francisco, CA: Jossey Bass, pp 3-32.

Bransford, J., Derry, S., Berliner, D., Hammerness, K. and Beckett, K.I. (2005) 'Theories of learning and their roles in teaching', in L. Darling-Hammond and J. Bransford (eds) *Preparing teachers for a changing world: what teachers should learn and be able to do*, San Francisco, CA: Jossey-Bass, pp 40-87.

Brown, A. L. (1992) 'Design experiments: theoretical and methodological challenges in creating complex interventions in classroom settings', *The Journal of the Learning Sciences*, vol 2, no 2, pp 141-78.

Cobb, P., diSessa, A., Lehrer, R. and Schauble, L. (2003) 'Design experiments in educational research', *Educational Researcher*, vol 32, no 1, pp 9-13.

Collins, A. (1992) 'Towards a design science of education', in E. Scanlon and T. O'Shea (eds) *New directions in educational technology*, Berlin: Springer, pp 15-22.

Department of Statistics Singapore (2011) *Singapore in figures 2011* (retrieved on 6 Dec 2011 from http://www.singstat.gov.sg/pubn/reference/sif2011.pdf).

Design-based Research Collective (2003) 'Design-based research: an emerging paradigm for educational inquiry', *Educational Researcher*, vol 32, no 1, pp 5-8.

Dewey, J. (1904) *The educational situation*, Chicago: University of Chicago Press.

Dimmock, C. (2012). *Leadership, capacity building and school improvement*. London: Routledge.

Dimmock, C. and Goh, J.W.P. (2011) 'Transformative pedagogy, leadership and school organisation for the twenty-first-century knowledge-based economy: the case of Singapore', *School Leadership and Management*, vol 31, no 3, pp 215-34.

Dimmock, C. and Tan, C.Y. (in press) 'Singapore's school improvement journey: how a "good to great" system has evolved a symbiotic relationship between the changing educational policy landscape and school leadership', *Leadership and Policy in Schools*.

Eidell, T. L. and J. M. Kitchel (eds) (1968) *Knowledge production and utilization in educational administration*, produced in cooperation by the University Council for Educational Administration Columbus, OH and the Center for Advanced Study of Educational Administration, University of Oregon.

Elmore, R. F. (2004) *School reform from the inside out: policy, practice, and performance*, Boston, MA: Harvard Education Press.

Fullan, M. (2007) *The new meaning of education change,* 4th edn, New York, NY: Teachers' College Press.

Fullan, M., Hill, P. and Crevola, C. (2006) *Breakthrough,* Thousand Oaks, CA: Corwin Press/Sage.

Goh, Chok Tong, (1997) *Thinking schools learning nation*, speech at the opening of the 7th International Conference on Thinking, Singapore, para 31.

Gopinathan, S. (1985) 'Education in Singapore: progress and prospect', in J. S. T. Quah, H. C. Chan and C. M. Seah (eds) *Government and politics of Singapore*, Singapore: Oxford University Press, pp 197-232.

Gopinathan, S. (2007) 'Globalization, the Singapore developmental state and education policy: a thesis revisited', *Globalization, Societies and Education*, vol 5, no 1, pp 53-70.

Gopinathan, S. and Hung, D. (2010) 'Research in the National Institute of Education since 1991', in A.Y. Chen and S.L. Koay (eds) *Transforming teaching inspiring learning: 60 years of teacher education in Singapore 1950–2010*, Singapore: National Institute of Education, pp 179-90.

Hargreaves, D. (2000) 'The production, mediation and use of professional knowledge among teachers and soctors: a comparative analysis,' in *Knowledge management in a learning society*, Paris: OECD, pp 219-38.

Hemsley-Brown J. and Sharp C. (2003) 'The use of research to improve professional practice: a systemic review of the literature', *Oxford Review of Education*, vol 29, no 3, p 449.

Hirst, P. H. (1966) 'Language and thought', *Proceedings of the Philosophy of Education Society of Great Britain,* vol 1, no 1, pp 63-75.

Hogan, D. (2007) 'Policy-driven research and evidence-based educational innovation in Singapore, in *Evidence in education – linking policy and research*, Paris: CERI, OECD, pp 131-44.

Hogan, D. (2011) *Interim Core 2 report on classroom pedagogy*, unpublished report, Singapore: National Institute of Education.

Hogan, D. (2012) 'Culture and pedagogy in Singapore: the fate of the Teach Less Learn More policy initiative in Singapore, 2004-2010', in S. Paris and K. Lee (eds) *Redesigning pedagogy* (forthcoming).

Hogan, D. and Gopinathan, S. (2008) 'Knowledge management, sustainable innovation and preservice teacher education in Singapore', *Teachers and Teaching: Theory and Practice*, vol 14, no 4, pp 369-84.

Hood, P. (2002) *Perspectives on knowledge utilization in education,* San Francisco, CA: WestEd (retrieved on 27 Feb 2011 from http://www.wested.org/online_pubs/perspectives.pdf).

Kapur, M. (2009) 'Productive failure in mathematical problem solving', *Instructional Science*, doi: 10.1007/s11251-009-9093-x.

Koay, S.L. (2010) 'Expansion and consolidation of postgraduate and research programmes', in A.Y. Chen and S. L. Koay (eds) *Transforming teaching inspiring learning: 60 years of teacher education in Singapore 1950–2010*, Singapore: National Institute of Education, pp 99-118.

Levin, B. (2004) 'Making research matter more', *Education Policy Analysis Archives*, vol 2, no 56 (available at http://epaa.asu.edu/epaa/v12n56/).

Levin, B. (2008) *Thinking about knowledge mobilization,* Vancouver: Canadian Council on Learning and the Social Sciences and Humanities Research Council of Canada (available at http://www. oise.utoronto.ca/rspe/Conference_Presentations_Publications/index. html).

Lewis, A.C. (1997) 'A new consensus emerges on the characteristics of good professional development', *Harvard Education Letter*, vol 13, no 3 May/June, pp 1-4.

Looi, C.K., So, H.-J., Toh, Y. and Chen W. (2011) The Singapore experience: synergy of national policy, classroom practice and design research, *International Journal of CSCL*, vol 6, no 1, March, pp 9-37.

Love, J.M. (1985) 'Knowledge transfer and utilization in education;, *Review of Research in Education*, vol 12, pp 337-86.

Luke, A. and Hogan, D. (2006) 'Redesigning what counts as evidence in educational policy: the Singapore model', in J. Ozga, T. Seddon and T. S. Popkewitz (eds) *Education Policy and Research*, London: Routledge, pp 170-84.

Luke, A., Freebody, P. and Lau, S. (2004) *Core program proposal: case for support*, Singapore: Centre for Research in Pedagogy and Practice.

Luke, A., Freebody, P., Lau, S. and Gopinathan, S. (2005) 'Towards research-based educational policy: Singapore education in transition', *Asia Pacific Journal of Education*, vol 14, no 1, pp 1-22.

MOE (Ministry of Education) (2010) *Essential statistics digest, 2010* (retrieved on 27 Feb 2011 from http://www.moe.gov.sg/education/ education-statistics-digest/files/esd-2010.pdf)

Mourshed, M., Chijioke, C. and Barber, M. (2010) *How the world's most improved systems keep getting better*, New York, NY: Mckinsey & Company (available at http://mckinseyonsociety.com/how-the-worlds-most-improved-school-systems-keepgetting-better/).

NIE (National Institute of Education) (2010). *TE 21 – a teacher education model for the 21st century*, Singapore: National Institute of Education.

Nonaka, I. and Takeuchi, H. (1995) *The knowledge creating company: how Japanese companies create the dynamics of innovation*, New York, NY: Oxford University Press.

OECD (Organization for Economic Cooperation and Development) (2000) *Knowledge management in a learning society*, Paris: OECD.

OECD (Organization for Economic Cooperation and Development) (2007) *Evidence in education: linking research and policy*, Paris: OECD.

OECD (Organization for Economic Cooperation and Development) (2010) *Education at a glance 2010*, Paris: OECD Eurostat Education Database (available from http://epp.eurostat.ec.europa.eu/portal/ page/portal/education/data/database).

Pathak, S.A., Kim, B., Jacobson, M.J. and Zhang, B.H. (2011) 'Learning the physics of electricity: a qualitative analysis of collaborative processes involved in productive failure', *International Journal of CSCL*, vol 6, no 1, pp 57-73.

Polanyi, M. (1967). *The tacit dimension*, London: Routledge and Kegan Paul.

Reimers, F. and McGinns, N. (1997) *Informed dialogue: using research to shape education policy around the world*, Westport, CT: Praeger.

Short, E.C. (1973) 'Knowledge production and utilization in curriculum: a special case of the general phenomenon', *Review of Educational Research*, vol 43, no 3, p 237.

Spillane, J. and Miele, D.B. (2007) 'Evidence in policy and practice: some conceptual tools for exploring the terrain', in P.A. Moss (ed) *2007 NSSE yearbook: evidence and decision making*, Malden, MA: Blackwell, pp 46-73.

Sternberg, R.J. (2006) 'Successful intelligence: toward a broader model for teaching and accountability, *Edge: The Latest Information for the Education Practitioner*, vol 1, no 5, pp 3-16.

Sternberg, R.J. and Horvath, J.A. (1995) 'A prototype view of expert teaching', *Educational Researcher*, vol 24, no 6, pp 9-17.

Stokes, D. E. (1997) *Pasteur's Quadrant: basic science and technological innovation*, Washington DC: Brookings Institution Press.

Timperley, H. and Alton-Lee, A. (2008) 'Reframing teacher professional learning: an alternative policy approach to strengthening valued outcomes for diverse learners', in G. Kelly, A. Luke and J. Green (eds) *Review of Research in Education*, vol 32, no 1, Washington DC: Sage Publications, pp 328-69.

Timperley, H., Wilson, A. , Barrar, H. and Fung, I. (2007) *Teacher professional learning and development: best evidence synthesis iteration [BES]*, Wellington, New Zealand: Ministry of Education (available at www.educationcounts.govt.nz/goto/BES).

Tushman, M. and O'Reilly, C. (2007) 'Research and relevance: implications of Pasteur's Quadrant for doctoral programs and faculty development', *Academy of Management Journal*, vol 50, no 4, pp 769-74.

Van den Akker, J., Gravemeijer, K., McKenney, S. and Nieveen, N. (2006) *Educational design research*, London: Routledge.

Wagner, J. (1997) 'The unavoidable intervention of educational research: a framework for reconsidering researcher–practitioner cooperation', *Educational Researcher*, vol 26, no 7, pp 13-22.

Wilson, S. and Berne, J. (1999) 'Teacher learning and the acquisition of professional knowledge: an examination of research on contemporary professional development', in A. Iran-Nejad and P.D. Pearson (eds) *Review of Research in Education*, vol 24, Washington DC: Sage Publications, pp 173–209.

Wong, L.-H., Boticki, I., Sun, J. and Looi, C.-K. (2011) 'Improving the scaffolds of a mobile-assisted Chinese character forming game via a design-based research cycle', *Computers in Human Behavior,* vol 27, no 5, 1783-93.

FOUR

Knowledge mobilisation in education in England

David Gough, Institute of Education, University of London

Introduction

This chapter provides an overview of knowledge mobilisation by universities in England. It first provides an introduction to the capacity of the education systems and the research structures, capacity and quality measures in the UK more generally. It then describes knowledge mobilisation issues in education in England, as one part of the UK – first in terms of recent historical developments since the 1990s, then in relation to new methods to enable accessing of research evidence, then new initiatives for using research, and finally describing new schemes to encourage the impact of research.

The UK has undergone considerable change in the last 10 years in its educational policies and in an interest in evidence-informed policy and practice. Many of these developments were stimulated by a New Labour government elected in 1997. In the Spring of 2010 a new Conservative–Liberal Democrat coalition was elected, which has embarked on its own radical reform agenda. It is not possible to describe all of these developments in this chapter. Discussion of some of the changes up to 2009 can be found in the country pages of the Strategic Forum for Research Evidence website[1]; more recent developments can be found in the education pages of the national media.

UK governance, population and education

The UK is made up of England, Scotland, Wales and Northern Ireland. It is a single democratic entity, yet contains four countries, and there are devolved national administrations with varying powers, policies and resources in Scotland, Wales and Northern Ireland. The UK is a member state of the European Union (EU). The UK has a population of 62 million, of whom about 20% are under the age of 16. The majority of the UK population lives in England, with approximately 5 million living in Scotland, 3 million in Wales and 1.7 million in Northern Ireland.

The UK population has increased by 8% over the last 20 years. In 2010 the working population was 38 million, made up of 23.8 million employees, 3.8 million self employed, 2.4 million unemployed and 8.2 million economically inactive.[2]

UK education

In 2009/10 there were 9.7 million full-time and part-time pupils in 33,137 schools. In 2008/09 there were 520,800 full-time qualified teachers in the UK. The average primary school had 228 pupils with a pupil–teacher ratio of 20:7. The average secondary school has 942 pupils with a pupil–teacher ratio of 15:3. Many other adults are employed as teaching assistants and other support staff.

At GCSE/NQ Standard Grade level, of pupils in their last year of compulsory schooling 68.7% gained five or more passes at grades A★ to C/1–3 (49.8% when this included English and Mathematics).

In 2008/09, 86% of 16-year-olds and 73% of 17-year-olds were in full-time post-compulsory education and government-supported training (GST), and 48.7% per cent of young people achieved two or more A level passes or equivalent.

The 2009 scores in the Programme for International Student Assessment (PISA) for England, Scotland and Northern Ireland were slightly above average for reading, average for mathematics, and above average for science. Wales scored significantly lower than the rest of the UK on all three measures (Bradshaw et al, 2010).[3]

England scored highly in the 2007 Trends in International Mathematics and Science Study (TIMSS), being outscored only by Asian Pacific Rim countries (Sturman et al, 2008).[4]

In 2008/09 there were 2.6 million (1.0 million part time) higher education students of whom 2 million were undergraduates and 542,500 were postgraduate students; 374,200 were overseas students. There were 127 universities, 37 other higher education institutions and 434 further education colleges (of which 93 were sixth form colleges). There were 117,000 full-time higher education academic staff and 60,000 full-time further education academic staff.

A total of 674,400 higher education qualifications were awarded in higher education institutions in the UK in 2008/09. Of these, 49.5% (333,700) were first degrees, 27.7% (186,900) were at Masters/other postgraduate level, 20.2% (136,100) were sub-degree qualifications and 2.6% (17,700) were PhDs or equivalent.

In England the main ministries responsible for education are the Department for Education (DfE) and the Department for Business, Innovation and Skills (BIS). The Scottish government has the Education Analytical Support Division (EASD) and a Director General for Education. The Welsh Assembly government (WAG) has a Department for Children, Education, Lifelong Learning and Skills (DCELLS). Northern Ireland has a Department of Education (DE) and a Department for Employment and Learning (DEL). The total expenditure on education and training in the UK for 2011/12 was £91.6 billion, which was 6% of GDP.

Education is a high-profile subject politically, with many changes of policy and funding, particularly in England. The previous Labour government made education a major area of policy and new initiatives. There was a focus, continued by the present coalition government, on not tolerating what were considered to be bad or failing schools. League tables were created to enable parents to make informed choices, although there have been concerns that this created perverse incentives of teaching to tests and thus an overemphasis on summative rather than formative assessment of students' work (Harlen, 2004). The DfE is accelerating the change of publicly funded schools from being maintained by the local authority (local government) to being academies established by sponsors from business, faith or voluntary groups working with partners from the local community. The academies are funded by and are accountable to central rather than local government. The coalition government has also created 'free schools'; this policy is a means to make it easier for parents and other groups to set up new academy schools. These changes also allow the private sector and profit making to have a greater role in the English education system.

As well as government concern about the quality of schools there has also been concern about the quality of teaching. There have also been major changes to initial teacher education with cash inducements to recruit new, highly qualified entrants to priority subjects, and special schemes such as Teach First, which provides for exceptional graduates to teach in challenging schools. The current government is also interested in increasing school-based teacher training rather than university-based training that scores highly on inspections but that the government fears to be too theoretical. Academies and free schools are also able to employ unqualified teachers.

In higher education, BIS has withdrawn the government subsidy paid to universities for UK and EU students so full-cost fees will be charged in England and Wales, supported by an expanded student loan system. In practice this is a doubling of fees paid by UK and EU students. Universities are concerned that student applications will fall, with consequent falls in their income. This is in addition to the fall in teacher training places arising from school-centred training of teachers.

University-based structures and research funding

Government infrastructure support for research by universities is allocated by Higher Education Funding Councils on the basis of quality assessments of previous research outputs in different discipline areas. The council for England (HEFCE) will distribute £1,558 million of such 'QR' funding in 20011/12. HEFCE will distribute £23 million of grants to 64 departments of education, with grants ranging from £1,000 to £6 million on the basis of the department's rating multiplied by the number of relevant included staff. This provides a major source of discretionary funding for universities (Evidence Ltd, 2005).

Some departments have no outputs judged to be of world-class standard while others have 35% of submitted outputs graded at that level. The QR system has been increasing the differential in funding between departments with high and low research gradings resulting in an increasing polarisation between research-intensive and research-limited departments (Pollard, 2006; Munn, 2008).

Size of academic department is also important. Some departments have only one or two active researchers, whereas the Institute of Education in London has approximately 200 academic researchers entered into the Research Assessment Exercise.

The DfE in England funds research directly to support its policy-making needs through commissioning specific studies and funding three research centres:

- Centre for Analysis of Youth Transitions (CAYT);
- Centre for Understanding Behaviour Change (CUBeC);
- Childhood Wellbeing Research Centre (CWRC).

In 2009/10 the Department for Children, Schools and Families (DCSF) – the precursor to the DfE formed on the election of the new coalition government in Spring 2010 – spent £13.3 million on research and analysis for research into education, children and families policy. It also invested in research centres, although they were more methodologically rather than topic based. There is an impression that DfE has significantly reduced its investment in research. A list of current projects dated November 2011 contained only three projects, with a total cost of £163,000, that had started in 2011.[5] On the other hand, the government has launched the £125 million Education Endowment Fund (EEF) to support and evaluate projects to raise the achievements of the most disadvantaged students in the most challenging schools and this will include funds for research as well as schooling provision. The government is using a similar strategy with early years by investing in an Early Intervention Foundation to provide advice and support to local commissioners on evidence and costs to assist them in choosing early intervention programmes. Overall, it is likely that there has been a reduction in the funding of educational research and thus also the number of education researchers working in universities and independent research organisations. This may be partly compensated for by increased applications from the UK for European Commission-funded research.

The UK government also funds research indirectly through the Economic and Social Research Council, which has an annual budget for research grants, studentships and knowledge transfer of approximately £180 million per year (ESRC, 2010). Education has to compete with other disciplines and has 8% success rate for research grant applications compared with 16% across social sciences (although this does not indicate the size of grants that are awarded).

The relatively low funding for research in education was made up for over recent years as a special government-funded initiative for research in education, the Teaching and Learning Research Programme (TLRP), funded over 100 specific projects and collaborative work and networking between 1999 and 2009. From 2007 to 2012 there was a further TLRP phase on technology enhanced learning (TEL).

Broader capacity issues

Most educational research in the UK is undertaken by universities, although there is a small but increasing number of private providers and the long-established charity, the National Foundation for Educational Research.

University academic staff in the discipline of education are estimated at 8,000 full-time equivalents (FTE). In 2007/08 nearly 40% were aged over 55, with under 10% aged below 35; 5% were non UK nationals (Munn, 2008; Mills, 2009; Oancea, 2009). Many of these staff do not have permanent positions or, even if technically permanent, do not have security of employment. There are many temporary lecturers and research officers supported by grant funding. EU legislation now requires employers to offer an open-ended contract to those who have been on a fixed-term contract for four years. In practice, however, staff with open-ended contracts are made redundant when grants end after that four-year period. The age profile of academics in education and the fixed-term nature of research posts may have long-term effects on research capacity in education (Fowler et al, undated). There also seems to be an increase in the amount of staff moving posts before government research assessment exercises as universities seek to recruit academics with strong research records to improve their institutional scores and therefore their research funding.

In the mid and late 1990s there were a number of critiques of educational research in the UK (Hargreaves, 1996; Hillage et al,1998; McIntyre and McIntyre, 1999) and a concern to increase capacity building in the sector. In the last 10 years there have been a number of initiatives to develop research capacity in education. By far the largest was the TLRP, which worked across the UK with a budget of well over £40 million.

In Scotland the Applied Educational Research Scheme (AERS) was funded at a cost of £2 million from 2004 to 2009 by the Scottish Funding Council and the Scottish government, to build collaborative research capacity across the seven universities in Scotland that provide initial teacher education, and to conduct research on the National Priorities in Education. AERS was a much smaller scheme than TLRP, with a budget of £2 million, although the scheme worked closely with the larger TLRP.

In Wales, in 2007, the Higher Education Funding Council (HEFCW), and the ESRC funded the Welsh Education Research Network (WERN). The Network aims to develop research capacity through collaborative partnerships with all the higher education institutions with education-related departments. One method has been to provide small bursaries to support cross-institution research grant applications. This network has been successful in building partnership between all higher education institutions in Wales to increase capacity in education research.

In Northern Ireland, again in 2007, the Department of Education (DE) commissioned a review of its monitoring, research and advice mechanisms, and the review recommended an education research forum (NIERF) be established to link the higher education institutions, the Education and Training Inspectorate (ETI) and both the DE and the Department of Employment and Learning (DEL) (Leitch, 2009).

A common feature of all these initiatives in the four countries of the UK was a concern to develop capacity through networking and collaboration rather than just specific research products.

Quality indicators

The main quality indicator for educational research is the previously mentioned research funding councils' assessment of quality for the distribution of QR infrastructure funding. This is essentially a peer review exercise with panels assessing the quality of the evidence submitted by university departments. Up until the last exercise in 2008 it was called the Research Assessment Exercise (RAE) but the next exercise in 2014 is to be called the Research Excellence Framework (REF). For the RAE, departments were rated for their research environment and all 'entered' staff submitted up to four research outputs (such as research papers) that were rated for excellence by a panel predominantly made up of other academics from the same discipline. The overall rating received by a department was multiplied by the number of staff entered so there was a tactical judgement to be made as to whether to maximise the overall grading or maximise the multiplier of number of staff submitted. The results for the 2008 RAE showed that the education panel rated on average 15% of outputs by 1,996 staff to be world class and a further 28% to be internationally excellent:

RAE 2008 education panel summary results for 1,996 staff

4★ Quality that is world leading in terms of originality, significance and rigour – 15%

3★ Quality that is internationally excellent – 28%

2★ Quality that is recognised internationally – 33%

1★ Quality that is recognised nationally – 19%

Unclassified Quality that falls below the standard of nationally recognised work – 5%

Many have criticised the RAE system for the crudeness of its approach and for increasing the number of academic papers published. However, the RAE does act as a powerful driver for universities to attend to the quality and quantity of academic outputs. The new REF system for 2008 is taking a similar model but is adding research impact (to research environment and research outputs) as an indicator of excellence, making up 20% of the grading, although this may increase to 25% in future

REFs. Impact will be assessed by expert review of case studies submitted. These may include any social, economic or cultural impact or benefit beyond academia and will be underpinned by research produced by the submitting institution.

Strategies and mechanisms for knowledge mobilisation

The UK uses many of the standard mechanisms for informing others of the outputs and relevance of academic research. These are largely focused at other academics through presentations at conferences, and publication of papers and books. This form of knowledge sharing is valued within academia and is often the basis for professional development and promotion. There is also growing awareness of more public dissemination of research with university press officers, media releases, and media training for academics. Pamphlets and brochures are also often produced to provide quality brand awareness to research funders and also to assist with student recruitment. All university departments of education have websites but these are often not very well developed and if there is any marketing initiative it tends to be focused on student recruitment rather than research findings. Some universities have knowledge transfer departments, although these tend to be focused at commercial exploitation of research with the private sector. This seems to occur predominantly in technological and biological sciences, even though there is a growing private sector provision in UK education.

There is also a demand-side aspect to research findings with policy makers, practitioners, and the media asking for research information. The most developed aspect of this is policy demands for research through asking for academic advice and through direct funding of research projects and research centres. Government departments in the UK employ research analyst professionals who both manage government research projects and also seek and interpret existing research findings.

Development of evidence-informed policy and practice

The change to a Labour party government in 1997 was followed by a White Paper on *Modernising Government* (White Paper, 1999) that emphasised the importance of evidence in developing public services and gave a central role to the Cabinet Office for social science research. In 2002, a Treasury Spending Review required evidence of the effectiveness of funded programmes. At the same time there was, as already mentioned, much criticism of educational research and the government commissioned a review of the direction, organisation, funding, quality and impact of educational research.

The review concluded that the relationship between research, policy and practice needed to be improved; that the research agenda was too supplier driven; and that with government-sponsored research there was too much emphasis on short-term evaluations at the expense of exploration and development of policy options (Hillage et al, 1998). Research that addressed issues relevant to policy and practice did not build sufficiently on previous knowledge and was too small scale to produce generalisable findings. The pressure on researchers to publish in academic journals limited the access of policy and practice to research findings. Hillage et al (1998) proposed that a more strategic approach be taken to planning research and synthesising and communicating evidence.

One response to the report was the setting up of the National Education Research Forum (NERF) in 1999 to develop a national strategy for research in education. In the first few years there was an intensive consultation and discussion phase, and from 2002 a focus on collaborative and developmental action to improve the quality and impact of educational research. NERF produced a number of working papers and proposed the development of some sort of knowledge centre structure to provide policy makers and practitioners with access to, and guidance on, educational research. NERF was set up as an independent body funded by government and closed when government terminated funding in 2006.[6]

Another response was the funding of a centre for evidence-informed policy and practice to develop capacity in the systematic reviewing of evidence in education in England from 2001 to 2009. This centre, the Evidence for Policy Practice Information and Co-ordinating Centre (EPPI-Centre), is based at the Institute of Education, University of London.

The interest in evidence-informed policy and practice in education was also a growing area of interest internationally. In 2002 the Centre for Educational Research and Innovation at OECD undertook a review of England's R&D system in education. The report made a number of recommendations but was broadly supportive of the government's aims and new initiatives in evidence-informed policy and practice (OECD, 2002).

At the same time as investing in evidence-informed education, the government was undertaking major reforms in the school system. A large section of the educational academic community saw their role as questioning and critiquing government; they saw the investments in evidence-informed policy as a means to exercise managerial control over research, limit its independence from government, and to prioritise a simplistic 'what works' research agenda and methodology (see, for example, Ball, 2001). There was clear resistance and hostility to some of the government investments including NERF. There was also limited engagement between the major investment in educational research of the TLRP programme and the evidence-informed policy and practice movement. The directors of TLRP did make very constructive use of the power of the combined research investment in engaging with policy and practice users, which showed some positive effects for uptake by practice but less so for policy, for all the common reasons such as turnover of policy staff and lack of fit between research focus and policy needs (Parsons and Burkey, 2011).

Overall, the Labour government put in place many of the component parts of an infrastructure for an evidence-informed policy and practice system in education. They created a strategic forum, capacity in systematic reviews, an overall increase in research funding, systems to enable teacher access to research resources and a general interest by government in using research in policy making. The system did not fully function. There may be several possible reasons for this. One reason may be that the separate components created by government were not sufficiently linked up. This may be partly because of some academic resistance and partly because the systems were so new and evolving. Another reason may be that a major necessary component of such a system – an evidence centre to help produce advice from research (suggested by both the Hillage report and by NERF) – was not fully enacted. The nearest the government came was the creation of the Centre for Excellence in Children's Outcomes funded by DfE for child welfare services. This includes user-generated research questions that are then addressed by academic semi-systematic reviews and the findings are then interpreted and communicated to practitioners at a local level. In other areas of social policy there are evidence centres (or intermediary organisations) such as the Social Care Institute for Excellence (SCIE) in social care and the National Institute for Clinical and Health Excellence (NICE) in health. A further possible reason that an evidence-informed system was not created for education was that most of the initiatives were in terms of the 'push' of production of research, rather than changing the organisational and individual professional drivers on the use of research. The involvement of users of research was largely limited to policy makers and teacher practitioners rather than a broader view of users of education in society, including students, parents, and specific groups. Think tanks were also not very involved, although some of these, such as the Institute for Public Policy Research and Centre Forum, have been very influential.

The new Conservative–Liberal Democrat coalition government that came into power in Spring 2010 has espoused an interest in educational research, but this has not been reflected by action. Although research councils and funding councils have had relatively modest cuts aimed at reducing the government financial deficit, direct research funding by government on education has largely been diverted to the Education Endowment Fund. In addition, the closure of some government agencies and a consolidation of government websites have meant that some research resources will no longer be updated. More worryingly, no government department has as yet agreed to partake in the new project of OECD's Centre for Educational Research and Innovation (CERI) on governing Complex Education Systems, which has two key elements of governance mechanisms and knowledge options. On the other hand, the National Endowment for Science, Technology and the Arts (NESTA), an independent but influential organisation close to government, has launched an initiative for the better use of evidence in decision making called an 'Alliance for Useful Evidence', with support from the ESRC. In addition, the DfE has indicated a new interest in experimental evidence from randomised controlled trials both through the creation of EEF (and other 'What Works' centres in other areas of social policy) and through commissioning a report in their favour by Ben Goldacre, a doctor and journalist, and critique of 'bad science'. The emphasis, however, is on the supply side of evidence rather than systems for the interpretation and application of that evidence.

The other big political influence has been the development of new ways of commissioning public services with an emphasis on local commissioners and on payment by results (PBR) rather than payment by activity (PBA). In a way, this is the ultimate test of evidence-informed policy and practice in terms of researchers being able to provide the evidence as to what services are most likely to be effective. However, debates will continue on the appropriate outcome measures for services in society.

New initiatives and resources for accessing evidence

In the last 10 years or so a number of new resources have become available to make research evidence more accessible. Some of these are briefly described in this section.

The UK government funded NFER to provide a free, online database of current education research called CERUK.[7] The database allows access to ongoing research rather than results of completed studies, which sometimes take considerable time to be published.

As already mentioned, the government funded capacity development in, and the production of, systematic reviews of evidence in education. This was achieved by funding review groups on various topics with training and quality assurance support by the EPPI-Centre[8] (Oakley et al, 2005). More recently there have been changes in the approaches used in systematic reviews, with greater acceptance of the complexity of many research issues. This has led to the broadening of systematic review methods to address all research questions rather than just efficacy and the incorporation of many forms of evidence to inform decision making (Gough, et al, 2012).

The Centre for the Use of Research and Evidence in Education (CUREE)[9] is an independent consultancy that supports evidence-informed educational practice. The aim is to help teachers make informed decisions about the most effective and efficient approaches to use in their own context. CUREE is commissioned by government agencies to support several evidence projects in education including research digests for practitioners. Another group, at the the DfE, produces research tools for teachers: Research Informed Practice Digests (TRIPS), Research Bites (summaries), and School Research News.[10]

The Training and Development Agency for Schools (TDA) produced the Teacher Training Resource Bank (TTRB), but the site is being archived by the new government.[11]

The General Teaching Council for England (GTCE) – with a timetable to be closed by the coalition government – provides on its website summaries of research findings and more detailed anthologies under the heading of Teaching and Learning Academy.[12]

The Institute for Effective Education[13] at the University of York work includes the conduct of systematic reviews of existing education research and runs the Best Evidence Encyclopaedia (the BEE) website to provide reliable, unbiased evidence on the effectiveness of educational programmes.

The UK Educational Evidence Portal (eep)[14] is a website that helps people find educational evidence from a range of reputable UK sources using a single search. The portal is run by a consortium of organisations with only limited core funding and no offices or ongoing staff. As evidence is so widely dispersed a group of organisations came together to create a central point of access to enable finding that evidence. This is being taken further by the EIPPPE capacity building project (discussed later) which is building search mechanisms similar to eep for accessing educational research in Europe.

New initiatives for use of research

A recent survey of activities in Europe linking research with policy making in education identified 76 such activities in the UK. The survey was not exhaustive but provides some information on the range of activities being used to enable evidence use. It also shows that this is a very active area of work in the UK (Gough et al, 2011). Some of these activities are focused on making research available for non-academic users of research (as discussed in the previous section) but others are concerned with mediation and use.

One long-standing initiative is the National Teacher Research Panel (NTRP),[15] which arises from a partnership between DfE, GTCE and National College for the Leadership of Schools and Children's Services and the Learning and Skills Improvement Service. The NTRP is an independent group of about 15 practising teachers and tutors who work towards ensuring that research is given a high role in decision making by all parties in education, that all research takes account of the practitioner perspective, and that there is an increased number of teachers and tutors engaged in, and with, the full spectrum of research activity.

The Coalition for Evidence-based Education (CEBE)[16] is an alliance of researchers, policy makers and practitioners who are interested in improving the way research evidence is used, and exchanged, across the sector. The aim is to bring together many of those working towards evidence-informed education to work towards the same shared goal and to increase the coherence across different elements of this evidence-using system. The two main paths of action are to encourage strategic collaboration between existing bodies and initiatives and to develop practical initiatives to identify, and fill, gaps in the current infrastructure. Current projects are aimed at: (i) increasing the use of evidence by the media; (ii) supporting the use of evidence by practitioners; and (iii) exploring developments of the use of evidence in policy making.

The Strategic Forum for Research in Education (SFRE) was an initiative led by the British Educational Research Association (BERA) and the Economic and Social Research Council (ESRC), with funding being provided by BERA, ESRC, DCSF (now DfE) and the educational charity CfBT. The SFRE supported multiple stakeholders in all four countries of the UK and many educational sectors in reflecting on how countries in the UK can improve the creation, mediation and application of evidence about education. In its final project report (Pollard and Oancea, 2010) SFRE structured its recommendations around the six elements in the development and mobilisation of knowledge in education:

1. *origination and planning* – including the conditions and provision for the facilitation and prioritisation of research activity;
2. *creation and production* – focusing on both the initiation and carrying out of projects in respect of each major type of research;
3. *assessment and validation* – including peer judgement, user and beneficiary validation and the processes, criteria and indicators specific to each assessment context and type of research;
4. *collection and interpretation* – concerning issues such as the processing of new knowledge in libraries and databases, empirical review and theoretical synthesis;
5. *mediation and brokerage* – addressing the multifaceted promotional and communication strategies that enable the supply of and demand for evidence to be bridged;
6. *use and impact* – considering the ways in which knowledge is used, scaled up and takes effect within policy and practice.

SFRE was led by the Director of TLRP and was in some senses a spin-off of TLRP. It could also be seen as covering some of the issues of the earlier NERF, although it was led more from the educational research community than by the ministry and so was less contentious for educational researchers.

Finally, the European Commission Directorate for Education and Culture has been encouraging evidence-informed policy and practice through publications and funding capacity building projects. Two recent projects have been led by the EPPI-Centre in the UK.[17] One aspect of the projects has been to identify practices linking research to use in education across Europe. The projects have adapted Levin's (2004) model on evidence use and have classified activities according to the mechanism by which they link research to use (Gough et al, 2011).

NERF and SFRE, for example, are classified as system level approaches (see **Figure 4.1**).

Figure 4.1: Evidence-informed policy and practice systems

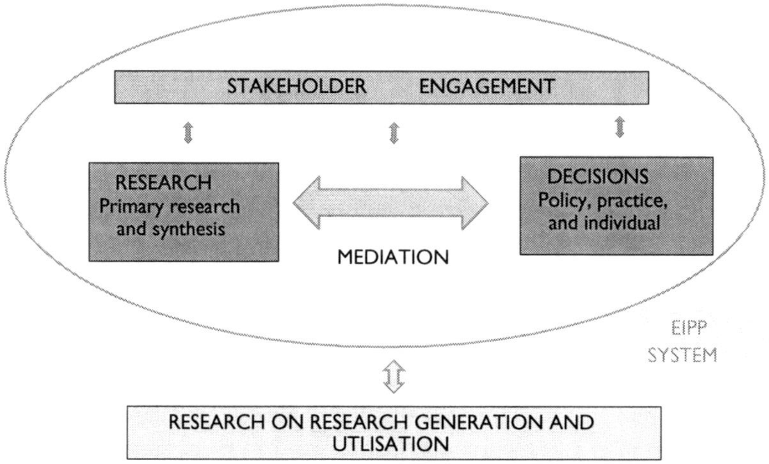

Source: Gough et al (2012).

Another aspect of the project has been to identify research on research generation and utilisation. Surprisingly, there is virtually none. There is research in disciplines other than education in Europe and research on education outside Europe, but very little research on education within Europe. The UK is fortunate to have the Research Utilisation Research Unit in Scotland, but the focus of their work is not primarily on education. The UK is also the base for the journal *Evidence and Policy*,[18] which is one of the few journals that examines evidence use.

Encouraging impact

Another aspect of evidence-informed policy and practice is the increased concern of government that research has impact. This is partly driven by a concern that research evidence should not stay in universities but benefit the wider society, including commercial development of research. Reference has already been made to the introduction by funding councils of impact as a measure in the REF exercise to determine infrastructure funding to universities for research. Although the new focus of the REF on impact is welcome, there has been little work to specify the meaning of impact and how the enlightenment effects of research can be measured to prove that this impact has been achieved, so justifying a high REF score and thus more QR resources from government (Weiss, 1977; Oancea, 2011).

HEFCE, which manages the REF, has also initiated the Higher Education Innovation Funding (HEIF) to encourage universities and colleges to engage in knowledge exchange activities. Universities receive an annual grant calculated by a formula related to institution size. The funds must be spent on knowledge exchange activities (detailed in each university's institutional strategy for knowledge exchange), but this can include infrastructure for coordinating research as well as more outward-facing activities such as strategies for public engagement in research.[19] This is reflected in a slowly increasing growth of knowledge activities by universities, such as the employment of knowledge brokers, the opening of knowledge offices and the use of social media to draw attention to university news.

Research Councils UK and its constituent government-funded research councils have also developed new policies and funding streams to encourage this. Holders of ESRC research grants, for example, are under much stricter rules to have dissemination plans and to submit details of research outputs onto the ESRC's online database. ESRC also has a raft of impact support schemes, including informing public policy, policy placements, policy fellowships, student policy placements, and follow-on funding to communicate research findings. The research councils label such schemes as evidence for public policy in that they aim to encourage the use of the research and knowledge to inform and improve public policy and services. The ESRC has also been a partner in several of the more recent developments such as the Alliance for Useful Evidence and the creation of new 'What works' centres in several areas of social policy.

Conclusion

The UK has undergone major political changes since the election of a Labour government in 1997, including a radical education reform agenda, and is now subject to a new set of radical policies from the Conservative–Liberal Democrat government elected in 2010. Education reform continues to be a major policy priority. Although many politicians speak of the important of evidence in policy making, the political agenda for their new policies is very strong and so may not be so amenable to contrary evidence. Despite this, the Labour government did invest in many structures and processes to develop capacity for evidence-informed policy and practice. The UK still has very many initiatives and energy to further develop this area of work.

One of the biggest changes over the last decade has been a general increase in awareness of the role of evidence. There are many discussions about science and evidence in the media, and it is not unusual for news reporters to ask those arguing for certain policy changes – including academics reporting research results – to be asked about the broader research knowledge. A current unknown is the effect that changes in the organisation and commissioning of educational services and of PBR policies in health and social care will influence research and research use in education.

The policies of HEFCE and the Research Councils on research impact are also likely to lead over time to major changes in the management of research evidence. Their funding of activities to increase the use of research and the requirements for impact in research grant funding represent a major development of government policy in the use of research evidence (even if this is not reflected in the support of other policies or infrastructure for the use of evidence in society).

One area of concern is what knowledge is being mobilised. It is often information from individual research studies rather than a considered synthesis of all that is known conceptually and empirically on a topic. Education as an academic and policy and practice arena is very different from the integrated system of health research in the UK – where there is policy and infrastructure to link primary research, reviews of research, stakeholder-engaged guidance from research and the interpretation and implementation of that guidance.

Notes

[1] http://www.sfre.ac.uk

[2] Much of the data reported here is available in DfE (2011) and in national statistics available at: http://www.statistics.gov.uk

[3] See reports at http://www.nfer.ac.uk/research/projects/oecd-programme-for-international-student-assessment-oecd-pisa/

[4] See reports at http://www.nfer.ac.uk/nfer/research/projects/trends-in-international-mathematics-and-science-study-timss/timss_home.cfm

[5] See http://media.education.gov.uk/assets/files/pdf/d/dfe%20current%20research%20projects%20-%202%20november%202011.pdf (accessed 30 January 2012)

[6] NERF papers are accessible on the UK Educational Evidence Portal (eep) website at *www.eep.ac.uk*

[7] http://www.ceruk.ac.uk

[8] http://eppi.ioe.ac.uk

[9] http://www.curee-paccts.com/

[10] http://www.education.gov.uk/schools/toolsandinitiatives/ tripsresearchdigests

[11] http://www.tda.gov.uk/support-staff/support-tools/teacher-development-hub.aspx

[12] http://www.gtce.org.uk/tla/rft

[13] http://www.york.ac.uk/iee

[14] http://www.eep.ac.uk

[15] http://www.ntrp.org.uk/

[16] http://www.cebenetwork.org

[17] http://www.eippee.eu

[18] http://www.policypress.co.uk/journals_eap.asp

[19] http://www.publicengagement.ac.uk/

References

Ball, S. J. (2001) '"You've been NERFed!" Dumbing down the academy: National Educational Research Forum:"a national strategy? consultation paper": a brief and bilious response', *Journal of Education Policy*, vol 16, no 3, pp 265–8.

Bradshaw, J., Ager, R., Burge, B. and Wheater, R. (2010) *PISA 2009: achievement of 15-year-olds in England,* Slough: NFER.

DfE (2011) *Education and training statistics for the United Kingdom 2010,* Reference ID:V01/2011. London: Department for Education.

ESRC (2010) *The Economic and Social Research Council annual report and accounts for 2009–2010,* Swindon: ESRC.

Evidence Ltd (2005) *Impact of selective funding of research in England, and the specific outcomes of HEFCE research funding: a desk-based review for HEFCE and the Department for Education and Skills,* Leeds: Evidence Ltd (available at https://www.education.gov.uk/publications/ eOrderingDownload/RW47.pdf).

Fowler, Z., Baird, A., Baron, S., Davies, S.M.B., Procter, R. and Salisbury, J. (undated) *Building research capacity in education: evidence from recent initiatives in England, Scotland and Wales* (available at www.dspace.cam. ac.uk/bitstream/1810/224926/1/3512.pdf).

Gough, D., Oliver, S. and Thomas, J. (2012) *An introduction to systematic reviews,* London: Sage.

Gough, D., Tripney, J., Kenny, C. and Buk-Berge., E. (2011) *Evidence informed policy in education in Europe: EIPEE final project report,* London: EPPI-Centre, Social Science Research Unit, Institute of Education, University of London.

Hargreaves, D.H. (1996) *Teaching as a research based profession: possibilities and prospects*, London: Teacher Training Agency (available at http://eppi.ioe.ac.uk/cms/Portals/0/PDF%20reviews%20and%20summaries/TTA%20Hargreaves%20lecture.pdf).

Harlen, W. (2004) 'A systematic review of the evidence of reliability and validity of assessment by teachers used for summative purposes', in *Research evidence in education library*, London: EPPI-Centre, Social Science Research Unit, Institute of Education, University of London (available at http://eppi.ioe.ac.uk/cms/Default.aspx?tabid=119).

Hillage, J., Pearson, R., Anderson, A. and Tamkin. P. (1998) *Excellence in research on schools*, Research report no 74, London: DfEE, pp x–xiv.

Leitch, R. (2009) 'Research capacity-building from a Northern Ireland perspective', in *Capacity building evaluations, initiatives and obstacles across the UK: reflections from England, Scotland, Wales and Northern Ireland*, Discussion paper 1 presented to the American Education Research Association Conference, San Diego, CA, 13-17 April.

Levin, B. (2004) 'Making research matter more', *Education Policy Analysis Archives*, vol 12, no 56, pp 1-20.

McIntyre, D. and McIntyre, D. (1999) *Capacity for research into teaching and learning*, (retrieved from http://www.tlrp.org/dspace/handle/123456789/330).

Mills, D. (2009) 'Scientising the social sciences? Demographics and the research economy', *Research Intelligence*, vol 108, p 13.

Munn, P. (2008) 'Building research capacity collaboratively: can we take ownership of our future?', *British Educational Research Journal*, vol 34, no 4, pp 413-31.

Oakley, A., Gough, D. A., Oliver, S. and Thomas, J. (2005) 'The politics of evidence and methodology: lessons from the EPPI-Centre', *Evidence and Policy*, vol 1, no 1, pp 5-32.

Oancea, A. (2009) 'Fixed-term employment in research: questions and experiences', *Research Intelligence*, vol 108, p 11.

Oancea, A. (2011) *Interpretations and practices of research impact across the range of Disciplines*, Final report, Oxford University.

OECD (Organization for Economic and Co-operation and Development) (2002) *Educational research and development in England: examiners' report*, CERI/CD, vol 10, Paris: OECD.

Parsons, D.J. and Burkey, S. (2011) *Evaluation of the Teaching and Learning Research Programme (second phase)*, Final Report of the Second Phase Review for the Economic and Social Research Council, Horsham: Host.

Pollard, A. (2006) 'Challenges facing educational research: Educational Review Guest Lecture 2005', *Educational Review*, vol 58, no 3, pp 251-67.

Pollard, A. and Oancea, A. (2010) *Unlocking learning? Towards evidence-informed policy and practice in education*, report of the UK Strategic Forum for Research in Education, 2008–2010, SFRE: London (available at www.sfre.ac.uk).

Sturman, L., Ruddock, G., Burge, B., Styles, B., Lin, Y. and Vappula, H. (2008) *England's achievement in TIMSS 2007: national report for England*, Slough: NFER.

Weiss, C. (1977) 'Research for policy's sake: the enlightenment function of social research', *Policy Analysis*, vol 3, no 4, pp 531-45.

White Paper (1999) *Modernising government*, Cm 4310, London: The Stationery Office.

FIVE

Knowledge mobilisation in Australian education research

John Polesel, Professor of Education, Melbourne Graduate School of Education, University of Melbourne

Acknowledgement

The assistance of Michael McBain, Kevin Yang and Clare O'Hanlon from the Melbourne Graduate School of Education (MGSE) in supplying data, setting up and implementing the online survey and conducting an internet search of knowledge mobilisation activities is gratefully acknowledged.

Introduction

This chapter examines the role of the objective of knowledge mobilisation – framed in much of the Australian literature in terms of 'engagement' and 'dialogue' – in Australian education faculties and the research activities they manage. It is based on a review of the relevant, though scarce, Australian literature, administrative data relating to the funding of education research through the Australian Research Council (ARC) competitive grants scheme, a search and analysis of the websites of all education faculties in Australian higher education institutions and data collected by a survey targeting research managers and associate deans (or equivalent) of research in faculties or schools of education in Australia.

It begins by describing the Australian higher education context and considering how knowledge mobilisation is conceptualised and discussed in the Australian policy environment and literature.

Overview of Australia

Australia may be described as a competitive, advanced market economy, which has weathered the recent global financial crisis relatively well. It has an unemployment rate of approximately 5% at the time of writing. It is a federal parliamentary democracy, consisting of six states and two territories, with the Australian Capital Territory accommodating Australia's capital city, Canberra.

Australia has a population of just less than 23 million people, living in the world's sixth largest country, in terms of land mass. This population is concentrated along the eastern and south-eastern coasts, with much of the inland area uninhabited. Nearly nine in 10 Australians live in urban environments. Australia has a relatively low birth rate (12.33 births/1,000) but a high net migration rate of approximately 6/1,000 migrants.

Australian higher education

The higher education sector in Australia consists of:

- 39 universities, of which 37 are public institutions and two are private;
- one Australian branch of an overseas university;
- three other self-accrediting higher education institutions; and
- non-self-accrediting higher education providers accredited by State and Territory authorities, numbering more than 150 as listed on State and Territory registers. These include several that are registered in more than one State and Territory. (DEEWR, 2011)

The Australian government (rather than the individual states and territories) has the main responsibility for funding higher education. It does so through the Department of Education, Employment and Workplace Relations (DEEWR), although the regulation and governance of higher education is shared with the states and territories and the institutions.

Australian government funding is provided through:

- The Commonwealth Grant Scheme, which provides for a specified number of Commonwealth Supported places each year;
- The Higher Education Loan Programme (HELP) arrangements providing financial assistance to students;
- The Commonwealth Scholarships; and
- A range of grants for specific purposes including quality, learning and teaching, research and research training programmes. (DEEWR, 2011)

In addition, students in Australian higher education institutions pay fees, although most only pay part of the cost of tuition, with the remainder paid by the Australian government through the schemes outlined above. Students may also defer payment of fees through a loan, which is repaid upon attaining an income threshold. Some courses are full fee-paying (that is, not Commonwealth supported) and receive no other direct government contribution towards their cost. Students may also receive subsidised loans from the Commonwealth government. International students are generally charged full fees for their studies in Australia.

A recent major review of the Australian higher education system (Bradley, 2008) found that, while the system had significant strengths, it also faced major challenges. These included declines in performance and investment in higher education, relative to other OECD countries. With respect to research specifically, the review found that government funding of research in universities fell 'significantly below the real costs' (Bradley, 2008, p xii), with unacceptable high levels of cross-subsidisation of research from teaching funds generated from domestic and international students and low funding for research infrastructure relative to funding provided through competitive grants. Lack of funding was also linked to predicted shortages of researchers in the future. The review made various recommendations relating to research, including major increases in infrastructure funding, increased Research Training Scheme places, increased funding for postgraduate awards and stronger support for international research students (including through scholarships). These findings and recommendations showed a concern that research be funded in a manner that reflected its true costs.

Views of knowledge mobilisation in Australia

The term 'knowledge mobilisation' is relatively unknown in the Australian context. Typically, 'knowledge transfer', 'knowledge exchange', 'knowledge utilisation and engagement' are the terms used for activities relating to the utilisation of knowledge outside teaching and research. A recent study by Wallis (2006) provides another related term – 'engaged scholarship'. This same source provides a useful definition framed around the concept of engagement as 'knowledge generation, use, application and exploitation outside academic environments' (Wallis, 2006).

Overall, the findings from a survey of the Australian literature on knowledge mobilisation and education research point to the importance of greater engagement with local learning communities (Selkrig et al, 2009), the need for academics to be involved in educational change and innovation (Ward et al, 2010) and greater collaboration between nations in global industry networks (Gardner, 2008), including the Asia Pacific region. There is a view that this kind of collaboration is needed in order to strengthen the research–policy nexus and improve educational policy making and practice across the macro-region (Keeves et al, 2003).

The broader Australian literature on knowledge mobilisation (not specifically related to education) also provides some useful theoretical and conceptual background. Harman (2001), for example, provides a balanced analysis of both the benefits and potential dangers of 'industry links and university commercialisation'. He argues that such links can provide a range of benefits, including the opportunity to apply the findings of theoretical research to practical problems and additional resources for research and the training of research students. On the other hand, he warns of the potential threat to researchers' autonomy and scientific freedom. Significantly, he argues that links with industry partners do not generally compromise academic independence and that the benefits of these links (especially increased funding) outweigh potential disadvantages, overall.

The other main theme to emerge in the Australian literature is the need for effective knowledge management in the structures, activities and processes used in universities (Blackman and Kennedy, 2009; Davison, 2009). The need for better management of knowledge mobilisation has been reflected in the findings of various international studies over time, for example Huberman and Levinson (1984), Amaratunga and Senaratne (2009) and Becheikh et al (2010), all of which argue the need for more effective linkages and processes between researchers and policy actors. Becheikh et al (2010) focus specifically on the need for 'linkage agents' (brokers) who can play a role in facilitating cooperation between researchers and the users of research. They go on to propose a framework for considering the role of these intermediary actors, which matches researchers and users of research and is able to identify and link specific kinds of knowledge with specific policy and practice contexts.

Outside the literature, it is evident that the term 'knowledge mobilisation' is rarely used in the Australian policy environment. This chapter will argue that, while education research plays an important role in Australian universities, there is considerable variation in the discourse relating to the concepts underpinning knowledge mobilisation and how they are applied in the governance and conduct of education research in Australia.

Knowledge mobilisation, for example, may be said to occupy a central place among the five key objectives of the Australian Research Council (ARC), which funds researchers and research training by means of a grants scheme that operates through a competitive peer review process. The three key objectives, as set out in the ARC's strategic plan published in 2012, are:

1: *RESEARCH*
To support excellence in research through funding for research and research training allocated through national competition across all disciplines supported by rigorous peer review processes.

2: *CAPACITY*
To build Australia's research capacity through support for the training and careers of researchers, critical research infrastructure and research in areas of national need.

3: *POLICY AND EVALUATION*
To provide informed high quality policy advice to Government and enhance research outcomes through effective evaluation by participation in policy forums and Government reviews, informed stakeholder consultations, evaluation and ongoing monitoring of performance. (ARC, 2012)

Of these, the third key objective – Policy and Evaluation – relates to the translation of research into policy advice and lists as its main policy development strategies:

3.1 Ensure policy advice is evidence-based, innovative and strategic
3.2 Monitor best practice international trends in research policy
3.3 Monitor and evaluate ARC research funding schemes to maximise their effectiveness
3.4 Review and monitor strategic areas to ensure the most effective allocation of resources
3.5 Engage with government, industry, research institutions, researchers and learned academies
3.6 Maintain dialogue with other funding agencies in Australia and internationally. (ARC, 2012)

These strategies suggest a two-way exchange of the knowledge generated through research, an exchange that explicitly includes dialogue and engagement, even though the term 'knowledge' is not used and even though the terms of this engagement and the identity of the policy actors are not defined.

With respect to quality, the systems currently in operation do not refer directly to knowledge mobilisation. Rather, they seem to focus on the issues of teaching and learning and the quality of universities as learning organisations. At the time of writing, the Tertiary Education and Quality Standards Agency (TEQSA) is the body that regulates and assures the quality of Australian higher education. Its mission is as follows:

> TEQSA registers and assesses the performance of higher education providers against the Higher Education Standards Framework. The Standards Framework comprises five domains: Provider Standards, Qualification Standards, Teaching and Learning Standards, Information Standards and Research Standards. The Provider Standards and Qualifications Standards are collectively the Threshold Standards, which all providers must meet in order to enter and remain within Australia's higher education system. (TEQSA, 2012)

Since January 2012, TEQSA has had the task of regulating university and non-university higher education providers. Its primary task is to ensure a high quality of education for students, rather than the monitoring of the practices or outcomes of research. An analysis of its role and functions reveals no reference to knowledge mobilisation (TEQSA, 2012).

Data relating to the outcomes of research are similarly difficult to locate, although a recent policy report released by the Group of Eight (eight of the oldest, most established and research-intensive universities in Australia) provided evidence of a concentration of research funding in these eight universities (Go8, 2012), accompanied by evidence that the major part of research activity classified as above world average was also concentrated in these universities. It cited further evidence that the commercialisation of research, as measured by invention disclosures, was also concentrated in this small group of institutions. Using this as an indicator (though limited and imperfect) of knowledge mobilisation, this suggests that the effective use of research findings in Australia, as well as the funding of research itself, may be concentrated in a relatively small number of elite institutions. The policy paper uses these findings to argue for a further concentration of resources in these institutions in order to ensure concentration of effort in those 'institutions which provide the best research environment' (Go8, 2012, p 12).

Methodology

The research underpinning this chapter consists of three main components. The first is an analysis of data compiled by the Melbourne Education Research Institute at the University of Melbourne. These data include research quantum generated through ARC grants during the period 2003–08. The second is an examination and analysis of the websites of faculties and schools of education in Australian universities, conducted in July 2010. The third is an electronic survey of research leaders and research managers in these faculties and schools, conducted in October 2010.

A total of 25 universities were identified as having faculties and schools with education programmes. These were targeted in both the website scan and the electronic survey. The website scan utilised a selection of terms identified by Sá et al. (2010) to examine research structures, processes and capacity, and to search for references to knowledge mobilisation. These terms included 'knowledge brokering', 'knowledge exchange', 'knowledge management', 'knowledge transfer', 'knowledge translation', 'knowledge utilisation' and 'knowledge to action'. More broadly, it included all references to research management. The electronic survey sought more specifically to identify attitudes and practices relating to research management and the utilisation of research in Australian universities. This electronic survey generated 12 usable responses.

Current state of university-based research in education

In Australia's federal system of governance, higher education is regulated by the Commonwealth government. However, systems of schooling and most aspects of vocational education and training are regulated by the individual states, as in other federal systems, such as the US, for example. Having noted this, the individual jurisdictions are more notable for the similarities of their educational governance structures, curricula and qualification frameworks than for their differences.

The funding of education research reflects this federal division of responsibilities. In Australia, the main funder of education research at the national level is the Commonwealth government, through the agencies of the Australian Research Council, the Ministerial Council on Education, Training and Youth Affairs (MCEETYA) and the National Centre for Vocational and Educational Research (NCVER). Of these, the ARC stands out, as it is the main source of university research funding other than health and medical funding, which is covered by a separate Commonwealth research funding organisation, the National Health and Medical Research Council (NHMRC).

At the state and territory level, educational research is also commissioned and funded by state government education departments, by the state Catholic Education Commissions, which administer Catholic schools, and by individual private providers of education, including independent schools and registered training organisations. Research may also be funded from 'internal' university sources, such as early career researcher grants or seeding grants designed to provide the impetus for academics to prepare a fully-fledged external research application.

The quantum (numbers of projects and amounts of funding) of the research commissioned is difficult to report accurately, as different state systems and conventions of reporting mitigate against consistency. The commercially sensitive nature of funding information relating to competitive grants also contributed to some reluctance among the respondents to the electronic survey in this study to disclose fully information relating to research income. However, publicly available data from national sources allows us to consider at least the quantum of research funded by the major source of university research funding – the ARC.

The ARC funds two main types of programmes – Discovery Grants and Linkage Grants. Discovery programmes are defined as 'fundamental research (sometimes called discovery, basic or blue sky research)', while Linkage Projects are 'collaborative research and development projects between higher education organisations and other organisations, including industry, to enable the application of advanced knowledge to problems'. Industry here may include government departments and other non-profit agencies.

Funding quantum relating specifically to research in education under these two programmes is reported in the following tables, which outline the number of grants for educational research funded each year from 2003 to 2008, the total yearly funding for educational research and what proportion of the overall funding within each scheme is educational research.

Two main issues arise from the data reported in **Tables 5.1** and **5.2**. First, education-related research forms a relatively minor part of the overall ARC budget – just 1.44% of all discovery grant funding (**Table 5.1**) over the period and 4.05% of all linkage grant funding over the period (**Table 5.2**). By contrast, the field of Engineering and Technology attracted 16.97% of all ARC discovery research funding and 22.36% of all ARC linkage funding over the same period. Moreover, as already noted, these figures exclude medical research, which is funded under a different scheme by the NHMRC.

Table 5.1: ARC discovery funding for education, 2003 to 2008

Year	Number of grants	Funding (AUS$)	Funding (% of total discovery funding)
2003	24	4,243,500	1.84
2004	15	2,297,000	0.97
2005	21	4,448,000	1.49
2006	20	3,966,683	1.45
2007	14	2,987,467	1.09
2008	21	5,179,979	1.76
Total	**115**	**23,122,629**	**1.44**

Source: Melbourne Education Research Institute data compilation

Table 5.2: ARC linkage funding for education, 2003 to 2008

Year	Number of grants	Funding (AUS$)	Funding (% of total linkage funding)
2003	29	4,673,748	4.65
2004	24	4,548,058	3.95
2005	22	4,570,927	4.10
2006	24	5,414,821	4.90
2007	21	4,714,569	3.94
2008	17	3,767,529	2.99
Total	**137**	**27,689,652**	**4.05**

Source: Melbourne Education Research Institute

Second, linkage grant funding was greater than discovery grant funding in the field of education, both in simple monetary value (AUS$27.69m, compared with AUS$23.12m) and as a proportion of all funding provided by the respective schemes (4.05%, compared with 1.44%). Given that Linkage Grants require industry or government partners and are more applied and collaborative in terms of research design and outcomes, it might be surmised that there is a greater demand for research that can be informed and utilised by non–university participants than for research that is more theoretical and is wholly conceptualised, designed and controlled by universities. This is not to argue that ARC discovery grant funding is limited to theoretical research, but rather to locate its origins relative to research conceptualised in cooperation with industry or user partners.

Table 5.3 reports ARC discovery grant funding in education by university. Of the 39 universities in Australia, the 25 listed above were allocated ARC discovery grant funding to conduct educational research during the period specified. The table shows that, of the 25 listed, five attracted well over 50% of funding allocated to educational research in this period. The same five attracted just over 50% of all the grants allocated. This is indicative of a considerable concentration of research, as these projects were conducted by a relatively small number of researchers in a relatively small number of institutions.

This is borne out by data reported in **Table 5.4**, although the concentration of effort with respect to the awarding of ARC Linkage Grants is not quite as great as that found in ARC Discovery Grants. In this case, a greater number of universities have been funded to carry out research – 32 of the 39. Moreover, 50% of the grants and a similar proportion of the overall funding are allocated across eight institutions instead of five. Nevertheless, a small number of institutions continue to attract a relatively large proportion of the national education research budget, and the same seven universities are ranked in the top seven places for both discovery and linkage funding over the specified period.

While four of the universities that are ranked in the top 10 for ARC research funding are Go8 institutions, the remainders are not, suggesting that educational research funding may be spread across a greater range of institutions than research funding more generally. It might be noted that the argument of the Go8 universities (noted earlier in this chapter) that research effort should be concentrated in those eight universities with the strongest research environments may not be applicable in the field of educational research, given the greater range of institutions engaging in this field.

Data on sources of funding were also collected as part of the electronic survey of research leaders in education schools and faculties, conducted in October 2010. It should be noted that the survey generated responses from only 12 respondents, although these included most of the larger

Table 5.3: ARC discovery funding for education, 2003 to 2008, by university

University	Number of grants	% of grants	Funding (AUS$)	Funding (% of total discovery funding)
The University of Melbourne	13	12.04	3,017,468	13.63
Queensland University of Technology	12	11.11	2,764,000	12.48
Monash University	11	10.19	2,440,000	11.02
The University of Queensland	11	10.19	1,930,683	8.72
The University of Sydney	8	7.41	1,581,182	7.14
Curtin University of Technology	6	5.56	1,215,000	5.49
University of Western Sydney	3	2.78	1,140,000	5.15
Griffith University	5	4.63	1,082,000	4.89
Deakin University	4	3.70	947,000	4.28
The University of Newcastle	4	3.70	695,600	3.14
RMIT University	5	4.63	686,500	3.10
Charles Sturt University	3	2.78	640,196	2.89
University of Wollongong	3	2.78	635,500	2.87
The University of Western Australia	3	2.78	562,000	2.54
The University of New England	3	2.78	475,000	2.15
Murdoch University	3	2.78	376,000	1.70
University of Technology Sydney	2	1.85	345,000	1.56
La Trobe University	2	1.85	310,000	1.4
Macquarie University	1	0.93	270,000	1.22
University of Tasmania	1	0.93	255,000	1.15
Edith Cowan University	1	0.93	225,000	1.02
University of Ballarat	1	0.93	200,000	0.90
Central Queensland University	1	0.93	150,000	0.68
University of the Sunshine Coast	1	0.93	150,000	0.68
University of South Australia	1	0.93	50,000	0.23
Total	**108**	**100.00**	**22,143,129**	**100.00**

Source: Melbourne Education Research Institute data compilation

Table 5.4: ARC linkage funding for education, 2003 to 2008, by university

University	Number of grants	% of grants	Funding (AUS$)	Funding (% of total linkage funding)
The University of Melbourne	13	9.49	2,686,074	9.70
University of Western Sydney	12	8.76	2,390,375	8.63
Queensland University of Technology	11	8.03	2,302,280	8.31
The University of Sydney	8	5.84	2,193,755	7.92
Curtin University of Technology	8	5.84	1,996,000	7.21
The University of Queensland	7	5.11	1,498,205	5.41
Monash University	8	5.84	1,395,980	5.04
Griffith University	7	5.11	1,302,850	4.71
Edith Cowan University	5	3.65	1,209,715	4.37
University of South Australia	5	3.65	1,087,822	3.93
University of Tasmania	4	2.92	1,073,776	3.88
RMIT University	3	2.19	878,000	3.17
Deakin University	5	3.65	813,124	2.94
The University of New England	4	2.92	703,764	2.54
University of Technology Sydney	4	2.92	625,000	2.26
La Trobe University	3	2.19	572,000	2.07
The University of Newcastle	1	0.73	550,000	1.99
Australian Catholic University	2	1.46	541,126	1.95
Charles Sturt University	4	2.92	492,882	1.78
Murdoch University	2	1.46	488,446	1.76
The University of Western Australia	1	0.73	390,000	1.41
University of Wollongong	3	2.19	384,100	1.39
Charles Darwin University	2	1.46	382,000	1.38
University of Southern Queensland	2	1.46	358,718	1.30
Southern Cross University	2	1.46	345,000	1.25
James Cook University	3	2.19	256,696	0.93
The Australian National University	2	1.46	222,414	0.80
The Flinders University of South Australia	1	0.73	198,000	0.72
Macquarie University	2	1.46	143,468	0.52
Central Queensland University	1	0.73	113,000	0.41
University of Ballarat	1	0.73	69,100	0.25
The University of New South Wales	1	0.73	25,982	0.09
Total	**137**	**100.00**	**27,689,652**	**100.00**

Source: Melbourne Education Research Institute data compilation

education faculties and schools. Furthermore, respondents were, for the most part, reluctant or unable to specify funding quantum, and many questions regarding funding were not answered.

However, a question seeking information regarding the main sources of funding for educational research generated eight responses from institutions, including the major education faculties. The responses to this item, reported in **Figure 5.1**, indicate that the ARC, internal university funds and state education departments were the most commonly cited sources for funding educational research in these universities. These were followed by the state Catholic Education Commissions, the NCVER, individual schools and non-education state government departments (for example, health, regional development and industry departments). In the category of 'other', one university added 'the Association of Independent Schools', an umbrella organisation that acts as an advocacy body for independent schools, and another added 'Private organisations'.

Figure 5.1: Number of times main sources of funding for education research were nominated by surveyed institutions

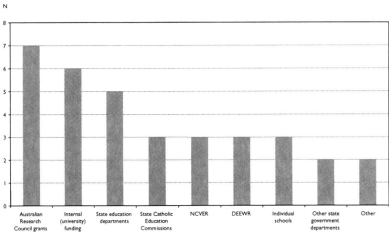

The survey also provided information on the proportion of funding obtained from each source within each university. This varied considerably from institution to institution. For example, ARC funding accounted for 60% of the education research funding in one of the universities surveyed and 0% in another. Similarly, state education departments accounted for as much as 50% of the research funding earned by one university and as little as 2% in another. **Figure 5.2** reports the average proportions of funding earned across the surveyed

Figure 5.2: Percentage of funding for education research from each of these sources (average response)

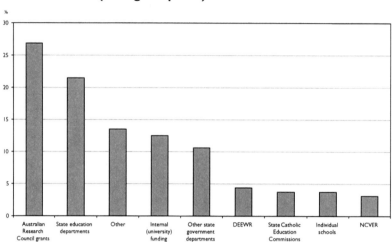

institutions from each of the funding sources. While these are only estimates and while the data do not include all universities, they allow us an indicative view of the importance of ARC funding, compared with other sources. On average, ARC grants remain the single largest source of funding for educational research. However, if we combine all the other sources, which include state and Commonwealth departments and agencies, schools, internal university funding and private bodies, the ARC grants, on average, provide only just over one quarter of educational research funding in Australia.

Research structures and capacity

Using a selection of terms collected by Sá et al (2010) a website scan was conducted in July 2010 to investigate research structures and capacity in education faculties and schools. This search found that most faculties had designated research leaders responsible for the direction and management of research. These ranged from associate deans to centre managers. In the electronic survey of research leaders, six of the eight academic leaders nominated were associate deans, while one was a deputy head of department and one was designated 'theme leader'. Five of the eight academic staff were at professorial level, three were associate professors and one was a senior lecturer. The level of seniority evident in the designation and level of staff leading these research structures shows a considerable commitment to research in these institutions. This finding is supported by the fact that eight of the nine institutions reported that they had a designated (non-academic) research manager and all nine reported that they had dedicated research support staff.

In terms of the structures within which research is actually conducted, however, there was considerable variation. The terminology used to describe these structures also varied and was not used in consistent ways. Terms included research institutes, research centres, clusters, groups and networks. A number of institutions also nominated particular research strengths, specialisations or interests. The term 'research institute', for example, which was used in 11 of the 31 websites examined, referred to overarching structures of research management in some universities but signified a body of actual researchers in others. The term 'research centre' was used in 22 of the 31 faculty websites and was the most common way to describe a body of researchers in education faculties. A total of 18 universities used more informal descriptions such as 'clusters' or groups, while five referred to 'networks' of researchers and five referred to research 'strengths'. Two universities in this part of the study did not refer to any kinds of research structures.

These findings suggest that there is considerable variation in the strength and formality of the structures that bring together individual education researchers in universities, not to mention between universities. The electronic survey, which included a more limited number of responses, casts further light on this phenomenon. Only three of the eight universities nominated research centres as loci of research, six nominated informal clusters or units, and all eight nominated individual researchers. The responses also allowed an estimate to be made of the proportion of educational research carried out by individuals, informal units or clusters and research centres in the surveyed universities. On average, these showed that most research (58.8%) was conducted by individual researchers, followed by informal clusters or units (28.8%), and the least amount was conducted by formally designated research centres (12.5%).

Strategies and mechanisms used to share and disseminate research

Using the search terms outlined above, the website scan also searched for evidence of knowledge mobilisation activities in education faculties and schools. Only two faculties were found to explicitly refer to such practices. However, most had research centres or networks that engage in the dissemination of research in the broader community. These were generally designed to provide overarching structures for the management of research funding and resources within the faculty/ school and to foster external partnerships. Some universities also have 'commercialisation' units designed to facilitate the dissemination of research through support or training.

A commitment to the utilisation of research for various purposes is evident in this scan. Faculties and schools of education clearly see the importance of utilising the findings of research to inform:

- the theoretical understanding of education policy and practice in the broader academic community (for example, the University of Technology Sydney seeks to disseminate the findings of research 'through books, journals, commissioned research reports and, from to time, in the media';
- the training of teachers (for example, the University of New England seeks to 'enhance teacher growth through research, preservice, inservice, community and overseas programs';
- engagement with schools (for example, Edith Cowan University's School of Education describes its research programmes as being 'conducted collaboratively with partners in the education sectors so that research findings can be applied and have immediate relevance to teachers, schools and the sectors';
- engagement with school communities and families (for example, RMIT University stakes a claim to making 'a difference to the economic, environmental and cultural well-being of the communities (they) operate within … in Australia and internationally through innovative research and research excellence';
- engagement with government agencies, school systems and industry partners in education (for example, Macquarie University promotes its links to education authorities such as Boards of Studies, state education departments and examination committees).

In addition, this scan also found evidence of practices designed to reward research staff for activities contributing to the broader community, including in the form of promotion criteria. For example, Central Queensland University has established a research incentive scheme to reward staff who win research funding and who publish the findings of their research in recognised outlets. Monash University offers a Dean's award for excellence in innovation and external collaboration in educational research. Queensland University of Technology includes Service among the criteria which must be addressed in applications for promotion. Few, however, made explicit in their public documentation the link between knowledge mobilisation and the evaluation of staff for review or promotion purposes by actually using terms such as knowledge mobilisation or knowledge transfer.

An exception is the University of Melbourne, which nominates knowledge transfer as a key indicator in staff performance development frameworks and as a legitimate component for inclusion in staff workload matrices, counting towards an individual staff member's overall workload, along with teaching and research. It is also one of the four criteria to be used by academic staff in preparing applications for promotion. For example, the guidelines for promotion to Level D/E (Associate Professor/Professor) outline the various activities that may be classified as knowledge transfer – 'artistic endeavour, professional practice, public engagement and commentary, engagement with industry and commercialization of research' – and specify the kinds of evidence needed to support claims of activity in these areas. The guidelines also provide a definition:

> Knowledge transfer is the use or development of intellectual capital through a two-way beneficial interaction between the university and non-academic sectors with direct links to teaching and research, and informed by social and global issues.

The University of Melbourne also presents its annual Vice-Chancellor's Engagement Awards (formerly known as Knowledge Transfer awards), which are designed to highlight and reward the achievements of University academics and students who 'engage with external partners and the wider community'.

Data from the electronic survey of research managers and research leaders largely confirm the findings from the scan of websites. The following were nominated by respondents as ways in which their universities shared and disseminated research:

- written report to commissioning body;
- policy recommendations;
- training programmes;
- workshops/focus groups;
- conferences/seminars;
- peer-reviewed publications;
- teaching.

Respondents identified links with policy makers, international and local research networks and teaching programmes as the principal media through which findings were shared and disseminated. However, because of the low numbers of responses to questions specifically regarding knowledge mobilisation, it was difficult to gain an understanding of the relative weight given to these activities and processes.

Three of the respondents nominated specific barriers to the successful implementation of knowledge mobilisation (KM) strategies and these provide an insight into which aspects of the knowledge mobilisation process may present challenges. Attitudinal or what might be deemed cultural factors were amongst these – 'divided attitudes and approaches among staff' and 'lack of sustained leadership for KM activities'. Also nominated were 'time constraints' and 'difficulty setting measurable targets and outcomes for KM'. Some respondents elaborated on these difficulties, suggesting both that there should be more research opportunities focusing on projects designed to translate results into practice at the school level and also that existing findings could be better applied to classroom practice.

These findings suggest that knowledge mobilisation practices are well understood in Australian universities, although described using a range of terms such as engagement, collaboration or knowledge transfer. They include many of the traditional ways in which academics have shared the findings of their research – through publications, conferences, policy recommendations and written reports – but there is considerable variation between universities in the priority given to mobilisation of research findings and the ways in which this is done.

Context of Australia's institutional framework for translating educational research into policy

The analysis of the key research objectives of the ARC funding programme presented earlier in this chapter suggests that the impact of research findings on policy should be key to practices and initiatives in the framing of education research. The impact of the proposed research is also a key element in the evaluation of any research proposal submitted for funding to the ARC.

Both ARC discovery and ARC linkage grant proposals require, in addition to the elucidation of aims, significance and approach, clear statements of the national benefits of the research and a plan for the communication of research findings. These usually include dissemination strategies and an outline of the expected and proposed impact of the research. Moreover, once a grant has been awarded, normal reporting requirements include documentation of dissemination activities – conference presentations, publications and reports to government and industry partners – and other impact.

Having said this, it is important to note that the ARC represents only a minor portion of the research funding allocated to education. Other research, commissioned by state education departments, Catholic education authorities and schools, may not necessarily contain these requirements. In fact, one of the survey respondents in our study suggested that the difficulty in translating research into practice had its origins in the structure of the funding opportunities themselves, with difficulties arising from the fact that much research is commissioned and narrowly conceptualised. This respondent called for more 'researcher-led activity rather than the high level of tender-based research undertaken at present'. This may relate to the data reported earlier on funding sources, which suggest that a significant proportion of educational research in Australia is commissioned research rather than research that has been conceptualised and submitted for funding by educational researchers themselves.

However, this argument also contains an assumption – that education research activity led by academics is more likely to translate into real change at the classroom or government policy level. Whether this is so would likely be disputed by state and Catholic education authorities (and schools), which commission much of the tender-based research. It might equally be argued that this commissioned research is, by its very nature, more 'applied' than most research conceptualised by university academics and therefore more closely linked in a policy sense to its potential users – the educational policy makers and the schools – than research that has been conceptualised solely by university researchers.

While resolution of this question lies beyond the scope of this chapter, it does raise the broader question of whether the organisations that fund research should also be required to 'audit' their use of the findings generated by research:

> (There) needs to be mechanism for greater accountability for use (of research findings) by funding bodies through a research translation or knowledge mobilisation auditing process at both state and federal level. (Electronic survey respondent, October 2010)

Conclusion

The review of the literature regarding knowledge mobilisation practices in Australian education research acknowledges the need for universities to engage more comprehensively and more successfully with the broader learning community and with policy makers. It also calls for university researchers to use the knowledge they generate to play a more active role in driving educational change and innovation. The literature warns of the potential dangers in this, as the threat to researchers' autonomy and intellectual freedom requires constant vigilance, particularly when so much of the research commissioned in the field is funded by governments and policy makers who may be influenced by broader or competing political and policy agendas. Having said this, the literature acknowledges the predominantly beneficial aspects of industry engagement, in the forms of increased funding and greater take-up of research findings.

This study notes the relatively limited amounts of funding allocated to educational research in Australia, with only 1.44% of ARC discovery funding and only 4.05% of ARC linkage funding going to education. There is, in addition, a relatively narrow range of educational institutions conducting this research, with five universities attracting over 50% of ARC discovery funding and eight attracting over 50% of ARC linkage funding. This funding is supplemented by other agencies that commission research, principally government and Catholic system education authorities based in each state and territory.

The electronic survey conducted as part of this study suggests that there is considerable variation in the structures adopted by universities to manage and disseminate research. The range spans from research institutes and centres to informal groups and individual researchers. There is some evidence that research conducted by individual researchers (rather than centres or formal groupings) may constitute the greater part of educational research activity in universities.

Finally, relatively traditional forms of research dissemination – written reports, policy recommendations, workshops, conferences and peer-reviewed publications – seem to dominate the discourse among research leaders and in public statements, such as those available on faculty websites. The broader concepts of engagement, discourse, two-way dialogue and, indeed, knowledge mobilisation are more difficult to find in this documentation. The electronic survey of research leaders raised the need for better monitoring of the ways in which knowledge generated by education research is used and disseminated.

All of these findings point to a higher education sector that is still coming to terms with the challenges and potential benefits of knowledge mobilisation in educational research in Australia. Given the importance of education in modern industrialised economies (OECD, 2010), it might be argued that research in this field is funded poorly in Australia. Certainly, it is limited in scope and number of proponents. The mobilisation of knowledge generated by educational research has yet to be coherently conceptualized, and its frameworks, processes and outcomes are rarely investigated.

The overview presented in this chapter suggests that the discourse among actors in this field, who include both researchers and users of research, has been thin. Further research into this field that investigates the needs and views of school practitioners and policy makers, that documents and analyses the processes and frameworks within which educational research is conducted in Australian universities and that explicitly investigates the links between researchers and users of research is required. Since Huberman and Levinson (1984, p 401) first observed that there was little in the way of 'hard empirical enquiry' into the connections between universities and users of educational research, it might be argued that little has changed. It is to be hoped that this chapter will provide an impetus for such research to be designed and conceptualised in the research community, for the policy and practitioner community to agitate for such research, and for the major agencies funding research to accord it the priority it deserves.

References

Amaratunga, D. and Senaratne, S. (2009) 'Principles of integrating research into teaching in higher education: built environment perspective', *International Journal of Construction Education and Research*, vol 5, no 3, pp 220-32.

ARC (Australian Research Council) (2012) ARC Key Objectives, Strategic Plan 2012–2013, Canberra: Australian Government (available at http://www.arc.gov.au/about_arc/strat_plan_12-15_key.htm).

Becheikh, N., Ziam, S., Idrissi, O., Castonguay, Y. and Landry, R. (2010) 'How to improve knowledge transfer strategies and practices in education? Answers from a systematic literature review', *Research in Higher Education Journal*, vol 7, pp 1-21.

Blackman, D. and Kennedy, M. (2009) 'Knowledge management and effective university governance', *Journal of Knowledge Management*, vol 13, no 6, pp 547-63.

Bradley, D. (chair) (2008) *Review of higher education: final report*, Canberra: Department of Education, Employment and Workplace Relations, (available at http://www.deewr.gov.au/HigherEducation/Review/Documents/PDF/Higher%20Education%20Review_one%20document_02.pdf).

Davison, C. (2009) 'Knowledge translation: implications for evaluation', *New Directions for Evaluation*, no 124, pp 75-87.

DEEWR (Department of Education, Employment and Workplace Relations) (2011) *Higher education overview* (retrieved 5 April 2011 from http://www.deewr.gov.au/highereducation/Pages/Overview.aspx).

Gardner, M. (2008) 'Research, innovation and knowledge transfer', in S. Marginson and R. James (eds) *Education, science and public policy: ideas for an education revolution*, South Carlton, Victoria: Melbourne University Publishing, pp 123-31.

Go8 (Group of Eight) (2012) Research performance of Australian universities, Policy Note 4 (available at http://www.go8.edu.au/__documents/go8-policy-analysis/2012/go8policynote4_researchperformance.pdf)

Harman, G. (2001) 'Australian university research commercialisation: perceptions of technology transfer specialists and science and technology academics', *Journal of Higher Education Policy and Management*, vol 32, no 1, pp 69-83.

Huberman, M. and Levinson, N. (1984) 'An empirical model for exchanging educational knowledge between universities and schools', *International Review of Education*, vol 30, no 4, pp 385-404.

Keeves, J., Watanabe R. and McGuckian P. (2003) 'Educational research in the Asia-Pacific region', in K Keeves and R. Watanabe (eds) *The international handbook of educational research in the Asia- Pacific region*, part 1, Dordrecht; Boston; London: Kluwer Academic, pp 123-40.

OECD (Organization for Economic Co-operation and Development) (2010) *Education at a glance 2010: OECD Indicators*, Paris: OECD Directorate for Education.

Sá, C., Li, S. and Faubert, B. (2010) *Faculties of education and institutional strategies for knowledge mobilization: an exploratory study*, unpublished discussion paper, University of Toronto.

Selkrig, M. and Keamy, K. (2009) 'Beyond borderlanders: universities extending their role in fostering creative partnerships within communities', *International Journal of Learning*, vol 16, no 3, pp 185-96.

TEQSA (Tertiary Education Quality and Standards Agency (2012) role and functions of TEQSA, Melbourne. TEQSA (available at http://www.teqsa.gov.au/about-teqsa).

Wallis, R. (2006) 'A dialogue of knowledge transfer and engagement funding: response in favour of broader knowledge exchange and community engagement indicators', published in the *4th Annual Higher Education Summit: the business of higher education: proceedings* [electronic resource], Sydney: Australian Financial Review.

Ward, M. H., West, S., Peat, M. and Atkinson, S. (2010) 'Making it real: project managing strategic e-learning development processes in a large, campus-based university', *Journal of Distance Education*, vol 24, no 1, pp 21-42.

SIX

Knowledge mobilisation in the Republic of Korea: linkages with economic, political and social development

Lynn Ilon, Seoul National University, Korea

Acknowledgement

In preparing this chapter I was supported by an extensive team. The research advisory board consisted of Professors Oh Nam Kwon, Heon Seok Oh and Jeong Cheol Shin. The team members are all professors at Seoul National University and helped from project conceptualisation to reviewing drafts. Two student research assistants gathered, formatted and translated all the data: Pan Deng (Lifelong Learning Programme) and Hyeok Jun Go (Global Education Cooperation Programme). In addition, my thanks goes to the following people for their considerable time spent in speaking with me about the policy/research process: Dr Shin Il Kim, Dr Chong Jae Lee, Dr Joo Ho Park, Dr Ki Seok Kim and Dr Dong Uk Jeong.

Introduction

The influence of research on educational policy within Korea[1] is as much a history of economic, democratic and social development as it is about the interplay of policy and research. Korea has moved rapidly from the 1950s until today to develop an educational system that has become the backbone of social progress.

Today's researchers are only part of the picture of policy development. The impetus for policy development and change arises as much from an ongoing policy dialogue within the media and among the general public as it does from researchers per se. With a highly educated population that values educational achievement for a number of cultural, economic, political and social reasons, the nexus of policy formation is broad and horizontal throughout the country, as much as it is vertical through research investigation.

Many top universities now require that incoming professors be already well published in the field before they can be considered for a professorial position. Thus, many younger doctoral graduates spend years within research institutes or ministries, building their résumés and networks before becoming professors within colleges of education. Indeed, nearly every professor involved in this particular piece of research had held positions within the Ministry of Education and within a top university and, sometimes, within a national research institute. Their influence in policy development variously took place while a professor, while seconded to the ministry, or before becoming a professor. The interplay of research between the institution that develops the policy (often the Ministry of Education) and the researchers is as much a story of movement between research centres and the ministry and among a network of professionals as it was formal collaboration for a specific piece of policy or research.

Educational policy context[2]

The question of knowledge mobilisation usually arises from a context in which research is supposed to influence policy. Within recent Korean history, however, research has been defined as much by the policy environment as the other way around. To understand this, it is convenient to examine three periods of educational policy in the last 60 or so years. In each period, the role of research and researchers was generally quite different, as was the policy environment for educational development.

1948 to 1960

This period was not generally research driven. It focused on the reconstruction of school infrastructure and on implementing free compulsory primary education. The Japanese colonial period was characterised by a high illiteracy rate (over 50%) and more than two thirds of the school infrastructure was destroyed during the Korean War. By 1960, the enrolment rate of primary education was above 95%.

1961 to 1980

This period was marked by rapid expansion of education. Nearly two million places were added to secondary level schools. At the same time, elementary school quality improved. A series of five-year economic development plans was implemented that specifically targeted educational goals. One such plan required that large class sizes be reduced. Students per classroom in elementary schools fell from 63 to 52, while students per teacher fell from 60 to 48. Grants for elementary and secondary education were enacted with a 13% domestic tax in order to improve educational quality. Salaries for elementary teachers were legally guaranteed.

During this period, the central government was the prime actor in developing, researching and implementing educational policy. Research ability at the Ministry of Education and within universities was still quite weak, as even university-trained researchers had weak training. During this period, two important policies were implemented. In 1969, the exam that served to restrict middle school entrance was dropped, effectively equalising most middle schools. A lottery system was implemented instead. This reduced the fierce competition for high school places and reduced the pressure on middle school students. The second policy, enacted in 1974, allowed municipalities to drop the high school entrance exam and replace it with a policy of equal high schools. This 'high school equalisation policy' remains in effect today and is discussed later in this chapter.

1981 to 2000

This period was marked by the push towards democratic institutions that guided educational research. The Constitutional Court stepped in to regulate educational inequities and spearheaded major education reform for a period. The focus of the reforms was largely on reducing the impact of private expenditure by parents of monies for private tutors and after-school classes. Such private expenditure was intended to give students a better chance of passing the important college entrance exam. Changing the structure of the exam was also a reform focus, with many changes designed to make the exam fairer or to have it less influential in the high school curriculum.

During this time period, the Ministry of Education became the primary actor in developing policy while senior researchers at universities helped to shape the policies. Tertiary education expansion was emphasised along with qualitative improvements in basic schools. Brain Korea 21 was a primary policy instituted by the ministry during this period and aimed at increasing instructional and research quality among top research universities. The Brain Korea 21 policy is discussed later in this chapter. A series of presidential commissions have often headed the educational reform efforts, and much of this involved substantial empirical research.

2000 to the present

This period is characterised by a push to restructure education for a knowledge-based society. Lifelong learning and human resource development have been major thrusts. The educational environment is increasingly competitive. Although the Ministry of Education is the major instigator of educational policy, the highly educated population is now broadly engaged in educational debates, policy suggestions and discussion. Major educational policies, while often formed from primary research contracted by the ministry, are often heavily debated through open public forums before they are implemented. Research derives not just as a contract from the ministry but from a wide range of actors, including independent researchers who critique and evaluate policies. The public is engaged in the debate, and policy design derives as much from this debate as from empirical research findings. The Lifelong Education credit system was developed in this period and is discussed later in this chapter.

University research

There is a strong link between research and educational policy, although typical direction of causation cannot be assumed. For example, two major higher educational initiatives, put in place at the ministry and executive levels, have had a profound effect on research. One policy, which has been funded since 1999, involves the creation of a strong environment for producing world-class graduate students capable of high quality research. That project, Brain Korea 21 (BK21) has funded many students within Korea's top universities and linked their academic work with research competence. Each institution and department designed its own project within BK21, but, in order to be funded, the goals of the individual projects had to link outcomes with increased publications and research.

By requiring that BK21 projects had research outcomes, the development of the BK21 policy changed the research environment of the universities. In a circular manner, though, it was the very research environment of these universities that conceived, designed and evaluated the BK21 policy.

There is a close association between professors, researchers and ministry personnel. Frequently, they are one and the same. For example, this research required the interview of two top scholars who had retired from the College of Education at Seoul National University. One had also served as Minister of Education, or as Deputy Prime

Minister, and both had headed major educational research institutes. During these periods of time, they were on leave from Seoul National University. One colleague at Seoul National University who assisted in this research had just joined the university after many years at the Ministry of Education, and two other professors on the advisory board for this research were also former ministry officials. All continue to do research for the government. Thus, the linkage between researcher, ministry officials and professors is very tight.

Colleges of education

Most of the education policy research not undertaken directly by the government derives from Korea's extensive network of universities. There are 45 universities with colleges of education; about a third of them are national universities and the other two thirds are private. **Table 6.1** shows this distribution.

Table 6.1: Overview of colleges of education

		National	Private	Total
Number of undergraduates				
	<1,000	7	22	29
	1,000–2,000	5	9	14
	>2,000	2	0	2
Total		14	31	45
Year established				
	1940s	4	1	5
	1950s	2	2	4
	1960s	3	9	12
	1970s	2	15	17
	1980s	1	2	3
	1990s	1	0	1
	2000s	1	2	3
Average number of faculty		83	40	
Average faculty to student ratio for UG		14	22	

Source: Ja-eok (2010)

National universities are generally older and larger than private universities. Both types produce substantial research, although the research emanating from colleges of education may not always be related to the field of education. Many faculties are employed to teach subject areas such as biology or mathematics. Students take many of their subject courses within the colleges of education. Thus, faculty members hired to teach these subjects may well be publishing in areas other than education. **Table 6.2** shows the quantity of publications coming from both types of universities.

Table 6.2: Research publication quantity, 1998

	Publications						Books		
	Domestic			International			Writing		
	Total number	Range	Average per faculty	Total number	Range	Average per faculty	Total number	Range	Average per faculty
National universitites	2,914	49–423	2.4	761	15–210	0.6	595	10–67	0.5
Private universities	3,495	14–435	2.6	1,631	2–202	1.2	825	3–200	0.6

Source: Seung-Hwan et al (2009)

The source study for these data divided results into various discipline categories. Education was included in the 'Social Science' category, and so numbers reported are for a larger spectrum than just education. Nevertheless, the relative distribution should be fairly accurate.

The table shows that the typical faculty member produced about three to four articles per year. About a fourth of these are published in international journals. Professors from private universities publish about a third more than those in national universities. A professor appears to write a book about once every four years. The range is quite high, with some universities out-producing others by a 10:1 ratio.

Government is heavily involved in funding research, as shown in **Table 6 3**. It funds about 28% of all research studies. But these research studies are well funded – comprising two thirds of all research funds.

Table 6.3: Sources of university educational research funding, 1998

Source	Number of research studies	Percentage of total	Total 1998 US$ (000s)	Percentage of total	Average funding per research (1998 US$)
Government-supported research	450	28%	20,247	66%	44,994
Local government-supported research	89	6%	3,778	12%	42,451
Privately supported research	69	4%	2,106	7%	30,524
Foreign supported research	2	0%	77	0%	38,475
Self-supported research	980	62%	4,520	15%	4,612
Total	**1,590**	100%	30,729	100%	19,326

Source: Seung-hwan et al (2009)

Professional societies and journals

There are 11 professional societies in the field of education that also put out scholarly journals on a regular basis. These societies work collaboratively on joint projects and meet collectively at an annual conference on educational research. **Table 6.4** lists their journals. Many of the local journals now include English language research articles and encourage articles from outside Korea.

The policy process – story of three policies

Following three educational policies from their ideas to their inception to their impact shows the very close association of research and policy in the field of education. The connection is strongest through the people involved – policy makers, researchers, and professors in a college of education. Some people have worn all three hats at various stages and with various policies. The policies themselves sometimes influence research both directly and by establishing a research or policy environment. The policies reviewed here demonstrate three overriding values expressed throughout the last half decade: (1) equity of educational

Table 6.4: Top 10 domestic journals in education in Korea

Journal	Issues per year	Articles in 2009	Website
The Journal of Korean Education	4	29	http://www.ekera.org/
The Journal of Education Administration	4	79	http://www.kssea.or.kr/
Korean Journal of Sociology Education	4	22	http://soe.or.kr/
The Journal of Educational Psychology	4	274	http://www.kepa.re.kr
The Journal of Educational Philosophy	3	44	http://www.pesk.kr/
The Journal of Anthropology of Education	2	18	http://www.kssae.or.kr/
The Journal of Educational Methodology	4	29	http://www.kaem.or.kr/
The Journal of Economics and Finance of Education	4	31	http://www.kosefe.org/
The Journal of Lifelong Education	4	40	http://www.kssle.net/
The Journal of Korean Society for History of Education	2	19	http://www.hisedu.net/
The Journal of the Korean Comparative Education Society	4	45	http://www.kcesstudy.org/

Source: Journal websites

opportunity, (2) a society that can and does learn continuously, and (3) economic growth through investment in education.

Lifelong learning credit system

Korea has a thriving lifelong learning community. It completed its fifth anniversary in 2010 (NILE, 2010). There are currently 922 programmes in 348 organisations representing 134 autonomous local governments participating in this system. It has doubled the number of participating organisations since 2006.

In 1995, Korea developed a system whereby individuals can receive credit for lifetime learning achievements that can be used towards an elementary, middle or high school qualification. It can also contribute to some university credits, a professional licence, and provide the basis for certifying volunteers, employee applicants and local government activities. Various adult education programmes can apply for accreditation under the scheme and their students can subsequently received credit for their work.

The learner applies to have a comprehensive record made of lifetime achievements including academic background, professional qualifications, lifelong educational achievement and individual activities. This comprises their learning record. At the same time, local and private organisations can apply to have learning centres accredited through the system so that participation in such centres is applied to the learner and/or can be officially used as credit upon admission.

The credit bank system was first researched in a comprehensive study that looked at systems throughout the world and how they provided credit for adults to attain degrees. The Ministry of Education financed this study. The prime researcher was a university professor who was on leave to undertake this study. After the research, the team wrote a policy paper and proposal for the credit bank system. A Presidential Commission on Education Reform agreed with the findings and drafted a law submitted for legislation. The law passed and an agency was established to administer the system. The National Institute for Lifelong Education (NILE) has recently separated from its former institutional home, the Korean Education Development Institute, and is now home to the credit bank system.

Table 6.5 shows that considerable research has been done on this policy through the years. The research derives from a wide range of universities and institutes. The Korean Institute for Educational Development produced five of these pieces of research. Publication occurred in a wide range of journals.

Figure 6.1 shows that research has grown in recent years on this topic. Previous to 2005, about two to three pieces of research were done each year. More recently, between five and 13 pieces have been produced each year.

Table 6.5: Research sources for credit bank system

Theses and dissertations	28
Local journal publications	27
International journal publications	2
Total number of authors represented	34
Total number of universities represented	19
Total number of journals represented	24

Source: Research and Information Sharing Service (2009)

Figure 6.1: Published research count for credit bank system policy

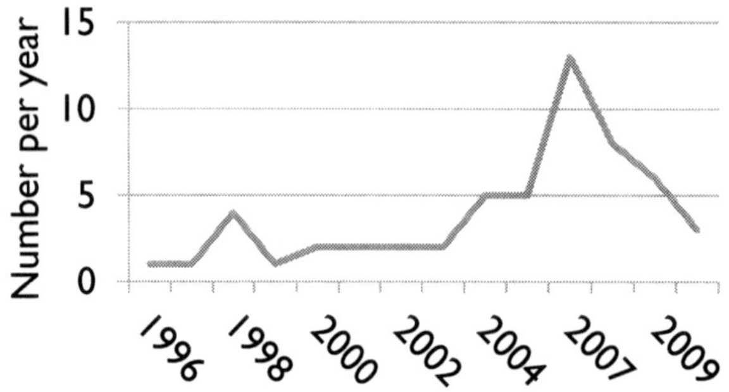

Source: Research and Information Sharing Service (2009)

Brain Korea 21

Brain Korea 21 (BK21) is a government-funded project aimed at developing world-class research-oriented universities. It was initiated in 1999 to produce global leaders who will help promote national competitiveness in the future. It completed its first seven-year period in 2005. In 2014, it will complete its second phase. In phase I, over 1.1 billion US$ was committed to the programme (Ministry of Education, 2007). It supported 564 centres and 90,000 students and researchers. During this period, published research both in international and in local Korean journals tripled.

The project began at the instigation of the Minister of Education for the country. He wanted to develop a project that would assist in raising the research capability of graduates from major research centres – largely at universities throughout the country. He felt that the time was right for Korea to have this as a goal and he felt he could garner financial support if he had the right plan. He began by forming a task force within the ministry to develop the project. This task force reported to him weekly on their progress during this development phase.

This advisory committee built a research team. They began with a list of scholars who might be included in the research, including foreign researchers. From this master list a research team was selected. Researchers included ministry officials, professors, foreign researchers and local researchers. The goal of the research team was not to support a policy per se, but rather to do empirical research to identify an effective policy design.

This development period lasted six months. Once it was completed, the proposed project was put out for public comment. Researchers attended hearings to explain their recommendations. One issue raised during these hearings was that the funding would not be equitable because it would go to the major research universities. Some people felt that the same money ought to be spread equally across all universities in order to raise research throughout the entire system. As a result of the public hearings, some details were changed, but the primary thrust remained unchanged.

The next phase was a budget phase. A proposed budget was drawn up at the Ministry of Education and sent to the National Assembly. It was approved and implemented. Later, Rand Corporation from the US was hired to do a major assessment of the project's outcomes, failures and successes (Seong et. al, 2008). As a result of this evaluation, the project was funded for a second phase.

Table 6.6 shows that the policy has received research attention. About 12 local journals have published something on this policy, with an average of two publications each. Local journals of educational administration and politics of education have published the most articles in this area (six and five, respectively). Most authors were from Youngnam (seven) and Yonsei (five) universities.

Figure 6.2 shows that the policy has been sporadically researched through the years.

Table 6.6: Research sources for Brain Korea 21 policy

Theses and dissertations	7
Local journal publications	24
International journal publications	7
Total number of authors represented	25
Total number of universities represented	22
Total number of journals represented	12

Source: Research and Information Sharing Service (2009)

High school equalisation policy

In 1974, the government introduced a policy meant to equalise high schools. The policy went into effect, initially in the two main cities – Seoul and Busan. The policy was in response to the pressure being put on sixth and ninth grade students to pass an exam that could determine their high school. Thus, high schools were differentiated by the levels of students who were admitted according to test scores. Since high school quality largely determined the probability to be admitted to a top university, and since such admissions could determine the quality

Figure 6.2: Research trend for Brain Korea 21 policy

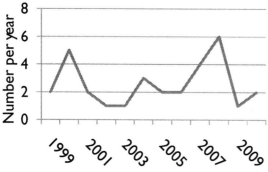

Source: Research and Information Sharing Service (2009)

of employment throughout an individual's adult life, the tests had great consequences. The pressure on adolescents was deemed to be too much. The new policy made assignment to high school on the basis of location. Also, every four to five years, teachers are rotated to ensure a more even distribution of teacher quality.

Private schools are included in the policy. Today, about three quarters of all children live in districts that have adopted this high school equalisation policy. To partly compensate for this equalising effect of high schools, the government has also provided for some special purpose high schools that are designed to provide education in a specialised area for students who have specific talents, such as foreign languages, science and arts. The policy is quite controversial but has remained intact for more than 30 years. It has reduced the competition for high school entrance and also eliminated the ranking system of high schools, which was previously determined through scores on the entrance exam.

The policy was first contemplated because of pressure from parents. They felt that the competition in the high school entrance exam was having a negative effect on their children's physical and mental health. About three quarters of parents felt something had to change (Kim, 2010). Prestigious schools argued to retain the high school entrance policy. As a result of parental pressures, several provinces began to lobby the national government for a policy that would satisfy parents and reduce the pressure on adolescents. The high school equalisation policy was proposed and was optional – provinces could elect to institute the policy or not.

Much of the current research examines the effect of the policy. Some research attempts to show that the policy is disadvantaging the best students in Korea, who are held back by lower-performing peers in their classrooms (Lee, 2004). There is some evidence that this may not be the case, as Korea's high school students continue to rank among the highest in international tests (OECD, 2010), and, according to OECD, Korea also has low systemic inequality. Despite rather constant pressure from some parties to revisit the policy, provinces retain the policy because of parental pressure. The central government is gradually giving schools more autonomy and allowing private schools to deviate from common resource allotments. This is decreasing the equalisation of high schools over time. The policy was not researched before it was adopted, but it has received considerable attention since that time. **Table 6.7** shows the published and unpublished research on this policy.

Table 6.7: Research sources for high school equalisation

Theses and dissertations	60
Local journal publications	58
International journal publications	8
Total number of authors represented	51
Total number of universities represented	35
Total number of journals represented	24

Source: Research and Information Sharing Service (2009)

The policy has been researched broadly across many authors, journals and universities. Ten of these publications were in the *Korean Journal of Sociology of Education*. The Korea Education Development Institute produced the most publications (eight) with Ehwa Women's University, Catholic University, and Seoul National University producing five or six publications each over this period. Ewha Women's University produced the most theses and dissertations on the topic.

Figure 6.3 shows that this policy is still well researched. In recent years, 10–12 publications have been appearing annually on the topic.

Educational research institutes

The government has three primary ways of funding research. First, it provides funding to government research foundations that issue grants for individual proposals based on national competition. Second, it funds large programmes that provide research support or incentives to build research capacity within universities. Third, it provides the base funding for several national research institutes within the broad field of education.

Figure 6.3: Research trend for high school equalisation

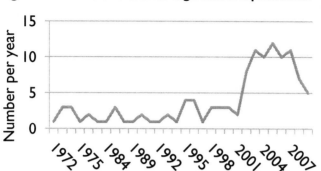

Source: Research and Information Sharing Service (2009)

There are five major think tanks or research institutes that are funded by government and have particular purposes and conduct considerable research. They are (1) the Korea Institute for Curriculum and Evaluation, (2) the National Institute for Lifelong Education, (3) the Korea Education Development Institute, (4) the Korea Education Research Information Service and (5) the Korea Research Institute for Vocational Education and Technical. Each will be described in turn.

Korea Institute for Curriculum and Evaluation

The Korea Institute for Curriculum and Evaluation (KICE) was established in 1998 (see www.kice.re.kr). The research carried out by KICE has covered not only the national curriculum and educational evaluation but also the improvement of teaching and learning methods, development and authorisation of textbooks and the implementation of national-level educational tests. KICE maintains close links with the government, academic circles and teachers and students through public meetings and seminars concerned with the dissemination of research findings in the context of educational policies. Many research staff members are also engaged actively in policy development and participate in international collaborative research projects.

National Institute of Lifelong Education

The National Institute for Lifelong Education (NILE; see www.nile.or.kr/) emerged out of the Korean Educational Development Institute (KEDI) to become a separate institution in 2008. NILE integrated the three major lifelong education functions that had been in operation: first, the Lifelong Education Centre, which had been administered under the KEDI since 2000; second, the Academic Credit Bank Centre, established under the KEDI in March 1998; and third, the Department of Bachelor's Degree Examination for Self-Education. NILE is beginning to tackle issues of literacy education and lifelong learning cities.

Korean Educational Development Institute

Since its inception in 1972, KEDI has been Korea's primary education think tank (see www.kedi.re.kr/). KEDI conducts scientific analysis and develops policy measures on Korea's current educational issues, such as lowering the expenditure on private tutoring, improving the achievement level of students, increasing autonomy in schools, and enhancing the quality of universities. It also helps in the development of innovative educational structures targeted at cultivating skills and competencies required for the future.

Korea Education Research Information Service

Since its establishment in 1999, the Korea Education Research Information Service (KERIS; see www.keris.or.kr/) has been responsible for Korea's educational Information and Communication Technology (ICT) development. Over the past 10 years, KERIS has striven to improve public education, raise national competitive power through ICT in higher education and learning, developed a national education information system, and build on global initiatives in e-learning. At the same time, in order to build strength for a statistics and research oriented approach, KERIS focuses on the unification of scattered information.

Korea Research Institute for Vocational Education and Training

The Korea Research Institute for Vocational Education and Training (KRIVET; see www.krivet.re.kr/) was established in 1997 and conducts research on technical and vocational education and training and human resources development (HRD). It supports and develops government policies for the purpose of developing the vocational capacity through Technical and Vocational Education and Training as part of an overall lifelong learning strategy. Since its foundation, KRIVET has conducted research on all of the following: national HRD and the establishment of information systems for vocational education and training, evaluation of vocational training institutions and programme qualification systems, the accreditation of private qualifications, occupations, and the provision of career guidance.

Getting research into schools

Although considerable amounts of research are done within universities regarding schooling and education in Korean universities and research institutes, the conversion of this research into school policy has a fairly narrow path. The Korean school system is fairly cohesive – its policies are relatively uniform and the structure and curriculum are largely controlled from a central ministry. Thus, the points of entry by which research affects policy are relatively easy to trace.

As was outlined at the beginning of this chapter, Korea has followed a fairly careful and largely successful path of education and economic development. In some 60 to 70 years it has progressed from one of the poorest countries in the world to one of the most advanced. It is at the top of the international tests in education, has nearly universal high school graduation, and, among its young people, nearly 80% go on to some form of higher education. This level of economic success accompanied by educational achievement is viewed to be, at least in part, the result of an educational system that has been guided by a cohesive national system of educational policies backed by research and sound management. Small windows of deviation and divergence are carefully considered because such divergence may lead to both inequities and lowering of quality.

Thus, most research that turns into classroom practice is done as a matter of careful consideration and carefully designed research. The KICE annual research report (KICE, 2010) is a good example of such research. The 2010 report lists 10 pieces of research, most of which are intended to be implemented in Korea's schools. The research for 2010 variously included looking at ways to improve achievement for different types of students, implementing curriculum changes and evaluation of a new teaching tool. All were research studies – all but one intended for implementation in schools. Most studies are conducted by professors in universities. The one piece not intended for implementation was an evaluation of the international PISA test results.

Many of these issues may well have been investigated by university researchers previously or will be done later, as the case studies contained in this chapter show. But the largely conformity of research implementation does have a cost in Korean school. The stresses are quite apparent. Students are under enormous pressure to pass the all-important high school exam that determines which universities students might be eligible to enter (Lee and Larson, 1996).The prestige of university placement is considered crucial to future jobs and social standing, and so students study 10-12 hours a day for years in order to maximise their score on this exam.They forgo athletics, socialising and other activities of youth. Korean society recognises that this is an enormous sacrifice of its youth but, at this point, is unwilling to forgo the exam, which is viewed as one means of assuring a fair way of sorting students into precious places at top universities.

Cyber-bullying is likely to be a symptom of these stresses, and an increasing number of youth suicides are being traced to the bullying that goes on in schools and outside of schools (Klomek et al, 2011). The pressure of this exam also means that schools are almost entirely focused on exam results and the society is beginning to realise that creativity is being lost among its young people (*Korea Times*, 2010; Hilburn, 2011). Curriculum planners are beginning to try to find ways of putting creativity back into the schools. Parents who can afford to do so are sending their high school or middle school children to the US for one or two years in order to give them a break from these pressures, expose them to native English and raise their test scores.

These types of stresses have several outcomes. One is that schools sometimes push for some autonomy. A recent policy was designed to give teachers in elementary school such autonomy (Jeong,et al, 2010). But many observers feel that such autonomy will be quite limited. When the pressure is high for students to pass the exam later in high school, even young students are focused on academic achievement, and teachers are under pressure to concentrate on the national curriculum or be highly criticised by parents.

Nevertheless, the public has considerable sway in Korea. The pressure on high school students is becoming an increasing concern for parents, who realise not only that much of their children's youth is being taken away, but also that the creativity needed for new innovation and knowledge jobs may not be growing.This pressure is in conflict with maintaining the high school exam as a means of sorting students fairly into coveted slots at prestigious universities. However, it is likely that the pressure will increase until a new solution is found. Already, considerable pressure is mounting to allow universities to admit student using criteria other than just test scores.

The need to achieve a high score on this exam narrows the range in which independent research can affect schools, as all schools are singularly focused on the exam. Even ministry policies intended to divert some energies away from constant studying are resisted. Recent ministry guidance that encouraged schools to integrate physical education (Schwartzman, 2011) into schools has been resisted by teachers and administrators because of parental pressure. Parents do not want their children's energies to be diverted from studying for the exam – even years before they will need to take the exam.

Thus, the policy environment in which educational research is implemented in schools has particular characteristics in Korea. First, the country has a strong, long-held belief that research can and should guide school policy. Although politics always has a role to play, given the level of education and its importance in the society, much of the national school policy has substantial and high-quality policy behind it. This research involves a rich mixture of professional researchers, professors and policy makers who, at various times, switch places and are close colleagues. The separation of university, ministry and research institutes is very thin – almost purposely so.

Nevertheless, the stream of research that reaches schools is narrow. Partly this is due to the nation's history and success in schooling. Having had such success in raising its own development through school and a cultural belief in education, a national attitude that education ought to be a national effort and not left to the ups and downs of market or social forces has proved to be a winning strategy. Also, the pursuit of educational equity has been shown to increase economic growth and diminish the old hierarchical bonds.

This nationally directed view of policy is reinforced by the control that the high school leaving exam has on the system. Teachers, politicians and policy makers are pressured to keep schools narrowly focused in order to maximise children's scores on this exam. Deviations that might have been derived from experimenting from research coming from universities are discouraged.

Nevertheless, this highly educated society is aware of the cost of this singular focus and on a national system that breeds considerable conformity. The Internet generation is creative, experimenting and inquisitive. Korea is likely to build new bridges into a more creative educational system in the future. Its university researchers are skilled and may be able to guide the way. But, at the moment, their research largely influences policy through official channels and when the areas of stress rise and bring forth a new area of research. Otherwise, university research outlines the possible but not always the likely.

Conclusion

University-based research is growing but serves as only one piece of extensive educational research informing policy. The strong linkages between educational policy and educational research derive not from their causality, but from the belief that education is a means of improving Korean society economically and in other ways. Education, in this view, is not sought as a separate goal nor is it viewed as an autonomous sector. Rather, policies reflect the firm integration throughout society's framework.

Thus, educational research does not so much inform educational policy as it measures the contribution or success of education in achieving larger social goals. In the last two decades, part of this vision is that of productivity driven by world-class industry, innovation and creativity. The emphasis on top research and on internationalising education is a means toward this end – to raise the quality of research and the variety of perspectives. But the vision of society neither begins nor ends with industry. A strong push to incorporate educational opportunities for all citizens, in all walks of life, throughout their private, social and economic life is demonstrated by the recently formed National Institute for Lifelong Education (NILE).

These goals continue to incorporate a value of equality for all citizens. Educational achievement is high and among the most equal in industrialised countries. Educational policy continues to support this goal with a renewed emphasis on closing achievement gaps.

The strongest link between educational policy and research are its scholars. Top researchers are employed in universities, research institutes and the Ministry of Education. Many begin employment in one location and move to another. Many take time away from the university to conduct a special piece of research for an institute or to work on an evaluation for the ministry. Individuals can wear all three hats at once and link with others who are likewise switching roles.

Funding is also integrated throughout. Government provides the usual funding for universities and funding of research institutes, such as the Korea Foundation for Research, which disperses research funds. But it also funds programmes that provide incentives or create environmental changes that spur research directly or indirectly. Students funded under the programmes must produce research with their professors. Professors, in turn, gain research assistants who are funded through their efforts.

It is fair to say that the environment is designed to reinforce the linkages among government policy, research, education, and social wellbeing. The system is not without its problems, controversies or even the occasional failure. But the overall attempt to integrate these elements is central to the philosophy. The challenge is to find the right balance through the proper integration.

Notes
[1] Korea is used as a short form for the Republic of Korea throughout this chapter.
[2] This section derived largely from an interview with Chang Jae Lee and from Kim (2001) and Lee et al (2006).

References

Hilburn, M. (2011) 'Seeking creativity, Asian educators look to US programs', *Voice of America*, 19 September (retrieved from: http://www.voanews.com).

Ja-eok, G. (2010) *2010 Teacher education assessment synthesis report*, Seoul: Korean Educational Development Institute.

Jeong, Y.K., Lee, K.H., Cho, K.P. and Park, J.M. (2010) 'Research supporting autonomy', in *School curriculum organization and implementation, KICE 2010 Research Report*, Seoul: KICE.

Kim, G.J. (2001) 'Education policies and reform in South Korea', in *Secondary education in Africa: strategies for renewal*, Africa Region Human Development Working Paper Series, Washington, DC: World Bank, pp 29-40.

Kim, K.S. (2010) Interview with Ki-Seok Kim about high school equalisation policy development and implementation.

Klomek, A., Sourander, A. and Gould, M. (2011) 'Bullying and suicide: detection and intervention', *Psychiatric Times*, vol 28, no 2, pp 1-6.

KICE (Korea Institute for Curriculum and Evaluation) (2010) *KICE 2010 research report*, Seoul: KICE.

Korea Times (2010) 'Korean education needs to foster more creativity', 20 February.

Lee, C.J., Jung, S.S. and Kim, Y.S. (2006) 'The development of education in Korea: approaches, achievement and new challenges', *The Journal of Educational Administration*, vol 24, no 4, pp 1-26.

Lee, J.H. (2004) 'The school equalization policy of Korea: past failures and proposed measure for reform', *Korea Journal*, vol 1, pp 221-34.

Lee, M. and Larson, R. (1996) 'Effectiveness of coping in adolescence: the case of Korean examination stress', *International Journal of Behavioral Development*, vol 19, no 4, pp 851-69.

Ministry of Education (2007) *Brain Korea 21*, Seoul: Ministry of Education and Human Resources.

NILE (National Institute for Lifelong Education) (2010) *NILE News*, Seoul: NILE, pp 13-14.

OECD (Organization for Economic Co-operation and Development) (2010) *PISA 2009 Results* (available at www.oecd.org/edu/pisa/2009).

Research and Information Sharing Service (2009) (available at www. riss.kr/).

Schwartzman, N. (2011) 'Korean schools reducing time spent on physical education', *Asian Correspondent*, 18 April (available at http:// asiancorrespondent.com).

Seong, S., Popper, S., Goldman, C. and Evans, D. (2008) *Brain Korea 21, phase II: a new evaluation model*, Santa Monica, CA: The Rand Corporation.

Seung-hwan, H., Sun-ro, C., Jeong-mo, Y. and Do-am, R. (2009) *A study on academic research and development activities in Korea*, Seoul: National Research Foundation of Korea.

SEVEN

Mobilising knowledge in higher education in Denmark

Claus Holm, Department of Education (DPU), Aarhus University, Denmark

Introduction

'Knowledge mobilisation' is not only a new expression in a Danish context, it is also an interesting concept to introduce and discuss. For doesn't modern knowledge mobilisation have to do with a new political will to mobilise the population by creating a connection between educational research and education (R&E)? On the basis of this chapter on the Danish efforts with respect to 'knowledge mobilisation', these questions can be answered affirmatively. The extent of knowledge mobilisation in relation to educational research depends on the political will for it. To what extent is it present in Denmark? On the one hand, it is wholeheartedly present in Denmark, where national competitive ability is formulated from an ideal of the population's competitive ability – a sort of popular competition state – that is to be realised by fulfilling the ambitions for comprehensive knowledge mobilisation through education.[1] On the other hand, Denmark is having a hard time finding a broad consensus when what is, in principle, supposed to be a common political will is to be translated into knowledge mobilisation. This lack of consensus can be traced to the political/administrative level and to the relationship between representatives of educational research and representatives of the education system. So, if the concept of knowledge mobilisation is not exploited in Denmark, it can be seen as a sign that until now the will for knowledge mobilisation has not been strong enough, in reality, to deserve the use of the term mobilisation. The other possibility is that what is conceptualised as mobilisation in other countries is conceptualised in Denmark by the use of terms such as transfer of communication and knowledge sharing. At any rate, the analysis in this chapter of the relationship between educational research and the education system during the period from 2000 to 2010 shows that a change has, in fact, taken place; a change from stressing transfer of knowledge, understood as one-way communication, to emphasising two-way communication, as in knowledge exchange, and knowledge sharing. I have chosen to use the concept of knowledge mobilisation to summarise these changes.

This chapter accounts for knowledge mobilisation through an analysis of the question of research affiliation of Danish universities with the centres for higher education (CVUs)/university colleges during the period from 2000 to 2010. The first reason why this analysis generally summarises the last decade of developments in Denmark is that the Danish University of Education – that is, the creation of the largest educational research environment in Denmark to date – became an effective reality on 1 June 2000. This led to a duty to transfer knowledge in the form of an obligatory research affiliation with the centres for higher education. The second reason is because this specific duty of knowledge transfer became a duty for all the Danish universities under the University Act of 28 May 2003 – an Act that in general stipulated the duty of universities to transfer knowledge to surrounding society.

The organisation of educational research and education in Denmark

Before beginning the analysis I will give a brief description of the Danish research and education system in the field of higher education before giving a specific description of educational research and education (R&E) in Denmark.

The institutions with responsibility for higher education in Denmark are the eight universities and the seven professionally oriented university colleges and two engineering colleges. The professionally oriented institutions offer basic, further and continuing education within the fields of health, education and didactics, engineering and business, social work education and creative education. The universities and university colleges differ in relation to the foundation for their knowledge production and in relation to their education programmes. The Danish universities are research based, focusing on knowledge production. In contrast, the task of Danish university colleges is to ensure that their education programmes have a knowledge base characterised by a developmental and professional orientation.

In relation to higher education programmes it is important first to underscore that they are the continuation of youth education and provide students with final vocational qualifications. Higher education programmes are categorised according to level and duration: short-cycle higher education includes, among other things, vocational academic education; medium-cycle higher education includes university bachelor programmes, professional bachelor programmes and other medium-duration higher programmes; while long-cycle higher education includes master's programmes (candidatus) and PhD programmes. Both the universities and the university colleges offer bachelor programmes. The difference is that the universities offer academic bachelor programmes, while the university colleges offer professional bachelor programmes. Both types of bachelor education are complete education programmes giving vocational qualifications as well as access to two-year master's programmes. The master's programmes and the superstructure to these, a research education leading to a PhD degree, are only offered by the Danish universities.

Turning to the description of educational research and education in Denmark, there is one aspect of this subject that needs to be mentioned in advance. The main material concerning educational research and its relation to education dates back to 1999 and 2004, when two research surveys described the resources, organisation and nature of Danish educational research (Hammershøj and Schmidt, 1999; Elbro and Rasmussen, 2004). Although a national committee on educational research issued a report in 2007 (Universitets- og Bygningsstyrelsen, 2007), the findings were mainly based on these two research surveys. The description in this chapter mainly uses data from the 2007 report. The figures are therefore not up to date, but the relative distribution of person-years at individual universities does not seem to have changed.

With regard to resources used on research, the report from 2007 (see **Table 7.1**) estimated that 386 person-years are used for educational research. You might consider – as did the OECD's national review of educational R&D in Denmark (OECD, 2004) – that this number may be underestimated as it does not include all funded research addressing issues relevant to education carried out in other disciplines. Nor does this number include applied R&D work carried out by the university colleges that includes teacher training.

With regard to the question about organisation, **Table 7.1** shows that the research is characterised by one large and many smaller research environments; the Department of Education (DPU) at Aarhus University clearly constitutes the largest Danish educational research environment, measured in number of person-years.

With regard to the nature of educational R&D in Denmark, it is relevant to repeat what the OECD review of educational R&D mentioned in 2004: namely, that in Denmark, in contrast to many other OECD countries, the initial training of teachers in teacher

Table 7.1: The number of person-years devoted wholly or partially to research in education, pedagogy and didactics, 2006

Institution	Number of person-years devoted wholly or partially to research in education, pedagogy and didactics
Copenhagen University	37
Aarhus University, DPU	205*
University of Southern Denmark	42
Roskilde University	60
Aalborg University	42
Copenhagen Business School	Not calculated

Source: Universitets- og Bygningsstyrelsen, 2007

*The number 205 is a composite of 187 person-years from the then Danish University of Education and 18 person-years from Aarhus University. The latter 18 person-years, however, does not include researchers with only minor connections to the field.

training colleges does not provide regular contact between teachers and researchers. This is still the case. The explanation is, on the one hand, that teacher training is not the responsibility of the Danish universities. When the Danish University of Education was created in the year 2000 by merging the Royal Danish School of Educational Studies, the Danish School of Advanced Pedagogy, and the Danish Educational Institute, this meant, among other things, that an university institution no longer had the responsibility to provide in-service training for teachers in primary and lower secondary schools. Instead this responsibility was assigned to the centres for higher education (CVUs) and then in 2008 to the Danish university colleges. On the other hand, the explanation is that there has been a continuing conflict between the universities and CVUs/university colleges about how to make cooperation between researchers and teacher training colleges work. This is what the following analysis of the conflicts about research affiliation in Denmark will show. At this point I will explain that it has to do with the conflicts surrounding the aim to create a use-inspired educational research.

The need for 'use-inspired' research

As already mentioned, the OECD review of educational R&D in 2004 stated that in Denmark, in contrast to many other OECD countries, the initial training of teachers in teacher training colleges did not provide regular contact between teachers and researchers. The

OECD recommended to Denmark that implementing contact between teachers and researchers would give greater weight to 'use-inspired' research (OECD, 2004).

We are familiar with the term 'use-inspired research' from the very influential book *Pasteur's Quadrant: Basic Science and Technological Innovation* (Stokes, 1997). Stokes' point of departure is the traditional distinction between pure basic research and pure applied research, but his aim is to make an argument against this distinction.

Pure basic research is characterised by the aim of extending our understanding of phenomena in specific research fields by producing general knowledge about it without thinking about how this knowledge should be applied in a practical setting. Pure applied research it characterised by the aim of generating knowledge and solutions to practitioners' known problems, but without thinking about generating a general, context-independent knowledge about these problems.

Stokes (1997) recognises the benefits of pure basic research, but he does not believe in a sharp and hierarchical distinction and linear approach to the relationship between pure basis science and pure applied science. Instead he emphasises Louis Pasteur as an exemplary researcher doing use-inspired basic research, which should inspire researchers of today to produce high-quality knowledge production in the form of research publications and simultaneously to make this knowledge usable, so that it is relevant for practitioners such as teachers improving the learning in their classrooms.

In this way you could say that giving Louis Pasteur as an exemplar is in itself a recommendation for cooperation between pure educational research, applied educational research, development work and practitioners about relevant problems in the field of education. However, for this cooperation to work, the partners have mutually to recognise that each of them makes a contribution that is equal to what the other parties are putting into the partnership. But the analysis of the conflicts in Denmark about research affiliation shows how difficult it has been to mobilise this mutual recognition.

The history of research affiliation in Denmark

Research affiliation was enacted in 2000 with the Act on the Danish University of Education (DPU), the Act that established the centres for higher education (CVUs), and the Act on Medium-Length Higher Education (MVU). From this overall complex of legislation, it appears that the DPU and the CVUs are mutually obligated to research affiliation. Research affiliation is described as a collaboration that has as its goal to 'contribute to an elevation of quality and a closer connection between research and practice' (Undervisningsministeriet, 2000, p 14), and that the DPU through research affiliation 'must help enhance CVU teachers' knowledge of pedagogy, didactics, learning, and competence development' (Undervisningsministeriet, 2000, p 17). With a new Danish University Act in 2003, the research affiliation obligation became a part of the duties of all 12 Danish universities at that time. However, despite this mutual obligation and common objective of research affiliation, there were difficulties in establishing genuine collaboration between Danish universities and the CVUs. Instead, a conflict arose about the character of research affiliation – including whether research affiliation meant the *transfer of knowledge* from universities to the CVUs. The interested parties in the conflict have been the scientific system, the education system, and the political system.[2] The conflict has played out among representatives of the universities, including the DPU, with the Danish Ministry of Science, Technology and Innovation as the ministry in charge, representatives of the CVUs, with the Danish Ministry of Education as the ministry in charge, and representatives of the political system. The DPU has been – and is – a significant interested party in the struggle over the definition of the concept of research affiliation and, later, collaboration. This is because research affiliation from a judicial perspective has been designated as a particular task for the DPU, first as an independent university and then as a school of education affiliated with Aarhus University. Similarly, this goes hand in hand with the fact that the field of pedagogy is a large part of the development and educational activities of the CVUs and university colleges at the present time.

Specifically, the conflict has to do with how the concept of research affiliation is to be defined. On one hand, we have a hierarchical understanding that links research affiliation with transfer of research-based knowledge and, on the other hand, a horizontal understanding that links research affiliation to a concept of equal communication.[3] Quite deliberately, I have divided the analysis of the struggle to define the content of research affiliation into three sections that correspond to three relatively distinct periods. The first period extends from the introduction of the concept of research affiliation in 2000 until 2003 and is analysed under the heading 'Level differences or equal two-way communication'. The second period extends from 2004 until 2007 and is analysed under the heading 'Research affiliation or knowledge-sharing'. Finally, I analyse the period from 2007 to 2010 under the heading 'Between rupture and collaboration'. In the fourth section, I assess the strategies and mechanisms that have been used over this 10-year period to create a transfer of knowledge or research communication between educational research and the education system represented, respectively, by universities, including especially the DPU at Aarhus University and the CVUs/university colleges.

Level differences or equal two-way communication

In 2001, the rector of the Danish University of Education (DPU), Lars-Henrik Schmidt, defined research affiliation as an affiliation between different hierarchical levels in the education system. This occurs by emphasising a difference between the level of education at the DPU, which is obligated to engage in research-based education, and the education level at the CVUs, which do not have this obligation. Lars-Henrik Schmidt drew the following conclusion from this distinction: 'when we talk about research affiliation, then the centre of higher education is linked to research, and the research-based teaching comes from the Danish University of Education, not the other way around. The traffic is one-way and takes place by invoice' (Schmidt, 2000).

Taking the contrasting view were the chairperson for the CVUs' Rectors' Conference Knud Munksgaard and the Danish Minister for Education Ulla Tørnæs. At a conference in 2003, Knud Munksgaard rejected the term research affiliation. Instead, he insisted that other terms were more appropriate for the concept of equality between universities and CVUs. The Danish Minister for Education Ulla Tørnæs backed this statement. At the Minister for Education's annual summer meeting with the world of education – the so-called Sorø conference – she said the following: 'However, it is already clear that the concept of research affiliation must not be understood as a one-sided process in which the exchange of knowledge occurs in a close-knit sender-receiver relationship' (Undervisningsministeriet, 2003, p 39).

The conflict between the Danish Ministry of Science and the DPU, on one hand, and the CVUs and the Danish Ministry of Education, on the other, culminated in 2003, when an inter-ministerial committee was appointed. The purpose of the committee's work was to enhance the function of CVUs as knowledge centres without thereby bringing them under legislation on research within the purview of the Ministry of Science (Undervisningsministeriet and Videnskabsministeriet, 2003, note 1). The result of the committee's work was that research affiliation was still to be considered as the foundation for CVU knowledge activities, and the committee stated explicitly that research affiliation was a concept 'still under development and should function as two-way communication in which universities and other research institutions and CVUs collaborate as equal partners in developing and sharing knowledge on the basis of basic research knowledge from universities and practice- and application-oriented knowledge from CVUs' (Undervisningsministeriet and Videnskabsministeriet, 2003).

Research affiliation or knowledge sharing

The decisive event in the period from the end of 2003 until 2007 was, without doubt, the OECD review of Danish educational R&D work (OECD, 2004). The OECD study was published in October 2004 and had great and immediate impact. This is because not only did the two ministries – the Ministry of Science, Technology and Innovation and the Ministry of Education – commission the review, but they also subsequently made the review and its recommendations into a reference point for a number of initiatives focusing on the question of research affiliation and, thereby, the relationship between the universities and the CVUs.

The overall conclusion of the OECD review was that an explicit national strategy was needed for the Danish R&D system in education that was understood by all the relevant participants and stakeholders. The assessment of the OECD review was that there was a lot to build on but a need for systematic and coordinated action. The OECD review proposed, therefore, that new strategies and mechanisms be developed for interaction between researchers and practitioners. Specifically, the OECD review suggested forming genuine partnerships: 'a genuine partnership representing a balance between the real needs of teachers and the concerns and expertise of the research community' (OECD, 2004, p 27). These sorts of dialogue-based partnerships were supposed to replace the conventional model of one-way communication, that is, meetings or materials that convey research findings to teachers and expect them to accept and implement the findings and their implications.

Thus, the ideal is a partnership between the universities and the CVUs – and, in particular, between the DPU and the CVUs. The review characterises the partnership mode of thinking with two-way communication as the ideal. Specifically, the review advocates the establishment of local fora consisting of teachers, researchers, and developers, which would balance teachers' needs with the expertise of the research community. The same type of partnership ideal is also found in the OECD review's proposal that a national forum be established in Denmark for educational research with the participation of researchers, teachers, politicians, and private foundations – a proposal that the two Danish ministries highlighted in a common press release upon the publication of the OECD review. Another central proposal in the OECD review was to establish a so-called clearing house for educational research. This was to perform the function of a professional knowledge centre that gathered together the most important research results and tried to ensure an effective transfer of research-based knowledge, so that practitioners had easier access to relevant research results.

The work to create a national forum for educational research and a clearinghouse began in the spring of 2006. The clearinghouse for educational research was established at the DPU at the end of 2006, but a national forum for educational research approved by the two ministries has not yet materialised. The debate on the establishment of these institutions between the scientific system represented by the DPU and the education system by the CVU Rectors' Conference showed that the disagreements about the collaboration were also intact in the second time period. The CVUs rejected the clearinghouse idea, since it did not live up to the ideal of equality but rather cemented a hierarchical conception of research affiliation in which the researchers were producers of knowledge and the CVUs as educational institutions were knowledge receivers and disseminators. As an alternative, the CVUs suggested that the concept of research affiliation be replaced by a duty of knowledge sharing between universities and CVUs with a mode 2 paradigm (see Nowotny et al, 2001) that emphasised that knowledge is developed by research and practice in common.

After the first period in the history of research affiliation, it was clear that the CVUs were not to engage in research. The analysis of the second period shows that the CVUs made a virtue of this decision in the sense that they attempted to replace the concept of research affiliation with the concept of knowledge sharing.

Between rupture and collaboration

The third period, from March 2007 until the end of 2010, was, in the first instance, characterised by the fact that during the collaboration between the universities and the CVUs both tried to break this collaboration.

The first rupture happened when the Danish government along with the Danish People's Party, the Social Democratic Party, and the Social Liberal Party entered into an agreement to form eight new cross-disciplinary and regional university colleges as replacements for the centres for higher education. The agreement came into force on 1 January 2008, when the Act on University Colleges for Higher Education became effective. The rupture occurred because university colleges, according to the new legislation, were no longer obligated to be affiliated with research.

The second rupture came from Aarhus University. In August 2007, Aarhus University – in conjunction with the merger with the Danish University of Education as of 1 June 2007 – announced an initiative to offer a five-year academic teacher education programme consisting of a three-year bachelor's degree and a two-year graduate programme. That is, 'a research-based teacher education that aims at a research-based professional practice presumes active research environments' (Aarhus University, 2007). This produced a sharp reaction from the CVU Rectors' Conference at that time. The reaction came in the form of a press release on 9 August 2010, which stated: 'Aarhus University's heralded application for a teacher education programme as of the next academic year is poorly timed and an expression of a denigration of other forms of higher education than that of the universities'.

Nevertheless, on 27 September 2009, Aarhus University submitted an application to approve a three-year teacher bachelor's degree, starting in September 2008. The education was granted accreditation by the Danish Accreditation Council, but at the same time the Accreditation Council asked the Danish Minister for Science Helge Sander to decide the extent to which the education could be approved from a socioeconomic point of view. This occurred with reference to section 10.3 of the Accreditation Act. Consequently, on 28 February 2008, Helge Sander announced that the Danish government, for its part, had 'decided that there should be an array of supplemental teacher educations, including research-based teacher educations, from 2009' (Videnskabsministeriet, 2008). On the other hand, there was a 'need to consider the socioeconomic consequences more before a supplemental teacher education can be approved' (Videnskabsministeriet, 2008).

As a result, Aarhus University was not allowed to offer teacher education from the summer of 2008. Instead, a working group was appointed consisting of representatives from the Danish Ministry of Science, the Danish Ministry of Education, and the Danish Finance Ministry, which was supposed to define the overall framework for the development of supplemental teacher education. In August 2008, this working group produced a report entitled 'The Overall Framework for the Development of Supplemental Teacher Education'. This report stated a general presumption that supplemental teacher education should not be assessed as inexpedient from a socioeconomic point of view; however, it also stated that an obligatory collaborative agreement between a university college and a university was a central premise for the approval of the Accreditation Council, since such a collaborative agreement would make sure there were no inexpedient socioeconomic consequences.

Thus, in principle, the Danish government through Minister for Science Helge Sander forced the parties – the universities and the university colleges – to collaborate as a precondition for offering supplemental teacher education. The need for political enforcement of a collaboration between the universities and the university colleges since then has gained more and more ground as the recognised way to make the collaboration work.

As an example of this recognition was the creation of a consortium between the DPU at Aarhus University and three university colleges in June 2010, when they issued a proposal, '4 Answers to 10 Challenges', to provide short-term and long-term solutions to raise the quality and competence of educational professions – teachers, pedagogues and managers – in Danish secondary schools. The proposal stated that they as 'partners are obligated to contribute in a coordinated, systematic, and directed way to raising professional quality levels' (DPU, Aarhus Universitet, 2010). Additionally, they stated that

> collaboration is a central presupposition, but it is a national task to raise the quality of the Danish secondary school. In order to address these challenges, a true partnership is required between the politicians in the Danish national parliament, civil servants at the Ministries of Education and Finance, the National Association of Local Authorities in Denmark, Danish School Managers, the Danish Union of Teachers, the Danish National Federation of Early Childhood Teachers and Youth Educators, the National Association of Parents and School Boards, the Confederation of Danish Industries, etc. The decisive question for all parties was: Is there, generally speaking, the political will, the managerial resolution and perseverance, to create a better secondary school for children and young people as we approach the year 2020? (DPU, Aarhus Universitet, 2010)

Simply the fact that this question was raised indicates an uncertainty in relation to the political will by the universities and university colleges. However, that the question was raised by the DPU at Aarhus University and three university colleges *together* is first of all an almost unique historic event in a Danish context, when one assesses the whole period from 2000 onwards. Second, it is also an indication of demand in Denmark for a stronger political – governmental – will to enforce collaboration between the parties.

Conclusion: the Danish way of mobilising knowledge

The analysis of the efforts at knowledge mobilisation between educational research done by Danish universities and the education provided by Danish CVUs/university colleges showed, first of all, that, from the year 2000, there has been a conflict between two rationales – a transfer of knowledge rationale and a communication rationale – that has prevented a comprehensive mobilisation. In fact, we have to go all the way forward to 2010 to find examples of the creation of a genuine and comprehensive partnership between the DPU at Aarhus University and Danish university colleges in the form of a comprehensive proposal for a short- as well as a long-term elevation of the quality and competence of education professions – teachers, pedagogues and managers – in Danish secondary schools. The point is that the last step from partnership contact to contract-determined collaboration has still not been taken in Denmark.

In the present situation, I assess the transition from partnership to a contractual relationship as essential for an effective knowledge mobilisation of educational research in Denmark. What I mean by this can be elaborated by using the differences between informal collaboration, partnerships, and contracts.[4] An informal collaboration is most often situation-conditioned and unique. As opposed to more formalised collaboration, informal collaborative partners are not bound to each other in the form of an explicit programme and an obligatory division of labour between the partners. In a formal partnership there is an agreement to structure the collaboration in a particular way. That is, the subject matter about which there is collaboration may be defined as a theme about which the partners may have different expectations, and the subject matter can, therefore, be developed dynamically within the framework of the partnership. Therefore, partnerships can also be called a possibility machine (Andersen, 2006), which indicates that it is more about the dynamic creation of expectations than about concrete agreements to realise these expectations. In a contract-determined collaboration, on the other hand, there is a formal specification of tasks, division of labour, procedures and rules, as well as provisions for solving tasks. Unlike an informal collaboration and a partnership, a contract can be valued and assessed objectively, so that it obligates the partners in a limited and clarified way.

On the basis of this distinction between informal collaboration, partnerships, and contracts, I want to reformulate my earlier assessment. A true knowledge mobilisation between educational research and the education system requires stabilisation around a particular contractual collaboration. And for this sort of collaboration to be realised it will take a much more wholehearted backing from the political system by providing earmarked means for it; that is, the political system must make access to universities' educational research and university colleges' education and knowledge production, respectively, dependent on engaging in formalised – contractual – collaboration.

The Danish way seen from an international perspective

Finally, the analysis of the Danish way of knowledge mobilisation can be placed in an international perspective, for which the reception of the tradition of Public Understanding of Sciences (PUS) development can be taken as an expression (Horst, 2003).

The first position within this tradition – traditional PUS – places the authority of research and the education of the population in the foreground. Research is privileged and sets the standard for what everyone should know. In this sense, traditional PUS represents a hierarchical and asymmetrical look at the communicative relationship between research and the surrounding society. In an extension thereof, conflicts between research and the surrounding society are explained as an expression of the fact that the surrounding society lacks information about research. Traditional PUS has been met critically internationally over last decade. Today, the critique itself constitutes the other position within the PUS tradition. Critical PUS may be identified with the fact that it raises a question about the idea that research-based knowledge should take a superior position. Instead, research acquires the status of being a social sphere among, and along the same lines as, other spheres. In addition, the society surrounding research is not considered to be relatively ignorant. Rather, within critical PUS, it can be observed that it is not the surrounding society that is to improve its lack of knowledge but, to the contrary, research that is to make its communication with its surroundings useful and relevant, accessible and comprehensible. Finally, the researcher Maja Horst (2003) has identified a third – and growing – position within PUS. She calls it *negotiated credibility in networks* (Horst, 2003). The premise for this third perspective is a critique – in fact, a dual critique – of the simple differentiations and value judgments of traditional and critical PUS. Horst (2003) proposes that the premise should be that it cannot be said in advance how the relationship between research and the surrounding society is to be constructed; instead, her suggestion is expressed by the thesis that the articulation of relations between different contexts is best understood as questions of usability, credibility, and influence (Horst, 2003).

In relation to these three positions that have developed within traditional PUS, one can follow a steady critique of the universities by the CVUs/university colleges in Denmark since the year 2000. The critique consists of placing a question mark on the authority of traditional research and research transfer of in favour of promoting a so-called mode 2 approach to research and knowledge production, which are assessed as more relevant and useful for university colleges as well as professional practitioners.[5] According to the CVUs/university colleges, a relevant knowledge mobilisation requires two interconnected measures – in part, a different research and knowledge production and, in part, a replacement of the concept of transfer of research-based knowledge by one of equal communication. The current question in a Danish context is whether we have actually reached a point at which representatives of educational research and university colleges will henceforth be forced by political conditions to negotiate solutions that have credibility and impact internally in the organisations within the different systems and also externally make an actual contribution to a comprehensive knowledge mobilisation in Denmark.

Notes

[1] It might be prudent to follow the Danish professor Ove K. Pedersen (2011) and recognise that the (Danish) welfare state is in the process of being replaced by a new type of state. This new state actively mobilises the people and enterprises to compete globally, rather than (as the welfare state did) compensate and protect the people and enterprises against the effects of fluctuations in the international economical climate.

[2] The use of the term 'system' refers to the fact that the analysis of the history of research affiliation derives from an analysis that was undertaken on the basis of Niklas Luhmann's sociological system theory. Parts of the analysis in this chapter can, in other words, be found in the book *Viden om uddannelse. uddannelsesforskning, pædagogik og pædagogisk praksis* [*Knowledge about Education: Educational Research, Pedagogy, and Educational Practice*] (Rasmussen, Kruse and Holm, 2007).

[3] The most important term for the CVUs/university colleges is equal communication. This term may be the proper translation of the Danish word *ligeværd* (equal worth), pointing to the phenomenon of 'having equal dignity', which refers to a Danish trademark, namely the cooperative movement and

the kind of educational philosophy that goes hand in hand with it in the form of a strong tradition of democratic, liberal education (Schmidt 2001).
[4] The description below is based on Anders la Cour and Holger Højlund's description of different forms of collaboration in the article: 'Samarbejdets dobbelte struktur' ['Collaboration's dual structure'] in the book *Luhmann and Organization* (la Cour and Højlund, 2008).
[5] The book *The New Production of Knowledge: The Dynamics of Science and Research in Contemporary Society* (Gibbons et al, 1994) introduces the concept of the mode 2 research approach, and it is further developed in the book *Rethinking Science: Knowledge and the Public in an Age of Uncertainty* (Nowotny et al, 2001). The authors distinguish between mode 1 research, which almost corresponds to traditional scientific knowledge production, and mode 2 research, which is a new way of producing knowledge.

References

Aarhus University (2007) *Ansøgning om godkendelse af ny akademisk lærerbachelor*, September, Aarhus.

Andersen, N. Å. (2006) *Partnerskabelse*, Copenhagen: Hans Reitzels Forlag.

DPU, Aarhus Universitet (2010) *4 svar på 10 udfordringer for folkeskolen*, Aarhus.

Elbro, C. and Rasmussen, J. (2004) 'Contribution to country background report on educational research in Denmark', Unpublished report.

Gibbons, M., Limoges, C., Nowotny, H., Schwartzman, S. and Scott, P. (1994) *The new production of knowledge: the dynamics of science and research in contemporary societies*, London: Sage.

Hammershøj, L.G. and Schmidt, L.H. (1999) *Danish research in education and educational theory and practices – a survey of the period 1994–99*, Copenhagen: The Danish National Institute for Educational Research.

Horst, M. (2003) *Controversy and collectivity: articulations of social and natural order in mass mediated representations of biotechnology*, Copenhagen Business School, Series 28.

la Cour, A. and Højlund, H. (2008) 'Samarbejdets dobbelte struktur', in J. Tække and M. Paulsen (eds) *Luhmann and organization*, Copenhagen: Forlaget Unge Pædagoger.

Nowotny, H., Gibbons, M. and Scott, P. (2001) *Rethinking science: knowledge and the public*, Cambridge: Polity Press.

OECD (Organization for Economic and Cooperative Development) (2004) *National review on educational R&D: examiner's report on Denmark*, EDU/CERI/CD, 2004(10), Paris: CERI.

Pedersen, O.K. (2011) *Konkurrencestaten*, Copenhagen: Hans Reitzels Forlag.

Rasmussen, J., Kruse, S. and Holm, C. (2007) *Viden om uddannelse:ud dannelsesforskning, pædagogik og pædagogisk praksis*, Copenhagen: Hans Reitzels Forlag.

Schmidt, L.H. (2000) *Forskningstilknytning betyder tilknytning til forskning*, unpublished manuscript, Copenhagen.

Schmidt, L.H. (2001) *The Danish way*, speech delivered at the Adam Smith Institute, London, 29 November.

Stokes, D. (1997) *Pasteurs quadrant: basic science and technological innovation*, Washington DC: The Brookings Institution Press.

Undervisningsministeriet (2000) *Forslag til lov om Danmarks pædagogiske university*, vol L188, Copenhagen: Undervisningsministeriet.

Undervisningsministeriet (2003) *Uddannelse: viden, vækst og velfærd et debatoplæg til Sorø-mødet 2003*, Copenhagen: Undervisningsministeriet.

Undervisningsministeriet and Videnskabsministeriet (2003) *Notat om CVU'ers videnrum*, Copenhagen: Undervisningsministeriet og Ministeriet for Videnskab, Teknologi og Udvikling.

Universitets- og Bygningsstyrelsen (2007) *Til gavn for uddannelserne: rapport fra udvalget for uddannelsesforskning*, Copenhagen: Ministeriet for Videnskab: Teknologi og Udvikling.

Videnskabsministeriet (2003) *Forslag til lov om universiter (universitsloven)*, vol L125) Copehagen: Videnskabsministeriet

Videnskabsministeriet (2008) *Arbejdsgruppen for supplerende læreruddannelser*, August.

————
EIGHT

Knowledge mobilisation in education in Canada and the role of universities

Jie Qi and Ben Levin, OISE, University of Toronto

Introduction

This chapter is organised around different dimensions related to research mobilisation in Canada, with a focus on the field of education and the role of universities. Major features of Canada as a country are described first to serve as a background to the chapter. The next section introduces the role of government, including current research funding agencies in Canada and issues of research quality indicators and research capacity building. Next, the chapter focuses on the strategies and mechanisms currently used by universities to share their research. The chapter concludes with a discussion about the key debates and considerations around education research mobilisation and identifies some unresolved issues that might help guide future research.

Overview of Canada

Canada is the world's second largest country in area. Canada is a large, rich, geographically and demographically diverse country with an advanced industrial and service economy. The term 'cultural mosaic' is commonly used to describe the multicultural nature of Canadian society. Canada has one of the highest immigration rates in the world (more than 1% per year). Nearly 20% of Canadians were born outside the country, a proportion that is increasing steadily, and these immigrants come from all parts of world (www12.statcan.ca/census-recensement/2006/as-sa/97-557/p2-eng.cfm). People who come from different origins and cultural groups are able to retain their religions and customs as well as languages.

Canada also has a high-achieving education system, consistently among the highest-ranking countries on international assessments such as PISA (Programme for International Student Assessment) or PIRLS (Progress in International Reading Literacy Study). Mandatory school age for young people is from 5–7 to 16–18 years old depending on the province. The adult literacy rate is 99%, although Canada does not score as highly on international assessments of adult literacy as it does for school-age skills (Conference Board of Canada, www.conferenceboard. ca/hcp/details/education.aspx). English and French are both official languages at the federal level.

Canada has a federal political system. Power is divided between the federal government and provincial or territorial governments. Canada's provinces range in size from Ontario, with 13 million people, to Prince Edward Island, with about 200,000 people; the territories have even smaller populations. Four provinces (Ontario, Quebec, British Columbia and Alberta) account for 30 million of Canada's 34 million people. In many fields of social policy, jurisdiction is shared between the provincial and federal governments but education is a responsibility of provinces. For schools, virtually all the responsibility rests with the provincial governments. In post-secondary education and training, the federal government has played a more significant role, particularly in regard to research (about which more later).

Although provinces and territories are responsible for education, and the coordinating mechanisms nationally are fairly weak, in general the differences in school systems or higher education systems across provinces are not large. The greatest divergence often occurs in Quebec, where the province's history and French-language nature has led to some quite different education policies, such as one year less of secondary education.

Schools in Canada are organised into districts that are governed by locally elected school boards. Although school boards are regulated by provincial legislation, they also provide schools with a political base in their local community, but one that is not part of municipal government. Canada now has fewer than 500 districts following a wave of consolidation in the last 20 years. Districts range from very large – as many as 250,000 students – to very small, with quite a few rural and remote districts having only a few schools and fewer than 1,000 students. The variability in districts presents some additional challenges to the effective use of research knowledge, as discussed later.

The Canadian university sector in education

Canada has approximately 70 universities, very diverse in terms of size, origins, and programmes. Canadian universities are primarily funded by provincial governments, with a significant contribution from student tuition fees. Universities are independent organisations with their own governing bodies and collegial systems of academic decision making. Freedom of expression for university faculty members is a deeply held value in Canada.

Across Canada there are more than 50 programmes or faculties of education (http://resource.educationcanada.com/foe.html) offering initial teacher education, graduate programmes in education, or both. Education is one of the largest fields of study in Canada, especially at the graduate level, since teachers are one of the largest groups in the Canadian labour force. In total there are perhaps something like 1,500 faculty members in faculties of education or education programmes across the country. Some faculty members in other disciplines, such as economics or psychology, also study education, though this number appears to be quite small. So in total the number of active researchers in education in Canadian universities is modest – though still larger than most other disciplines. The Ontario Institute for Studies in Education (OISE) research team's current study of those holding significant grants for education research suggests that there are perhaps 300–400 active researchers (defined as those who have held external research grants) in education faculties across the country, and those cover all areas of education, so the number of researchers in any one sub-field is almost always quite small. Moreover, Canada's geography means that researchers are separated by large distances. Bringing together a national seminar or network involves people spending many hours on aeroplanes. Still another complication is that the Quebec research community, which is about 25% of the Canadian total, operates primarily in French and often has stronger links with other francophone researchers around the world than with English-speaking Canada.

Canadian faculties of education use the academic ranks of assistant, associate and full professors and award tenure after five or six years of successful service. Tenure and promotion for the most part still use traditional measures of academic activity – notably publication in refereed journals. Universities are struggling with how to recognise research dissemination work and how to account for the growing importance of electronic publications, especially since the latter can often have far more impact than the former.

Major research funding agencies and organisations in education

In this section, we sketch a general picture about research funding agencies and other relevant organisations with a focus on the education sector. Research funding is certainly one critical part of the research mobilisation enterprise.

Around 30 billion Canadian dollars (C$) per year, or about 1.88% of Canada's GDP, is allocated to research and innovation in all fields (www40.statcan.ca/l01/cst01/scte01a-eng.htm). Canada does not rank highly in this area by international standards. In 2007 more than 40% of this spending came from the business sector, governments provided about 25%, and universities about 15%.

Total research in universities is estimated at about C$10 billion, or about a third of total research and development (www.aucc.ca/policy/quick-facts_e.html). Externally funded university research is around 50–60% of all university-based research activities. All sectors in Canada increased their investments for research in universities in the past 15 years, especially the federal government. Canada ranks the first among G7 countries for private sector investment for university research (www.aucc.ca/policy/quick-facts_e.html).

Most university research funding in Canada for social sciences comes from the federal government; provincial government research funding is much smaller and private sector funding is very small (Johnes, 1994). The total amount of funding for education research in Canada is unknown.

Federal research funding is allocated primarily through three research funding agencies, which are agencies of the federal government. They have their own governing councils but their CEOs are public servants, they report through a federal minister, and they are subject to federal government rules in areas such as human resources and finance. The three councils are:

- Natural Science and Engineering Research Council (NSERC), with a research funding budget around C$1 billion in 2010 (http://www.nserc-crsng.gc.ca/_doc/FactsFigures-TableauxDetailles/QuickFactsonFunding);
- Social Sciences and Humanities Research Council (SSHRC), with a 2010 budget of C$335 million (http://www.sshrc-crsh.gc.ca/about-au_sujet/facts-faits/budget-eng.aspx);

- Canadian Institutes for Health Research (CIHR), with an annual research budget around C$900 million (http://www.cihr-irsc. gc.ca/e/22953.html).

These budget figures include not only direct research funding but also costs of various programmes such as indirect research costs and graduate student support.

SSHRC is the most important single source of funds for university-based research in the area of social sciences and the humanities, including education, in Canada. SSSHRC's programme architecture changed somewhat in 2011, but the emphasis on knowledge mobilisation has remained.

The largest single share of SSHRC research funding, some C$136 million annually, is awarded competitively to interest-driven research based on peer reviews. Most of these grants are for three years and provide funding for graduate students, direct research costs and, occasionally, release time for researchers. Each application is reviewed by external referees and all the applications in a given field are then collectively rated by a panel of researchers chosen by SSHRC. A typical three-year grant in education would be in the area of C$100,000 to C$150,000.

In addition, SSHRC has funded several other kinds of research grants, and will continue to do so in future, though the programme names and criteria are due to change. SSHRC has funded a small number of much larger grants to teams of researchers working in priority areas. For example, from 2000 to 2005 SSHRC operated the 'Initiative on the New Economy', which provided funds for studies related to the changing Canadian economy. SSHRC has also funded 'Community-University Research Alliances' (CURA), which have sought to build bridges between university researchers and community organisations. These grants, typically for five years, have supported a number of education initiatives such as the new project launched in 2009 to examine how northern Ontario communities and First Nations (aboriginal people) work in partnership to foster economic growth. Another recent CURA project at the University of Waterloo focuses on supports for community mental health in a diverse community. Yet another looks at building relationships in Montreal between a new hospital and its local community. In March 2010, SSHRC announced four Major Collaborative Research Initiatives (MCRI), each worth about C$2.5 million.

SSHRC funding for research in education has fallen well short of demand. Each year a significant number of applications are rated as deserving of funding by the reviewers and panels but are not funded because of lack of budget. So SSHRC is only able to support a relatively small number of university researchers in education (Hanson, 1994). In fact, the success rate for applications in education has been falling; in 2008–09, SSHRC provided more than C$4 million in grants in the area of education, and only about 25% of applications in that area were funded (http://www.sshrc-crsh.gc.ca/results-resultats/stats-statistiques/postdocs_2008.xls).

Only a few provincial governments, notably Quebec, have any significant funds for education research on an open competition basis, though most provinces fund research on a contract basis, at least to some degree. Still, our team's analysis of websites of Canadian provincial ministries of education showed that in most cases research had little or no prominence (Qi and Levin, 2010). Canada also has relatively few philanthropic foundations or other third-party organisations that fund research, particularly in comparison to the US, and those that do exist are generally small. This is largely a result of the lack of federal government involvement in education, so that national organisations and think tanks are also few in number and fairly weak. For example, national organisations of school boards, teachers and administrators are all much weaker in Canada than are their provincial counterparts. The Canadian Education Association is one of the very few pan-Canadian organisations in education with a national scope and an interest in research, but it is small and does not have very much funding. The Canadian Council on Learning, set up in 2004 to promote research and knowledge exchange in education, was terminated five years later, leaving a significant gap. Even in national education data Canada is quite weak, leading to weak participation in many international projects and a lack of comparable national data about education, providing further constraints to research.

In the 1990s, the federal government took several steps to improve university-based research and development. It created the National Centres of Excellence (NCE) programme that created national research networks in high-priority areas (nce.nserc.ca/Index_eng.asp). Most of the NCEs are in the sciences, and neither of the two that have some connection to education – one on information technology and one on language and literacy – had their funding renewed after the initial five years.

In 2000, the federal government also launched the Canada Research Chairs programme and established the Canadian Foundation for

Innovation (CFI) as well as providing funding directly to universities to offset some of the overhead costs of research (AUCC, 2003). The Canada Research Chair programme and the CFI between them have provided funds to support salaries and other costs for 2000 Research Chair positions at universities across the country with the aim of allowing universities to attract and retain top researchers. However the vast majority of the chairs, as with the overall funding for research, have been allocated to science, medicine, engineering and related areas, and there are probably fewer than 20 across the country in education (Tunzelmann and Mbula, 2003, pp 41–2).

The Canadian research granting councils, including SSHRC, have for the last 15 or 20 years also supported the creation of national research networks, linking researchers across the country and from different disciplines doing related work. A number of networks of this kind were created in education, but often the funding expired after a few years and the momentum was lost. Still, the connections did help create more lasting links across the Canadian research community.

Creating public support for research funding and ensuring accountability for the money spent remains a considerable issue, especially in the social sciences and humanities. In a general climate of scepticism about public spending, research programmes are also under pressure to demonstrate value for money, leading to increased reporting and other accountability requirements. This can be a particular pressure in education. Whereas in the sciences most lay people do not understand the titles or content of much academic research, in the social sciences it can be easy for anti-taxation groups to score political points by issuing press releases suggesting that funded research projects are esoteric or silly or both, a process sometimes helped by project titles that are heavy on academic jargon.

Research mobilisation in education

The focus on greater sharing, use, dissemination, transfer, exchange or mobilisation (all these terms are used in the literature) is not new (see, for example, Weiss, 1979) but has certainly been a field of growing interest in the last 10 years or so (Cooper et al, 2009; Levin, 2010). This movement has perhaps been strongest in health (Weel and Rosser, 2004) but has been occurring in many other fields as well (Pfeffer and Sutton, 2006). It has been increasingly recognised by practitioners as well as policy makers that better transfer and use of new information and knowledge from research are key to achieving high-quality results in most fields. As a result, the ideas of 'evidence-based decision making' and 'evidence-based practice' quickly gained popularity in many fields.

In education, the trend of promoting applied and practice-based research by governments and other organisations also reflects growing interest in how to utilise research knowledge effectively (Furlong and Oancea, 2005). Ideally, the development of research mobilisation efforts should go hand in hand with the research on dissemination, as the former need to be guided by the latter (Kerner et al, 2005).

There has been much discussion concerning effective approaches to sharing research in the field of education (Levin, 2004, 2010) Various empirical studies have been conducted on effective sharing of educational research (Levin, 2008, 2010). A range of barriers to, and facilitators of, research use have been identified, such as the accessibility of material in academic journals to non-academic audiences, lack of encouragement or support given to researchers around dissemination to practitioners, and absence of time and support to help practitioners access research.

Canadian researchers have contributed significantly to the understanding of knowledge mobilisation (KM)-related issues. Cooper and Levin (2010) reviewed some of the important Canadian studies. Mitton et al (2007) found that more than half of the authors engaged in the issues related to KM are in Canada. Landry et al (2001) studied the research dissemination efforts of Canadian university-based researchers in the social sciences. Surveys were collected from 55 Canadian universities. Of the researchers in social sciences who responded, 55% stated that they disseminate their research findings quite often, while 35% reported they are rarely or never concerned about research dissemination. However, one would expect that in the decade since then these numbers might have shifted, given the emphasis on KM. Landry et al (2001) hold that research use varies in different disciplines and they emphasise that 'knowledge utilization, depends much more heavily on factors related to the behavior of the researchers and users' context than on the attributes of the research products' (Landry et al, 2001, p 347).

The Research Supporting Practice in Education (RSPE) team at OISE (www.oise.utoronto.ca/rspe) is undertaking a series of studies and projects around KM activities across different aspects of education. Our team uses an organising framework for research mobilisation with a focus on education research, as exemplified in **Figure 8.1** (Levin, 2010).

This framework provides an overall approach to the mobilisation of research knowledge that can be assessed at the organisational or system level over a period of time. It draws attention to the key roles

Figure 8.1: Conceptual framework for research knowledge mobilisation (KM)

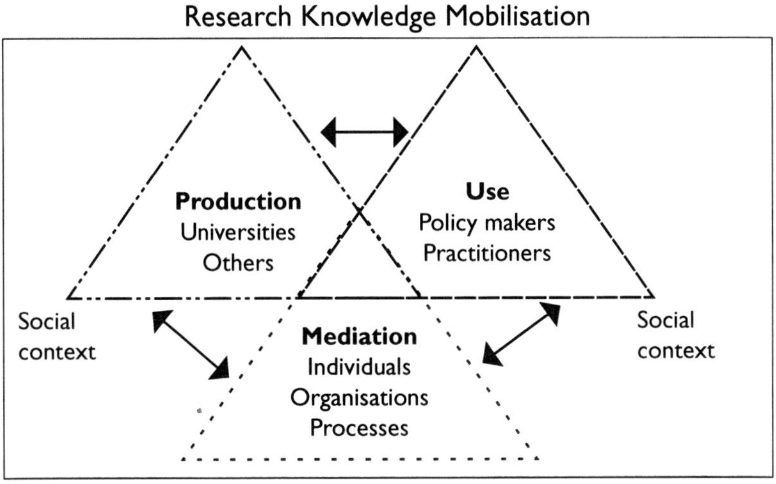

Research Knowledge Mobilisation

Production
Universities
Others

Use
Policy makers
Practitioners

Social context

Mediation
Individuals
Organisations
Processes

Social context

The triangles represent functions, not necessarily structures. Some people or groups operate in more than one context. Arrows represent strength of relationships. KM occurs where two or more of these contexts or functions interact.

of knowledge production, use and mediation while recognising that these roles can overlap particular organisations or individuals.

Our team's work has drawn heavily from the broader research on KM, including work by Lavis and colleagues (Lavis et al, 2003; Lavis, 2006) and Landry and colleagues cited earlier (a fuller discussion can be found in Levin, 2010). Our empirical work has investigated research use in secondary schools across Canada (Levin et al. 2009), patterns of online research use (Cooper et al, 2010, Edelstein et al, 2011), and KM strategies in educational organisations based on their institutional websites (Qi and Levin, 2010). Our work on universities is reported more fully below.

We find, as do those working in other fields (Nutley et al, 2007), that the evidence for KM practices is still quite limited, and that current practices are not always consistent with the evidence that does exist. In education, many key institutions such as government education departments do relatively little in this field, while schools and school systems generally lack the capacity to find, share and use relevant research knowledge (Levin, 2010). Universities provide a particularly interesting and important instance of the potential and limits of research knowledge mobilisation.

The role of universities in knowledge mobilisation

Universities are very important knowledge creation institutions and remain at the centre of the knowledge production system in most societies. Universities sit between the communities of practice they serve and the federal and provincial governments that largely fund them (Godin and Gingras, 2000). In many fields, including education, they are the largest single source of research, and other relevant institutions working on or with research are often linked to universities at least to some degree.

As Furlong and Oancea (2006) point out, traditional indicators of research quality, such as trustworthiness, contribution to knowledge, ethical propriety and careful reporting, while still relevant, are no longer sufficient. In an applied field such as education, a particular emphasis needs to be put on the potential contribution research can make to practice; in other words, how well a research project relates to the needs of policy and practice. A significant literature has now grown up in this area (for example Nutley et al, 2007; Cooper et al, 2009; Levin, 2010) and many interesting ideas are being proposed and attempted, although health continues to be the leading field for this work. However, in our view the overall research effort in Canadian universities is only now starting to change significantly to support greater knowledge mobilisation.

Education researchers in Canada do make many efforts to share their findings. Data from our new study in this area show that many researchers do write in professional publications, build partnerships with schools and other professional organisations, conduct workshops for educators, and use new dissemination mechanisms such as websites and videos. However, these efforts depend on individuals and are not matched by institutional support and commitment at either the faculty or university level.

SSHRC grants are the single most important financial support for research in education in Canada. SSHRC requires researchers to include in all proposals an indication of plans for dissemination of their results and, at the end of their grant, to submit productivity reports that address the significance of their research results and the efforts made to share their research with professionals and the public. However, which activities should be counted as research dissemination efforts is not entirely clear. So far these reports are used for administrative purposes and there is currently no public analysis of the content related to research dissemination activities, so there is no consistent and objective data concerning the impact of research supported by SSHRC (Hanson, 1994).

Evidence for our contention that university KM efforts are still modest at best comes from studies done by the KM research team at OISE. We first analysed the KM practices of a range of Canadian and international organisations using information from the organisation's websites (Qi and Levin, 2010). Our current sample of about 100 organisations includes provincial ministries of education as well as faculties of education, school districts, various professional organisations, and comparison organisations in fields such as health. We developed inductively a rating system to evaluate the extent and quality of KM activities as evidenced on each institution's website.

A second study has assessed the KM strategies of five schools of education in Canada and eight at research-intensive universities in other countries (Sá et al, 2010). The study focuses on institutional efforts to encourage and support the dissemination of research knowledge to a broader range of potential users, as opposed to individual initiatives. We used information from institutional websites and also interviewed deans or other senior leaders in each institution around their KM policies and practices.

More recently we have surveyed more than 100 researchers who have held SSHRC grants in education in recent years, asking about their KM work (Cooper et al, 2011).

Faculties of education have taken a variety of steps to encourage and support knowledge transfer. These strategies can be summarised under three headings: using traditional knowledge dissemination channels (particularly academic publications and conferences), establishing connections between researchers and potential users, and providing institutional supports and incentives. However, our results in both studies show that most institutions are not well equipped to share existing research information quickly or effectively and usually encounter substantial difficulties when trying to do so (Sá et al, 2010). Although the internet is now a primary vehicle for knowledge sharing, including research knowledge, most universities have not exploited these possibilities in organised ways.

In our analysis of KM practices based on institutional websites, although faculties of education had among the highest ratings in this study compared with other kinds of organisations, with about 50 points on average, their scores were still far from the potential maximum of 72 points, meaning that quite a few important features of a comprehensive KM strategy did not seem to be in use. In particular, university KM strategies on websites focused largely on making available various products such as reports, or providing short releases or audio or video commentaries by or about particular studies. We found much less use of active approaches such as the building of interpersonal networks between researchers and potential users, even though new information technologies make such approaches much easier. The sharing strategies tend to be non-comprehensive; it is often hard to find out what research is being done at a given institution. Website materials often provide results of individual studies, seemingly in an effort to promote the status or prestige of the institution, rather than defining issues of interest to practice and bringing cumulative institutional knowledge to bear on these. In very few cases could a practitioner easily find research in a form useful to policy or practice on a faculty of education website, whether in Canada or abroad. Moreover, our research also shows that even when online resources are available the take-up of these is not very strong (Edelstein et al, 2011).

In our study of university KM practices we found significant variation across institutions. Most of the deans with whom we spoke did recognise KM as an important function, but they also reported few practices at the institutional level to support this work. In most universities tenure and promotion policies do not recognise KM work, although this appears to be changing slowly, and there is still heavy weighting in the academic world towards academic rather than professional or lay publications. So, to a considerable extent, involvement in KM work continues to depend on the interest of individual faculty members. Notably, there is no equivalent in education almost anywhere to the well-organised processes that most universities have in place to support technology and knowledge transfer in the sciences or engineering or medicine (Sá et al, 2010).

A few institutions were more advanced in their KM work, especially where the external policy environment or funders put pressure on, and provided support for, greater efforts around knowledge sharing. However, this work continues, in most faculties of education, to have a relatively low priority compared with more traditional functions of teaching and research. Additionally, the opportunity to use graduate students as vehicles for knowledge mobilisation is rarely exploited in any organised way. Recently Canadian deans of education published an 'accord' on research laying out some common ideas and priorities (educ.ubc.ca/sites/educ.ubc.ca/files/FoE%20document_Research_Accord_FINAL_01-19-10.pdf).

Of course, the performance of Canadian universities is affected by many external factors, such as the availability of funding for research and for knowledge mobilisation. Canadian national scholarly organisations are weak because the country is so large yet so sparsely populated. Moreover, living next to the US, Canadian researchers are deeply influenced by the much larger US academic world, and our public policy is often influenced by US public policy, even though our countries are very different. As an example, more Canadian education researchers typically attend the annual meeting of the American Educational Research Association than attend the Canadian equivalent, the Canadian Society for the Study of Education. Equally, it is harder for Canadian education journals, whether academic or professional, to survive because of small numbers and large distances, just as it is harder to build research networks across the country. Given the lack of infrastructure to support knowledge mobilisation at national, regional and local levels, the current level of performance is not surprising.

The province of Ontario has just launched an interesting effort in this regard, called the 'Knowledge Network for Applied Education Research' (Levin, et al, 2011; see also www.knaer-recrae.ca). This initiative, funded by the Ministry of Education and led by two universities, is an attempt to strengthen research–practice connections in Ontario by bringing researchers and practitioners together to share knowledge and work on its application. It is unusual in that the work is not supporting research itself, but the more active sharing of research, particularly by building networks among the parties.

Future possibilities

Obviously the effective sharing of research knowledge with the profession and the public presents challenges for universities. As awareness of the importance of KM grows, more and more university researchers are interested in promoting the use of their research results. The institutional processes to recognise and support these researchers are slowly being improved. Encouraging and rewarding research dissemination efforts are crucial for this work, as young researchers may otherwise be penalised by the tenure and promotion standards in universities. Also, universities need to build up intra-university communication channels to make sure that faculty members and graduate students are aware of the research sharing opportunities available. Universities could also provide better platforms for networking among university researchers and practitioners who work on enhancing the impact of their research results. To overcome these challenges, universities need to have a strong leadership not only from individual departments or faculties but from the university as a whole. This capacity building cannot be only at one level, it needs to embrace different levels such as research leaders and information management (Weel and Rosser, 2004).

At the organisational level, universities need better institutional information systems. A starting point would be for external audiences to have easy and effective access to the research being done and its implications for practice. A second important step would be to improve support for building networks between researchers and practitioners for conducting research collaboratively and for sharing results and implications, since we do have evidence that interpersonal connections are much more powerful than is the simple dissemination of information (Nutley et al, 2007).

The research dissemination system should do the following:

- provide support for different uses of research knowledge including creation, dissemination as well as retrieval of existing research evidence;
- reflect a wide range of research users and their working contexts;
- embrace both social and instrumental dimensions of research knowledge;
- make full use of conventional and new media to build research infrastructure;
- set up consistent standards to fit different aspects of research mobilisation together not only within institutions but across institutions.

As Hemsley-Brown and Sharp (2004) summarised:

> ... research findings should be more accessible; the reward structures should be reframed; alternative publishing venues should be developed to target users; and academic jargon should be reduced. Authors of opinion papers frequently argue that teachers and policy-makers do learn from research but research utilization works best in settings of collaboration and mutual support.(p 12)

Graduate students in Canada represent another important and untapped resource to improve knowledge mobilisation, since they are mainly practitioners who are now also being initiated into the world of research. In general, graduate education programmes in Canada do not pay enough attention to building bridges between the students' practice experiences and their graduate study. If graduate students could connect their research to the real issues of practice, or support partnerships between researchers and school systems, they could play important roles as research mediators and more value would be gained from graduate research projects instead of just letting the thesis sit on the library's shelf after months and months of hard work.

Canada faces the challenge of improving its infrastructure for research impact in education while lacking a national system and national support for doing so. Health organisations have been investing a great deal of time and money in transferring research knowledge to inform policy making and practices in health. Detmer (2003) proposed the idea of a national health information infrastructure (NHII) through which the quality of research knowledge and relevant data can be improved and used to inform decisions at different levels. NHII is defined as 'an information and communications infrastructure [that] exists to connect users – to each other, to information, and to analytical tools – and to enable management and generation of knowledge' (Detmer, 2003, p 10). Canada has built some of this in health through the Canadian Institutes for Health Research (one of which is entirely focused on research mobilisation) and through organisations such as the Canadian Institute for Health Information (CIHI). However, the provinces and territories in Canada are generally resistant to federal government initiatives in education yet are also generally unwilling to create their own pan-Canadian systems, so the prospects for anything similar in education are not good. The Canadian Council on Learning, created with federal government funds in 2004, was terminated in 2009 largely as a result of opposition from the provinces. It is possible that SSHRC, as the major granting organisation, could further strengthen efforts around knowledge mobilisation but it is also struggling with multiple demands, including pressure from researchers to be less directive both in setting priorities and in pushing for research application. Still, initiatives such as the CURAs have had a significant positive impact.

Of course, we need to recognise that there are diverse views about research knowledge itself, and complicated issues regarding research methods plus varying disciplinary perspectives make this job very difficult. The idea of research mobilisation challenges the traditional distinction between 'pure theoretical research' and other types of research. To emphasise the actual take-up of research knowledge in the world of practice is not to say that the continued contribution to pure theoretical knowledge is less important. Knowledge that contributes to theory can also contribute to changed practice and is, indeed, essential to that end in the longer term (Furlong and Oancea, 2006).

Future research

The study of knowledge mobilisation is also at an early stage. More research is needed on almost every aspect of the elements illustrated in **Figure 8.1**. For example, we do not know nearly enough about the roles of principals, district consultants, superintendents, and classroom teachers in research knowledge use. Teacher research (or action research) is another potential means to build research use capacity, although the degree to which this strategy can operate at a large scale remains uncertain. In other words, much detailed descriptive work is needed in order to understand how various research users acquire information, innovate and produce new information in the research mobilisation process. User preferences in terms of research format, type of language, and search patterns may differ and these differences can have a large influence on the ultimate degree of research use.

Our journey to understand and improve the mobilisation of research in education is a challenging undertaking, as the concept of 'research use' itself is embedded with considerable complexities (Nutley et al, 2007). Fortunately, there is a growing interest worldwide. Canadian researchers and policy makers are more engaged in working to increase the uptake of research outcomes. We can expect, with confidence, that improved knowledge mobilisation will benefit education and other fields of the society.

References

AUCC (Association of Universities and Colleges of Canada) (2003). *Research without (southern) borders: the changing Canadian research landscape, a national roundtable on new directions in international research in Canada*, Ottawa: AUCC.

Cooper, A. and Levin, B. (2010) 'Some Canadian contributions to understanding knowledge mobilization', *Evidence and Policy*, vol 6, no 3, pp 351-69.

Cooper, A., Levin, B. and Campbell, C. (2009) 'The growing (but still limited) importance of evidence in education policy and practice', *Journal of Educational Change*, vol 10, no 2, pp 159-71.

Cooper, A., Rodway, J. and Read, R. (2011) 'Knowledge mobilization practices of educational researchers in Canada', paper presented to the Canadian Society for the Study of Education: Fredericton, New Brunswick.

Cooper, A., Edelstein, H., Levin, B. and Leung, J. (2010) 'Use of web-based research materials in education: is uptake occurring?', paper presented at the Canadian Society for the Study of Education, Montreal, Quebec.

Detmer, D.E. (2003) 'Building the national health information infrastructure for personal health, health care services, public health, and research', *Medical Informatics and Decision Making,* vol 3, pp 1-12.

Edelstein, H., Shah, S. and Levin, B. (2011) 'Mining for data: empirical data from the use of online research project', paper presented at the Canadian Society for the Study of Education, Fredericton, New Brunswick.

Furlong, J. and Oancea, A. (2006) 'Assessing quality in applied and practice-based research in education: a framework for discussion', *Review of Australian Research in Education,* April, pp 89-104.

Godin, B. and Gingras, Y. (2000) 'The place of universities in the system of knowledge production', *Research Policy,* vol 29, pp 273-8.

Hanson, R. (1994) 'Allocation and evaluation: the approach at the Social Science and Humanities Research Council of Canada', *Higher Education,* vol 28, no 1, pp 109-17.

Hemsley-Brown, J.V. and Sharp, C. (2004) 'The use of research to improve professional practice: a systematic review of the literature', *Oxford Review of Education,* vol 29, no 4, pp 449-70.

Johnes, G. (1994) 'Research performance measurement: what can international comparisons teach us?', *Comparative Education,* vol 30, no 3, pp 205-16.

Kerner, J., Rimer, B. and Emmons, K. (2005) 'Dissemination research and research dissemination: how can we close the gap?', *Health Psychology,* vol 24, no 5, pp 443-6.

Landry, R., Amara, N. and Lamari, M. (2001) 'Utilization of social science research knowledge in Canada', *Research Policy,* vol 30, pp 333-49.

Lavis, J. (2006) 'Research, public policymaking, and knowledge-translation processes: Canadian efforts to build bridges', *Journal of Continuing Education in the Health Professions,* vol 26, no 1, pp 37-45.

Lavis, J.N., Robertson, D., Woodside, J.M., Mcleod, C.B. and Abelson, J. (2003) 'How can research organizations more effectively transfer research knowledge to decision makers?', *The Milbank Quarterly,* vol 81, no 2, pp 221–48.

Levin, B. (2004) 'Making research matter more', *Education Policy Analysis Archives,* vol 2, no 56 (available at http://epaa,asu,edu/epaa/v12n56/).

Levin, B. (2008) 'Thinking about knowledge mobilization', paper presented at conference of Canadian Council on Learning and the Social Sciences and Humanities Research Council of Canada, Vancouver.

Levin, B. (2010) 'Theory, research and practice in mobilizing research knowledge in education', *London Review of Education,* vol 9, no 1, pp 15-26.

Levin, B., Cooper, A. and Macmillan, R. (2011) 'The Ontario Knowledge Network for Applied Education Research', paper presented to the Canadian Society for the study of Education, Fredericton, New Brunswick.

Levin, B., Sá, C., Cooper, A. and Mascarenhas, S. (2009) *Research use and its impact in secondary schools,* CEA/OISE Collaborative Mixed Methods Research Project Interim Report.

Mitton, C., Adair, C.E., McKenzie, E., Patten, S.B. and Perry, B.W. (2007) 'Knowledge transfer and exchange: review and synthesis of the literature', *The Milbank Quarterly,* vol 85, no 4, pp 729-68.

Nutley, S., Walter, I. and Davies, H. (2007) *Using evidence: how research can inform public services,* Bristol: The Policy Press.

Pfeffer, J. and Sutton, R. (2006) *Hard facts, dangerous half-truths and total nonsense: profiting from evidence-based management,* Boston, MA: Harvard Business School Press.

Qi. J. and Levin, B. (2010) 'Strategies for mobilizing research knowledge: a conceptual model and its application', paper presented at the Canadian Society for the Study of Education, Montreal, Quebec.

Sá, C., Faubert, B. and Li, S. (2010) 'Knowledge mobilization in faculties of education', *Journal of Higher Education,* vol 61, pp 501-12.

Tunzelmann, N.V. and Mbula, E.K. (2003) *Changes in research assessment practices in other counties since 1999,* Bristol: Higher Education Funding Council for England.

Weel, C.V. and Rosser, W.W. (2004) 'Improving health care globally: a critical review of the necessity of family medicine research and recommendations to build research capacity', *Annals of Family Medicine,* vol 2, pp 1-12.

Weiss, C.H. (1979) 'The many meanings of research utilization', *Public Administration Review,* vol 39, no 5, pp 426-31.

NINE

Knowledge mobilisation in education in South Africa

Johan Muller and Ursula Hoadley, University of Cape Town

Introduction

In this chapter we consider both the notion of knowledge mobilisation and practices associated with it in the South African context. The chapter begins by providing an overview of the education system in South Africa, including the higher education policy and funding context. We then go on to trace the evolution of the concept of community engagement (the more common term denoting knowledge mobilisation in South Africa). We argue that the multiple sources from which the current term is derived have left some confusion as to what 'engagement' entails and what constitutes the 'community'. Surveying some examples of local practices relating to knowledge mobilisation, the chapter argues that knowledge mobilisation in education specifically suffers from the same conceptual disorientation, as well as a poor quality knowledge base available for mobilisation. In many senses the field remains in a pre-evidence mode, tending still towards the opposition and critique that characterised engagement pre-democracy. The chapter concludes with some suggestions around how we may go forward, drawing on Cooper's (2011) notion of a 'development oriented' discourse of engagement.

Education system overview

The legacy of apartheid education presented enormous challenges to the government at South Africa's transition to democracy in 1994. A total of 18 racially separated departments of education for different race groups had to be integrated. A new assessment, qualification and certification structure and new accountability and support structures were deemed necessary. In terms of financing, wide disparities in the per capita allocation for students of different race groups had to be addressed. The school curriculum was outdated, both in terms of formal knowledge, but also in terms of the racial and gender biases it contained. The infrastructure of most schools and many higher education institutions was in a dismal state and required considerable capital investment. The task of transforming education was undertaken in the years following transition. Resting upon the crucial South African Schools Act of 1996 for schools, and the White Paper of 1997 for higher education, a unitary, non-racial system of education provision was created, with one national and nine provincial departments responsible for overseeing the delivery of education.

Although there have been significant gains in access to schooling, access to higher education and the quality of educational processes and outcomes in both schools and higher education institutions has remained a problem. South Africa's performance on local and international standardised tests like TIMSS (Trends in International Mathematics and Science Study) and PIRLS (Progress in International Reading Literacy Study) has been poor and the vocational and higher education sectors are struggling to graduate sufficient numbers of appropriately skilled people to meet the social and economic demands of the country. Wide disparities still exist between different provinces and between schools and universities that were previously established for different race groups. The system is still characterised by very unequal provision for students from different racial and social class locations.

The higher education landscape

The public higher education sector consists of 23 institutions, including 11 universities, six comprehensive universities and six universities of technology. The private higher education sector in South Africa is small but growing. Universities offer a combination of programmes, including career-oriented degrees and professional programmes, general formative programmes and master's and doctoral programmes. Universities of technology are focused on professional and vocational education, though not exclusively. Comprehensive universities offer programmes across the spectrum, from research degrees to career-oriented diplomas. The public university sector is marked by large institutions, with a high intake of students and a reputation for generating a substantial amount of the total research produced in the country.

The two main *statutory bodies* in the higher education sector are the Council on Higher Education (CHE) and the South Africa Qualifications Authority (SAQA). The higher education institutions are also represented by Higher Education South Africa (HESA), a loose network that coordinates the views and interests of member institutions. The CHE is responsible for advising the Minister of Education on higher education matters, and contributes to quality assurance in higher education through institutional audits (see detail later) and processes of accrediting the programmes offered in higher education.

The higher education policy context

The 1997 White Paper sets out an agenda for the transformation of higher education from the segregated, inequitable and inefficient apartheid institutions, towards a single national system. Along with teaching and research, community engagement is cast as one of the pillars of this system. Universities are called upon to 'demonstrate social responsibility … and their commitment to the common good by making available expertise and infrastructure for community service programmes'. A key objective is to 'promote and develop social responsibility and awareness amongst students of the role of higher education in social and economic development through community service programmes' (Ministry of Education, 1997, p 10). This policy position is reaffirmed in asserting the priority of enhancing 'responsiveness to regional and national needs, for academic programmes, research, and community service' (Ministry of Education, 2001). Further, and appropriately, the Higher Education Quality Committee (HEQC), a sub-structure of the CHE, identified 'knowledge-based community service' as a basis for programme accreditation and quality assurance. In order to make this policy operational, the HEQC required specific reporting on community engagement in its institutional audits (CHE, 2004).

Considered in the context of international policy and practice, South African policy is both clear and progressive. The understanding of what engagement entails, however, remains a contested issue, with a particular history in the South African context.

The concept of engagement

Having sketched in broad strokes an overview of the education system, and higher education landscape in particular, in this section we provide a very brief genealogy of the notion of 'community engagement' in the South African academy. Here we hope to indicate in what ways 'engagement' as a value has been taken up by the academy, and why it is critical to consider historical context when considering the notion in the South African case.

In a refreshingly candid introduction to a recent volume on university engagement and 'relevance', Alan Scott and Alan Harding (2007) comment that, in the new competitive higher education climate, research relevance is an insistent refrain in the rhetoric of institutional self-promotion.

> Whether they consider themselves 'world class' and in possession of an 'international reputation' ... or as essentially 'national' or 'civic' institutions with fewer international credentials ... most claim to produce eminently useful knowledge that can be utilized by a huge range of 'communities' but is especially valuable to those living, metaphorically speaking, on the university's doorstep. (Scott and Harding, 2007, p 2)

So it is in South Africa too: universities represent themselves as having the answers to the pressing problems of the communities they serve. In this way, they seek to legitimate themselves to an ever wider set of ever more diverse, and unfortunately, sceptical constituencies. 'Communities' are in practice more or less anything that is in the university's external environment, and 'relevance' can be anything from engaging in policy on national priorities, regional engagements with development projects, to local engagement with poor communities, new links with firms, and simply disseminating results of research. A brief historical review of the concept of community engagement is useful to understand how it has come to be currently configured.

In the mid 1980s, academia in South Africa was a politically turbulent place. The debate around what academics should be doing about apartheid was fierce, and it was conducted at the institutional level (how should the university be more responsive to 'the community') and at the individual level (how to be committed and helpful without becoming unwittingly intrusive, or alternatively, handmaidenly 'useful idiots', in Lenin's prescient phrase).

A number of entailments of the late-apartheid period are worth recording since they cast a long shadow over work done up to the present. Most notably, there was a critical shortage of researchers qualified to produce powerful educational knowledge. The universities had turned out activists skilled in critique, but not in advanced statistics or economics of education. This was the case not only in education, but in the social sciences in general. This shortcoming had the consequence that when the African National Congress party (ANC) came to power, they were simply not supported by an existing nationally produced body of powerful knowledge that made it possible to govern from an informed knowledge base. This lack of capacity continues today, especially with regard to larger-scale quantitative studies.

During the first decade of democracy in South Africa, a new, somewhat de-politicised idea of engagement entered the educator's lexicon. 'Community engagement' as a constitutive idea, in the form enthusiastically promoted by US foundations (see, for example, Kellogg Commission, 1999), was imported to South Africa in the 1980s, especially by the Ford Foundation (Fehnel, 2007). The idea has an elective affinity with the 19th-century land-grant ideal of 'service to the community' (Lohmann, 2004), but also with American volunteerism, as exemplified by the Peace Corps. Much of the discourse of 'service learning' was thus brought to South Africa by well-meaning grant-making officers of these US foundations, though without much conspicuous success, at least by their own assessment (Lohmann, 2004, p 160).

As the Mouton and Wildschut (2007) evaluation of a national service learning project argues, in South Africa's 'service decade', roughly up to the mid 2000s, it was the students and their tutors who were benefiting most; what 'the community' was getting was far less clear. We infer that 'service learning' as a form of community engagement always has to struggle with the fact that students are neophytes, not adepts, and with the fact that all too often exactly who the community recipients are or should be is hazy to them.

Another notion of 'engagement' entered the lexicon during the deliberations of the National Commission on Higher Education (NCHE, 1996). This was the notion of 'mode 2' research (Gibbons et al, 1994; Nowotny et al, 2003). Mode 2 as an organising idea was a sub-set of 'borderless world' globalisation optimism, transposed onto research and innovation. It forecast that all research would in future be done in transdisciplinary teams, in a context of use or application, where producers and users would labour together in collaborative harmony. Mode 1, that is, basic research as conventionally practised in the universities, would wither and die, and all research would in future be 'engaged' – so went the Gibbons thesis. These ideas had a major impact on the National Research Fundation grant allocation policy, which for a while allocated grants only to multidisciplinary projects with demonstrable relevance, starving the non-applied sciences and humanities alike, and directing education in a top-down fashion.

The vogue for mode 2 has since abated. In the end, the mode 2 progenitors did too little too late to distance themselves from epistemological populism and from being used by marginal academic constituencies in their battles for status and standing. Small wonder that the idea caught on everywhere except among the mainstream scientific community at which it was directed. In South African academia the word is still used on occasion, but the idea that basic research will give way to applied research in a simple linear fashion has gone out of fashion (Hall, 2010).

A number of different trajectories thus contributed to multiple understandings of what universities' 'engagement' with communities entailed. The earlier activist orientation, service learning and mode 2 engagement have all contributed to a diversity of responses to current policy directives. In the next section we consider what it is that universities are doing in the name of community engagement. We start by looking at the outcomes of national audits of these institutions carried out by the HEQC.

Engagement in higher education institutions – the HEQC audits

The HEQC is a standing committee of the Council for Higher Education (CHE), charged through legislation with programme accreditation and audits of higher education institutions. With regard to community engagement, the HEQC advises that community engagement (including service learning) should be linked to institutions' quality management policies. In turn, community engagement should be related where possible to teaching and learning and research, and be given institutional recognition (CHE, 2004).

Two of the 19 audit criteria are particularly relevant to community engagement. Criterion 1 requires that 'the institution has a clearly stated mission and purpose with goals and priorities which are responsive to its local, national and international context and which provide for transformational issues'. The HEQC's guidelines to institutions to meet this requirement include engagement with local, regional, national and international imperatives in order to establish the fitness of purpose of the institution, and adequate attention to transformational issues in the mission and goal-setting activities of the institution, including issues of community engagement. Criterion 18 is dedicated to community engagement, and specifies that 'quality-related arrangements for community engagement are formalized and integrated with those for teaching and learning, where appropriate, and are adequately resourced and monitored'.

While there may be a general understanding of what teaching and research is in the audit guidelines, there is no such consensus as to the meaning of either 'community' or 'engagement', or of how knowledge generated by such activities is to be understood or transmitted. It is therefore not surprising that no clear patterns have emerged in the detailed responses to Criterion 18 in the institutional audits that the HEQC has conducted to date. Audit reports show a range of conceptualisations of community engagement. In most cases, a broad range of activities is reported, including both curricular and extra-curricular, sometimes incorporating research activities, and sometimes not. Most reported activities are ad hoc, although in a few cases community engagement is reported against a focus that connects with institutional mission and geographical location. Investment of resources is highly uneven. 'Community' was understood in a wide range of ways: as a form of democratisation, tolerance and pluralism; all stakeholders outside the university; industry and the labour market; local and provincial government; as a place of origin and identity; as debt and accountability; and as anything 'other' (CHE, 2008). Again, this diversity of responses is not surprising.

This preliminary scan of the outcomes of the institutional audit process (Hall, 2010) suggests that little of systematic value has been learned of the ways in which public higher education institutions are contributing to the public good as envisaged in policy. This is unsurprising, for, as always, meaningful measurement depends on clearly defined and generally understood definitions of that which is to be measured.

We will show later, in the consideration of education research specifically, that the understanding of community engagement is diffuse, and knowledge mobilisation practices are difficult to identify and measure adequately. First we give some context to education research in general in South Africa.

Scale and funding of education research

Funding for research comes from three main streams: the Department of Higher Education and Training, the Department of Science and Technology and the National Research Foundation (NRF). The NRF is a central administrator of funding for research to higher education. It is an independent government agency that promotes and supports research in key focus areas relevant to South Africa's development (but see also later in discussion). It provides services to the research community, especially at higher education institutions and science councils, with a view to promoting high-level human capital development. Increasingly, the Department of Science and Technology makes targeted grants to institutions, bypassing the NRF. The NRF is, in consequence, increasingly a junior funding partner in the research and development landscape, except when it comes to scholarships for master's and doctoral students, and has nowhere the same funding muscle as, say, the Economic and Social Research Council (ESRC) in the UK.

Research activity and consequently research funding is not evenly spread throughout the system. Over 75% of higher education expenditure on research is spent in six universities (Pandor, 2010). Similarly it appears that not many of the substantial research and development grants from the Departments of Science and Technology and of Trade and Industry go to formerly black institutions or technology universities. The low research capacity base and hence low research output record of these institutions is thus caught in something of a vicious circle.

Thus both the capacity to do research in education, and the emphasis placed on research, varies substantially between institutions (Kruss, 2008). Measured in terms of publication output, the most productive institutions are formerly white institutions – namely the University of South Africa, the University of Pretoria, the University of Stellenbosch and the University of Witwatersrand – and the majority of former black institutions produce less than 10 articles in education per year and in some cases none (Kruss, 2008).

The main funder of education research in higher education institutions has been the NRF. Other significant funders of education research include: Ford Foundation, Carnegie Corporation, Rockefeller Foundation, Kresge Foundation, Norwegian Agency for Development Cooperation, Swedish International Development Agency, Interfund, World University Service, United Nations Children's Fund, Canadian International Development Agency, Royal Netherlands Embassy, Norwegian Embassy, British Department for International Development, Kellogg Foundation, United Nations Educational, Scientific and Cultural Organization (UNESCO).

These donors often set up projects with the aim of knowledge mobilisation built into the project criteria. So, for example, when Ford Foundation funded the CHET/HERANA project (more on this later) an initial research agenda was extended to ensure that the research was used to promote information sharing across the continent and to empower various bodies to utilise the data for monitoring and evaluation, and advocacy purposes. In its funding, the Kellogg Foundation also places a strong emphasis on partnerships. Its Innovative Education Practices research agenda aims to encourage innovative education and learning practices – and partnerships between schools, families, communities, government and business. A more general emphasis on collaboration, especially between institutions in the interests of strengthening research capacity and generating more robust findings is found across funders.

In the 1990s, the NRF began to stipulate 'relevant' research foci in its call for proposals. This greater stipulation of criteria for funding arose from a systematic enquiry by the NRF into education research called 'Setting a Framework for Education Research in South Africa' in 2009. The enquiry entailed a survey of education research (see later), and the elicitation of concept papers from the education research community in all regions to identify research issues/directions. Grants thus became dependent on research meeting particular criteria. In the 2011 funding cycle, only proposals submitted by consortia were accepted. Proposals were to include at least three different institutions in South Africa. This follows the global trend towards fostering partnerships and collaborative research. It also indicates that the 'mode 2' ideal has not completely died away in the education sphere.

Educational research centres

A number of structures, including centres, institutes and units, exist within or are aligned to education faculties and departments for the purposes of conducting or managing research.[1] Many of these research units within higher education institutions were formed just prior to the 1994 democratic elections or shortly thereafter, with the primary focus being the development and implementation of policies and strategies for effective post-apartheid education. A number of units also house resources such as databases, documentation centres and subject specific libraries, and a few units take responsibility for the publication of academic journals.

There are a number of non-governmental organisations (NGOs) in South Africa whose main purpose is also education research. The main ones include Centre for Higher Education Transformation (CHET), Southern African Regional University Association, Southern African Association for Institutional Research, Centre for Education Policy Development, Evaluation and Management (CEPD), Joint Education Trust (JET), South African Institute for Distance Education and the National Business Initiative. One of the four national science councils – the Human Sciences Research Council (HSRC) – conducts extensive research in education. Of the little large-scale research that is undertaken in education in South Africa (see later), most of it is undertaken in these institutions with external donor funding. Higher education institutions neither attract sizable grants to do this work, nor have the institutional capacity, support and experience to undertake it.

Strategies for sharing research and increasing impact

A number of the research units and NGOs have established policy briefs, networks, centres and initiatives in order to disseminate research findings and involve various stakeholders in understanding their research and implementing recommendations. A few examples are given here. The HSRC has a number of research dissemination strategies, including its Policy Analysis Unit which has been set up specifically to generate policy recommendations based on research evidence. Its strategy known as Getting Research into Policy and Practice (GRIPP) focuses on three priority areas, namely social policy and poverty, social protection and health, and education and social innovation. It works with a range of partners to enhance the implementation and evaluation of social policy, most notably national government. Other NGOs also have specific strategies aimed at knowledge mobilisation. JET has an Education Evaluation and Research Division focusing on research that informs the national education agenda. Most recently this research has focused on large-scale school effectiveness studies (Taylor, 2007). The CEPD has a series entitled *Issues in Education Policy*, which comprises a number of booklets on key issues in education. Each booklet deals with one key issue and aims to give the reader an overview of the topic, the main findings of research and policy evaluations and their implications for various stakeholders.

There are also a number of projects directly concerned with the link between research and policy, either as their central aim or as part of a broader project. CHET has established the Higher Education Research and Advocacy Network in Africa (HERANA). Alongside its research component is an advocacy strategy that aims to disseminate the findings of the research projects, better coordinate existing sources of information on higher education in Africa, develop a media strategy, and put in place a policy dialogue (via seminars and information technology) that facilitates interactions between researchers, institutional leaders and decision makers in and out of government (see http://www.herana-gateway.org).

More recently, and reflected in the NRF's funding priorities cited earlier, there has been an attempt to increase the reach and impact of education research by forming consortia and engaging in research collaboration. An example is the self-initiated, long-term research programme entitled the Education Policy Consortium (EPC), made up of the CEPD and the university-based Education Policy Units. The aim behind the consortium is to contribute to policy debates by 'introducing critique and theory into the discourse of public policy and by adopting a perspective of engaged scholarship'.[2] This entails providing a critique of social policies nationally and in comparative international situations, encouraging policy dialogue and consequently influencing policy makers (Motala, 2008).

Knowledge mobilisation strategies in university education faculties

A survey of all 23 university websites was conducted in order to consider evidence of knowledge mobilisation strategies in departments, schools and faculties of education. On their main web pages, almost all 23 universities refer to community engagement/social responsiveness/ knowledge transfer as an explicit part of the institution's activities. Few provide clear definitions of what is meant by these terms, and even fewer indicate projects that exemplify the practice. As indicated earlier, there is a conceptual muddle as to what the activity entails, who the community is, and very little hard evidence of impact. Only seven of the departments, schools and faculties of education websites refer to some form of knowledge mobilisation strategy. Most refer to 'community engagement', and usually this refers to outreach activities, student volunteerism or community service learning, or some combination of these. Unlike some of the projects and units referred to earlier, none refers to policy influence directly, nor clarifies the link between research and community involvement. In fact, the relationship between research and its mobilisation is poorly articulated in most instances. An example is from the University of Pretoria, where 'community engagement' is framed as 'enriching' on the one hand, and as part of a pedagogical strategy on the other: 'Community engagement is integrated into teaching and learning, and into research to enrich the knowledge base. The faculty's mission includes a commitment to ensuring that all undergraduate and postgraduate students have the opportunity to participate in curriculum- and research-based community engagement as part of their learning experience.'[3]

It is clear from the examples given above, that the importance of the dissemination and 'mobilisation' of research knowledge is acknowledged. Although a number of strategies and structures can be identified in projects, there is limited evidence of best practice in mobilising knowledge or strategies that work. So although in the higher education sphere, and in research units and centres and projects, there are strategies in place to foster the broader dissemination of research, how much actual transfer is going on, what is transferred and how, remains opaque. There is also a question mark hanging over the quality of the research to be 'mobilised'. Before considering this question we turn briefly to the ways in which users of research mobilise knowledge.

User-driven research mobilisation

There is limited evidence of how users of research, such as schools and government agencies, themselves mobilise research. Many of the strategies are highly localised and many are idiosyncratic or very small scale. A number of networks within schooling have, however, made attempts to harness research knowledge to enhance their understanding of practice. One such example is the South African Principals' Association. Another is the South African School Governing Body Coalition. The Principals' Association holds an annual conference in an attempt to present some of the most recent advances in education research. Bodies such as the South African Council of Educators and the Education Labour Relations Council also commission research from time to time. A large-scale nationally representative study on teachers' workload and time use is one such study that was initiated from the Labour Relations Council (Chisholm et al, 2005).

Because self-generated attempts to mobilise knowledge have been rather half-hearted this should not suggest that educational knowledge and expertise has failed to make any impact on policy. One of the more indirect ways in which government mobilises research in the South African education sphere has been through a series of Ministerial Committees (or Mincoms). These committees are set up by the minister with a specific mandate. Though not always representative, these Mincoms generally include a number of academics able to harness current thinking and research on a particular issue, which they bring to bear on the issue in question, by collating the existing primary research in the area. Mincoms have focused on curriculum, on school management and on further education and training (FET) colleges. Several Mincoms have been tasked with conducting primary research themselves, for example on racism in higher education, and on 'schools that work' in socially marginal communities (Christie et al, 2007; Soudien et al, 2008).

The Mincoms have been conducted with varying degrees of success. What is interesting about them is the way in which research, through members, is potentially brought directly to bear on policy decision making, in the form of the inevitable recommendations that flow from the Mincom report, and thence into a governmental Green or White Paper.

The national and provincial departments of education also commission research from the education research community. One of the problems encountered in this regard is the limited capacity from within government to identify and frame the appropriate questions on the one hand, and the ability to interpret research and its implications on the other. Both these aspects – Mincoms and government processes of commissioning research – would be fruitful avenues for further research in considering the question of knowledge mobilisation.

We return in the next section to the question of the quality of the research base in education in South Africa, a crucial question when thinking through the mobilisation of that knowledge.

Research quality

Deacon et al (2009) is the most up-to-date overview of recent education research output in South Africa. The study was commissioned by the NRF with the aim of compiling a comprehensive database, and undertaking an analysis, of any research projects that had anything to do with education research in South Africa over the 12 years between 1995 and 2006.

Of the 10,315 texts in the database, 45% are journal articles,[4] 25% are conference papers and proceedings, 14% reports, 7% chapters in books, 6% are theses, and 3% books. Up to 35% of all the research is authored by more than one person.

Of the journal articles, approximately 73% were published in South African journals of education, and only 27% in international journals. In other words, the extent of international publishing, and hence exposure of the research to the international peer community, is limited.

The study found that 48% of education research in South Africa focuses on the classroom level, 38% on the systemic level, 11% on the institutional level and 3% on the out-of-school experience. Considering *scale*, 94% of education research has been small-scale research, and usually qualitative in nature. Very little large-scale research has taken place, with only 1% of the database falling into this category. Most large-scale education research is at the systemic level, while most case studies are of classrooms. In terms of *educational sector*, formal schooling makes up 48% of the database, with the higher education sector following at 32%. The researchers argue that there has been hardly any large-scale or quantitative research in educational research over the past 12 years, but a great deal of small-scale and qualitative research, generally unfocused, unstructured and uncoordinated. The paucity of generalisable empirical research has resulted in a corpus of limited value for either pedagogic practice or policy making.

Some concluding issues

Despite a relatively rich history of engagements with 'engagement', the South African educational research community has not moved effectively into the domain of evidence-led research and effective knowledge mobilisation practice. Some of the reasons for this, explored earlier, include the following:

- The size of the research-active community remains comparatively small, as can also be seen from the relatively small corpus of published journal articles per annum.
- The capacity of the community is thus relatively restricted, and the range of research work produced is overwhelmingly small scale, school rather than system based, practitioner oriented, and qualitative. The corpus is thus fragmented and non-cumulative. The amount of quantitative research is vanishingly small (Taylor, 2007).
- There is no clear idea about what 'research engagement' might mean, let alone 'research mobilisation'. There is evidently some work to be done in this regard.

The travails of the research community aside, there are also some exogenous forces which might restrict the possibilities even further. A premier candidate is the direction research funding seems to be taking globally. In a recent UNESCO publication edited by Meek et al (2009, p 20), Marie-Louise Kearney worries about a potential exclusive 'focus on application-driven project funding or on problem-oriented research cooperation to the exclusion of basic, "blue skies" research' and goes on to warn that 'The familiar catch words of relevance and utility need to be treated with caution. Relevance is vital, but truly useful knowledge can be discovered in various ways.' The debate around relevance has not been particularly sophisticated or helpful (see Hall, 2010; Muller, 2010), and tends to get stuck in the either-or dichotomy of basic or applied. An interesting alternative is provided by the longitudinal empirical and analytical work of David Cooper (2011), which draws together a number of strands that herald the emergence of a third way, more helpfully 'development'-oriented discourse of engagement in South Africa.

Cooper introduces the idea that if we think in very long wave cycles, we can discern, also in South Africa, that the world entered a 'third capitalist industrial revolution' in the 1970s, led by ICT, biotechnology, fibre optic technology, material science, nanotechnology and the like. Symbiotically coupled to this he notes the emergence in the 1980s of a 'third university mission' (the first two being teaching and research), namely, a mission to contribute to the socioeconomic development of society. What this has meant in practical terms is a huge growth in industry and government funding for university-based research. What kind of research Cooper (2011) set out to discover.

He chose 11 university-based research groups, collecting data from them three times in a seven-year period. Although he chose all but one of the groups on the basis of their applied orientation, he was surprised to find that not only were they doing applied research, but that a good proportion of their work could far better be regarded as 'use-inspired basic research', after Stokes (1997). Moreover, he also came to see that what industry and government bodies sought from university-based research centres was either use-inspired basic, or even just basic, research. From universities of technology, they sought orthodox applied research. Cooper (2011) concludes that the emerging national system of innovation requires, and will increasingly demand from research-based universities, the fundamental good ideas which in-house research and development operations cannot supply. This applies equally to government and industry, and probably to community groups too.

We should not imagine that this form of engagement with the world outside the university will always be smooth, or produce virtuous effects. In African universities, where the 'academic core' is relatively small, and with consequently only a small number of research-active staff, donor project funding tends to draw the African scholars out of the university instead of providing means for strengthening the academic core inside the institution. The result seems to be a persistent de-institutionalisation in the very places where the institution is in need of being shored up. This should act as a general warning: external networks are good, but only if they do not prosper at the expense of the nurturing institution.

Finally, university-based 'epistemic communities' (Haas, 1992) have increasingly to deal with competition from NGOs that compete with them for epistemic influence over policy makers and users like schools (Schwartzman, 2010). Some of these NGOs are international and backed by powerful funders. The advice given by these NGOs is less fastidious about epistemic niceties and more concerned with interest-driven agendas. The terrain of knowledge mobilisation is set to become far messier in the future.

Notes

[1] Including Wits Education Policy Unit (EPU), Centre for Higher Education Development (CHED), Centre for Research on Evaluation, Science and Technology (CREST), Centre for Higher and Adult Education, Centre for the Study of Higher Education (CSHE), Centre for Evaluation and Assessment, School for Education Research and Engagement, Centre for Education Practice Research, Institute for Education Research (IER), Centre for Higher Education Studies and Development (CHESD), Centre of Higher Education Studies (CHES), Centre for Higher Education Research, Teaching and Learning (CHERTL).

[2] http://www.cepd.org.za/?q=node/7 (accessed 5 December 2010).

[3] http://web.up.ac.za/default.asp?ipkCategoryID=276&subid=276&ipkloo kid=6 (accessed 6 December 2010).

[4] It is interesting to note that the majority (49%) of these articles were published in a *single* South African-based journal of education.

References

CHE (Council on Higher Education) (2004) *Criteria for institutional audits*, Pretoria: Council on Higher Education.

CHE (2008) *Proceedings of the CHE/NRF Workshop on community engagement*, 22 August, Pretoria.

Chisholm, L., Hoadley, U. and wa Kivulu, M. (2005) *Educator workload in South Africa,* Cape Town: HSRC Press.

Christie, P., Butler, D. and Potterton, M. (2007) *Schools that work*, report to the Minister of Education (accessed 4 January 2011 from http://www.sbmmetsouth.co.za/Schools_that_work_ministerial_ committee_report.pdf)

Cooper, D. (2011) *The university in development*, Cape Town: HSRC Press.

Deacon, R., Osman, R. and Buchler, M. (2009) *Audit and interpretative analysis of education research in South Africa: what have we learnt?*, Pretoria: NRF.

Fehnel, R.A. (2007) *Dick Fehnel: lessons from Gravers School – memoirs of R.A. Fehnel*, Wynberg: CHET.

Gibbons, M., Limoges, C., Nowotny, H., Schwartzman, S., Scott, P. and Trow, M. (1994) *The new production of knowledge: the dynamics of science and research in contemporary societies,* London: Sage.

Haas, P. (1992) 'Introduction: epistemic communities and international policy coordination', *International Organisation*, vol 46, no 1, pp 1-35.

Hall, M. (2010) 'Community engagement in South African higher education', in *Kagisano no 7: debating community engagement*, Pretoria: Council on Higher Education.

Kellogg Commission (1999) *Returning to our roots: the engaged institution*, Washington DC: National Association of State Universities and Land Grant Colleges.

Kruss, G. (2008) *Teacher education and institutional change*, Cape Town: HSRC Press.

Lohmann, S. (2004) 'The political economy of the university: a research programme', *Economics of Governance*, vol 5, pp 8-13.

Meek, V.L., Teichler, U. and Kearney, M-L. (eds) (2009) *Higher education, research and innovation: changing dynamics*, Kassel: UNESCO Forum on Higher Education Research and Knowledge/International Centre for Higher Education Research.

Ministry of Education (1997) *Education white paper 3, a programme for higher education transformation*, Pretoria: Ministry of Education.

Ministry of Education (2001) *National plan for higher education*, Pretoria: Ministry of Education.

Motala, E. (2008) in Malcolm et al (eds) *Democracy, human rights and social justice in education*, papers presented at a conference of the Education Policy Consortium, March 2007, Braamfontein: CEPD.

Mouton, J. and Wildschut, L. (2007) *An impact assessment of the CHESP initiative: high-level findings*. Johannesburg: JET Education Services.

Muller, J. (2010) 'Engagements with engagement: a response to Martin Hall', in *Kagisano no 7: debating community engagement*, Pretoria: Council on Higher Education.

NCHE (National Commission on Higher Education) (1996) *A framework for transformation*, Pretoria: Ministry of Education.

Nowotny, H., Scott, P. and Gibbons, M. (2003) 'Mode 2 revisited: the new production of knowledge', *Minerva*, vol 4, pp 179–94.

NRF (National Research Foundation) (2010) *Call for proposals – educational research in South Africa*, Knowledge Fields Development Directorate, 9 June, Pretoria: NRF.

Pandor, N. (2010) Address by the Minister of Science and Technology, Naledi Pandor MP, at the Higher Education South Africa (HESA) Research and Innovation conference, CSIR, 12 March, Pretoria.

Schwartzman, S. (2010) *Changing universities and academic outreach*, Rio de Janeiro, Brazil: Mimeo.

Scott, A. and Harding, A. (2007) 'Introduction: universities, 'relevance' and scale', in A. Harding et al (eds) *Bright satanic mills: universities, regional development and the knowledge economy*, Aldershot: Ashgate.

Soudien, C., Michaels, W., Mthembi-Mahanyele, S., Nkomo, M., Nyanda, G., Nyoka, N., Seepe, S., Shisana, O. and Villa-Vicencio, C. (2008) *Report of the ministerial committee on transformation and social cohesion and the elimination of discrimination in public higher education institutions*, Pretoria: Department of Education.

Stokes, D. (1997) *Pasteur's quadrant: basic science and technological innovation*, Washington DC: The Brookings Institute.

Taylor, N. (2007) 'Equity, efficiency and the development of South African schools', in T. Townsend (ed) *International handbook of school effectiveness and improvement*, Dordrecht: Springer.

TEN

Knowledge mobilisation and education policy making in China

Chengwen Hong, Leiyu Mo, Yan Meng, Yipeng Tang, Xianming Xia and Yijuan He, Beijing Normal University, China University of Mining and Technology

Acknowledgement

This chapter could not have been finished without support from the faculty of education, Beijing Normal University (BNU). The chapter is a team effort. We would like to give our thanks to the Department of Development at BNU for the provision of data. We are grateful to all the people who have provided support. We are grateful to Professor Camel from Queensland University of Technology, Australia, for designing the topic of knowledge mobilisation and to Professor Julia Pan from OISE, University of Toronto for her hard work in editing the chapter. Special thanks are given to two professors from Beijing Normal University, Professor Zuoyu Zhou and Professor Jiayong Li.

Introduction

This chapter uses the lens of knowledge mobilisation (KM) to look at issues in education in the People's Republic of China. The authors try to answer the following questions. What is the current state of KM work in China? What are the characteristics of education policy making in China and how does KM relate to it? The chapter is divided into five sections. The first part provides some background about the Chinese education system, research capacity and the major achievements of recent education reforms. The second part examines education research institutes to see how they have been influencing policy, especially at the national governmental level. In the third part, the features of KM in China are portrayed. The fourth section describes four challenges China is facing. In the last part, a general picture of KM is outlined.

The Chinese education system and education research

An important background point to keep in mind about China is size and scale. China has a population about four times as large as the next largest country in this collection – the US. It is also geographically large and ethnically diverse. All of this creates huge challenges in delivering high-quality higher education and research in a country that 60 years ago was desperately poor. It also means that the numbers involved in anything national are massive. Compare Canada's few thousand education researchers and faculty members with the 230,000 or so in China.

A second important issue is language. While a very large number of Chinese are studying English and other foreign languages, the unique nature of Chinese as a pictorial rather than an alphabetic language creates a larger challenge for Chinese people to become highly competent in foreign languages (and foreigners in Chinese), making international work somewhat more difficult.

Despite these issues, research in science and technology plays a critical role in China's development and international competitiveness. Confronting increasingly fierce competition among countries, most of the OECD economies have planned thoroughly and spent large amounts of money to keep their cutting-edge advantages in the ever-changing world. Examples include the *Higher Ambition* report from BIS (2009), the recent changes to the Research Assessment Exercise in the UK (Manifredi et al, 2009), *FIRST* planning by the Japan Society for the Promotion of Science (2010), and Canada's National Centres of Excellence project (Government of Canada, 2010) and so on. Meanwhile, middle-income countries (most notably Brazil, Russia, India and China (BRIC)) and many other developing countries are making concerted efforts to improve their national scientific research competence as well as to construct comparative advantages in a scientific and technological world (Postiglione, 2010).

China has also been aware of the great importance of research in international competitiveness. Project 211 and Project 985 can be seen as two of the most important strategic choices in the nation's long-term drive to build its first world-class universities. Project 211 dates back to the Eighth Five-year Plan (around the 1990s), when the central government invested heavily in the higher education system to create a group of leading disciplines within about 100 top universities nationwide. In the late 1990s, the Chinese government initiated another important university project, called Project 985. The aim of the project is to speed up university development, with the aim of creating some world-class universities in China. Since then an unprecedented investment has been put into selected universities. The 39 universities designated so far as 'universities of 985' have received 30 billion RMB (about US$5 billion) in funding. Both Project 211 and Project 985 have had positive results, as demonstrated by the steady climb of Chinese universities in the international rankings.

An increase in research investments

China's education research funding system is mainly supported by several central funding agencies, both governmental and non-governmental. Natural science funding is usually separate from the social sciences, although they may overlap with each other in some fields. Investment in education research is growing steadily. In 2006, the three-year total investment reached 105 million RMB (about US$16 million). Annually, education research receives more than 35 million RMB (about US$5.4 million). The funding is mainly from three sources: National Educational Science Planning, Humanities and Social Sciences and Psychology project, and Provincial Educational Science Planning. As a result of increased research funding, most projects are now better funded than in past, and some key projects receive large amounts of funding (see **Table 10.1** and **Figure 10.1**).

Table 10.1: Major research funding agencies and funding quota

Sponsor	Launch year	Total funding (in 2008) RMB	Beneficiary	Amount per grant (thousand RMB)
National Natural Science Foundation	1986	3.4 billion	Various research institutions	Over 200
National Social Science Foundation	1983	0.3 billion	Research Institutions	80–600
Humanities and Social Sciences in Colleges and Universities	1986	0.3 billion	Universities	30–800
Scientific Planning of National Education	1983	20 million	Education Sector	10–300

Source: *China Education Statistical Yearbook* (Government of China, 2010)

Figure 10.1: Funds for national education science planning from the 'Sixth Five-year Plan' to the 'Eleventh Five-year Plan'

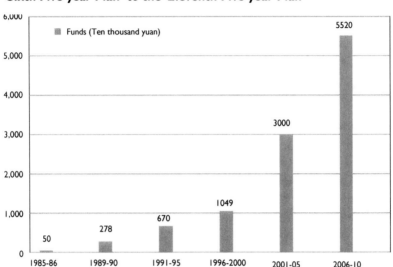

An increased number of education researchers and research-based products

With the accelerating growth of Chinese higher education and research funding, the number of education researchers has grown dramatically. In China, most education researchers work in a limited number of highly reputed research institutions. Higher education institutions produce more research than any other institution. Faculty and administrative staff in these institutions form one of the largest bodies of education researchers in the world. As a result, the talent pool for education and scientific research has been enhanced, programme structures have been adjusted, the knowledge base has improved, both the quantity and quality of research productivity has been notably enhanced, the extent of multidisciplinary cooperation has increased, and the scope of research in education has also increased to a great extent (see **Figure 10.2**).

With the development of education research, numerous research reports, advisor reports, teaching materials, learning tools and teaching software products have appeared. Through media such as newspapers, radio and television networks, audiovisual aids, and so on, these research findings are shared both by government officials and the public. Based on scientific knowledge, as well as artistic and technical methods, new education ideas are generated, new education plans developed, and institutional mechanisms and educational models designed. At the time

Figure 10.2: Quantity and position of postgraduate advisors in Chinese universities between 2006 and 2009

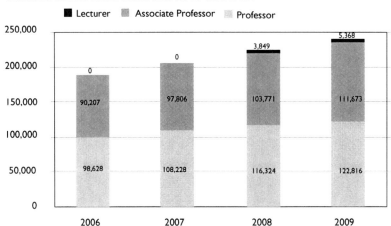

of writing, there are 625 academic journals in China, which publish 80,000 articles annually. There are over 500 academic publishing houses, which produce more than 2,000 books every year. Both academic articles and books exert influence over education policy making and educational practice (see **Figure 10.3**).

Figure 10.3: Education research articles published in academic journals between 2006 and 2008

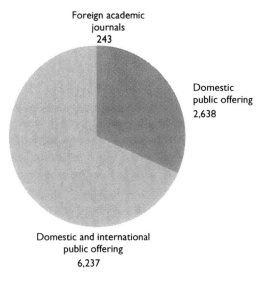

Inside universities, the scope of education research has grown into several disciplines including education foundation, the history of education, psychology of education, comparative education, moral education, educational management, educational information technology, K–12 schooling, higher education, vocational and technical education, adult and continued education, physical health and aesthetic education, national education, national defence and military education – and this is by no means a comprehensive list. The Chinese system has also developed a culture of sharing so that now all kinds of institutions share their intellectual potential in various projects (see **Figure 10.4**).

Figure 10.4: Distribution map of National Education Science

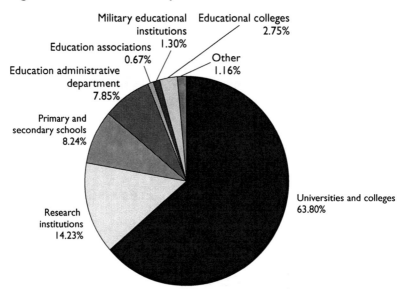

Although significant progress has been made in China in education research, compared with the requirements of education reform and development, there is still a large gap between the knowledge producers and practical needs. One of the great needs in research is for large-scale interdisciplinary studies, which entail more cooperation between institutions from different regions. High-quality findings are still in short supply, so knowledge production is not yet optimal.

Research contributions of higher education institutions: case studies

In China, education research institutes both inside and out of universities tend to develop large policy advisory teams. Many consultants have become experts and scholars in specialised areas, accumulated a large amount of education policy consulting experience, and played a key role in education decision making. Meanwhile, the advisory bodies continue to modify their own talent pools, form multidisciplinary and interdisciplinary teams, and make use of the talents of both younger and older people. This not only lays a good foundation for the future development of education research and advising, but also provides support for the development and improvement of educational policies. With the increase in experts and research-oriented policy makers, the effectiveness and efficiency of educational decision-making are improving.

In China, unlike most other countries (though not dissimilar from other Asian countries), the majority of research workers in education are both policy makers and education researchers. Not only do these professionals have excellent research capabilities in educational matters, but they get highly involved in national policy making. For example, universities and research institutions are the main source of the members of the State Council Academic Degrees Committee, Ministry of Education Social Science Committee, and National Education Science Planning Subject leaders. The following sections present case studies of four highly reputed institutions to illustrate the ways in which these institutions influence education policy and practice in China.

Beijing Normal University

Beijing Normal University (BNU) is one of the top research universities in China. An exploration of the contribution of BNU's research can illustrate the role of Chinese universities in knowledge mobilisation.

One way to look at BNU's research contribution is through its funding. The university's research funding is divided into two categories: humanities and social sciences, and natural sciences. **Figure 10.5** shows the rapid increase in humanities and social science research funding from 2000 to 2008, from less than RMB 10,000,000 (US$1.5 million) to RMB 60,000,000 (US$9.2 million). BNU has increased funding in this area far more than any other university. BNU has been hugely successful in competing for natural science research funds, and in turn it is noticeable that BNU saw a rapid increase in the numbers of humanities and social sciences research projects – an increase as high as 50% per year (see **Figure 10.6**).

Figure 10.5: Humanities and social sciences research funding in BNU, 2002 to 2009

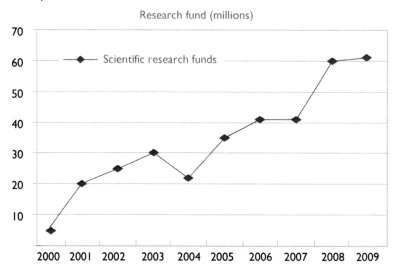

Figure 10.6: Humanities and social sciences research projects in BNU, 2002 to 2009

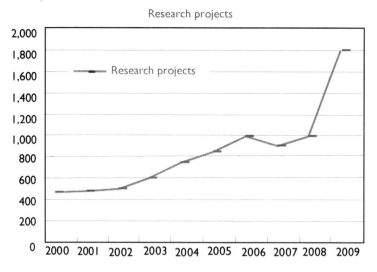

It is not difficult to come to the conclusion that BNU has a powerful place in the production of social science research and knowledge. Abundant research funding, numerous scientific research projects, and fruitful achievements in scientific research are some of the indicators. Those advantages have laid a solid foundation for BNU to have considerable influence in educational decision making at both national and local levels.

Research institutes are an efficient way for universities to build platforms for knowledge mobilisation. These research platforms are more or less targeted to specific policy areas. **Figure 10.7** shows the research platforms BNU has created in the past few years. The platforms have strengthened the links between BNU, governments and other policy-making entities. BNU makes full use of the advantages of team cooperation for research sharing. It now contains six creative teams that work with the Ministry of Education and various working groups. All of these are aimed at providing policy advice on important issues highly related to progress for the country, as well as innovative research for the future.

Among these platforms, the China Institute of Education Policy (CIEP) was created by BNU together with the central committee of the China Association Promoting Democracy, an important political body. CIEP takes part in education policy investigations as well as

Figure 10.7: Research platforms of education faculty in BNU

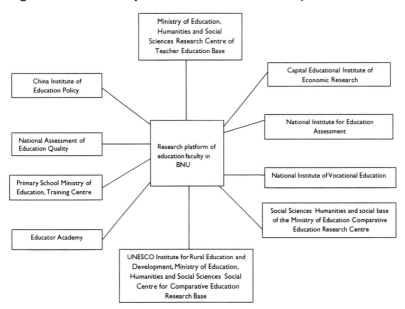

participating in various symposiums organised by the government. Some key research areas in which the institute engages include education development, regional education policy, and educational tactics at different study stages, critical education topics in modern society, comparative education, and basic theories of education policy (China Institute of Education Policy, 2010).

The National Assessment of Education Quality (NAEQ) was established on 16 November 2006. The institute, housed within BNU, is coordinated and supported by the vice president of BNU, Professor Qi Dong. This pioneering effort focuses on the Chinese basic education assessment system with the goal of improving basic education reform and development. At the same time, basic empirical studies are also done in this organisation

The mission of NAEQ is outlined as:

- compile and enact standards for the assessment of education quality;
- devise instruments for the assessment of education quality;
- put the work into practice as requested by the Ministry of Education;
- provide technology support and business guidance for schools and local education administrations.

Recently NAEQ has focused on the task of measuring moral character and civic literacy, the level of both physical and mental health, academic level and literacy, art literacy, practical ability, awareness of creativity and the education environment that affects the development of pupils.

Another platform is called The China Institute of Private Education (CIPE). Established in late 2011, CIEP has a three-fold mission: offering ideas for research consultancy; constructing databases to support school operations; and training leaders, administrators, and teachers in private schools and universities. The Institute is in part recognition of the growing importance of private education institutions in China.

The fourth platform is the National Institute for Education Assessment (NIEA). It is supported by the Ministry of Education and organised by BNU. Established on 26 January 2010, the task of NIEA is to support reform and development of national education, to compile research sources at home and abroad, to undertake important projects related to education assessment, and to distribute useful research products. The Institute's research and policy work supports effective strategy for the educational administration department to put forward comprehensive service. For example, the education commission of Fangshan district in Beijing held a forum on education quality and balanced development. Members of the Institute who come from the

BNU surveyed students' reading, mathematics and science achievement levels in the district, looking as well at the correlation between academic level and socioeconomic status. These findings informed the district's reform programme (Ministry of Education, 2010). NIEA also formed a workforce to compile a planning strategy for the Ministry of Education's State Assessment Centre (NSA).

All of these platforms are targeted to the real and practical issues of education. What is special is that they don't just conduct research inside labs but also translate the research findings into documents and recommendations for the different departments of the Ministry of Education.

BNU has a 100-year history of teacher training and related research. On the campus there are dozens of senior professors who are so renowned that they can offer advice directly to senior officials and policy makers at various levels of government. Of these, 19 professors are members of the National Academy of Science, 22 are Yangtze River Scholars, and 112 young scholars are titled as New Century Talents. These professors are not only researchers, but they also have opportunities to bring their ideas and proposals directly to key policy makers, connecting policy making directly with scientific research.

The State Council (SC) has also established an advisory organisation of its own, called National Advisory Chamber (NAC). NAC conducts independent research, which can have a strong influence on the SC. There are four member of NAC who are BNU professors. BNU has a larger number of senior consultants than any other university in China.

Outstanding alumni also contribute to linking research with policy. BNU has a large number of outstanding graduates. Many of them have become the elites of various fields in education, technology, business, politics and social sciences. One of BNU's graduates, Professor Guiren Yuan, is currently the Minister of Education. He and other famous alumni will attend the sixth National People's Congress, where they will submit their policy proposals for education.

The official text of *National Long-term Education Reform and Development Plan (2010–2020)* was released on 29 July 2010. It is the first grand educational plan of the 21st century and will guide national education reform and development in the next decade. In the process of producing these guidelines, BNU played a key role as 'brain trust' and 'think tank'. Two or three dozen BNU scholars in various fields were invited to take part in the discussion and drafting of the draft plan.

As a national educational flagship university, BNU plays an important role in teacher training and the development of education research. BNU has cultivated a large number of front-line education experts, master teachers all over China. They take the initiative to undertake the important tasks of teacher training, and participate extensively in the formulation of such national education policies as drafting and revising of the education laws and regulations, such as the recent policy waiving tuition in teacher education or the 'Interim Measures for the Regulations of Academic Degrees of the People's Republic of China'. Cooperating with various education groups and research institutions, BNU created a series of research platforms to support the development of education. BNU continues its historic mission of enhancing the strength of educational science and also serving the practice of educational reform and development.

BNU has had a strong impact on education practice, which has occurred through six channels. They are:

- *Compiling textbooks and supplementary materials*: Professors of BNU not only edit college texts, but also textbooks for primary and secondary schools. The textbooks published by BNU are of great influence and are highly valued and quite popular among teachers. Moreover, BNU is one of the main sources of supplementary materials for national primary and secondary schools, helping teachers to prepare lessons and students to learn.
- *Teacher training and development*: BNU is responsible for training up to 10,000 teachers each year, mainly through training 'backbone' teacher development providers. This work is done in the Faculty of Education and the School of Continuing Education. When these teachers return to their local schools, the majority of them become model teachers and most of them will be teacher mentors.
- *Principal training*: The institution responsible for school leadership training is the Ministry of Education Primary School Principal Training Centre, School of Continuing Education, in the Teacher Education Research Centre of BNU. Every year BNU provides more than 50 training courses and more than 5,000 school principals receive in-service training. Moreover, BNU has engaged in the training of principals and teachers from Hong Kong and Macao Special Administration Regions.
- *Experimental school projects for the application of education theories*: Right now, BNU has 10 affiliated schools in the region of Beijing Municipality, among them seven high schools, one junior high school, one primary school, and one kindergarten. Outside of Beijing, BNU collaborates with local government, jointly managing more than 30 affiliated schools. These schools play a positive role

in improving the quality of local education and contribute to the improvement of educational and teaching models.

• *Extensive cooperation with local education authorities in some special administration regions (SARs)*: BNU has signed agreements with several cities or districts to help build their educational programmes. These reform projects offer integrated services in which BNU staffs work with local officials in areas ranging from school development planning, to teacher professional development, to student study guides.

• *Research projects related to experimental schools*: Many Professors of BNU who undertake research projects work with various schools on this research. In a typical year more than 2,000 schools will be connected to BNU research projects.

East China Normal University

East China Normal University (ECNU) is another institution that exerts a strong impact on national policy making in education. ECNU is located in Shanghai, the frontier of China's open-door policy. Since it was founded in 1951, ECNU has experienced successful mergers with several other institutions and become well known in the area of teacher training and education research. Now, it has become a cutting-edge education research hub for China. In a recently published work *Portrait of Chinese Universities in the 21st Century* (Hayhoe et al, 2011) Professor Ruth Hayhoe, a famous Canadian comparative educator, praised ECNU as the 'leading education-related university in China'. The report titled *Reports on Chinese Outstanding Humanist and Social Scientist 2011* (available via www.ccaa.net) includes 12 educators from ECNU on the list, which reinforces this university's high academic status in China. Compared with BNU, ECNU places more emphasis on education practice, especially in K–12 education.

In 1989, ECNU established its training centre for school leaders. It is one of the six headquarters for the training of principals supported by what was then China's Education Commission (currently the Ministry of Education). In 2003, this centre was restructured into a unique centre for secondary school leaders, making itself a national base for leadership training across the country.

Between 1999 and 2001, ECNU established two leading education research institutes. One is the Institute of Basic Educational Reform and Development (BERD), directed by Professor Lan Ye, a well-known education theorist and practitioner. The other is the Institute of Curriculum and Instruction (ICI), led by Professor Qiquan Zhong, a top curriculum expert. Since then, ECNU has been paying more attention to connecting its education research directly to practice. The year 2009 witnessed the foundation of the Ministry of Education Key Laboratory of Spoken and Auditory Sciences, which caters for the needs of children with spoken and auditory disadvantages. Additionally, a new centre concerning youth health evaluation is currently being developed.

Overall, in areas from basic education to special education, and physical education, ECNU has played an important role in affecting both policy making and practice in education. For more than 60 years ECNU has continued to develop, and its history is also a reflection on Chinese educational transformation and reform generally, as well as a continuing example of mobilisation of research knowledge. However, as with any institution, it has challenges. For one thing, in spite of its strengths, the institutional setting is rather chaotic and complicated, resulting in both redundancy and waste of resources. Given the international tendency to make higher education more streamlined and efficient, ECNU needs to make some changes. For example, several sub-fields are largely ignored, such as higher education and private education.

Xiamen University

There are many reasons why we selected Xiamen University as a case study in this section. One is because of the university's strong higher education research team and their influence on higher education policy. Xiamen University was established 90 years ago, with the mission statement of 'Strive constantly for self-improvement and for perfection'. It is a comprehensive university that covers a wide range of disciplines, with excellent faculty staff and classified as a first-class university in China. Xiamen University now enjoys a worldwide reputation. So far, Xiamen University has successively fostered more than 200,000 undergraduates and graduate students, and more than 60 academicians of The National Academy of Science and Engineering are alumni of Xiamen.

In the field of education research, Xiamen University established its first specialised research institution focusing on higher education. It is the first university in China authorised to grant master's and doctoral degrees in higher education. Professor Maoyuan Pan is the founder of the higher education institute and is one of the leading policy consultants of higher education in China.

The Higher Educational Development Research Centre (HEDRC) of Xiamen University is the sole research base of humanities and social sciences designated by the Ministry of Education. As a 'think tank', HEDRC has offered many recommendations for the country's educational development and for national educational decision making.

Established in 2000 by Xiamen University, HEDRC became the humanities and social research base of the Ministry of Education with regard to higher education studies. The institute has cultivated excellent scholars and organises high-level scientific research for the national educational development strategy as well as addressing major theoretical and practical issues in the field. As China's economy and society have changed, the centre has produced many innovative achievements, acted as an academic exchange centre with other countries and provided assistance to many newly established universities. Its work gives special attention to suggestions and advice useful for educational decision makers in universities and governments.

Besides HEDRC, Xiamen University has several other related education research institutes, such as the Private Institute of Higher Education, the Higher Education Quality and Assessment Research Institute, the Educational Economics and Management Research Institute, the Educational Theory Research Institute and so on. They provide a large number of reports and recommendations for educational decision making as well as policy implementation.

At Xiamen University, there are several senior experts and scholars. Professor Maoyuan Pan is one of the pioneers in Chinese higher education. His academic achievement has been recognised by his counterparts in China and abroad. He has played a major role in the founding of higher education study and the development of higher education in China.

Professor Pan's first important policy proposal was to advocate the establishment of the discipline of higher education. This suggestion was adopted into national policies and regulations. In 1978, Professor Pan published a paper titled 'Theoretical research on higher education is a must' in *Guangming Daily*, one of the leading newspapers for the academic sector. His aim was again to support the establishment of the discipline of higher education. In 1983, under the impetus of Professor Pan and with the efforts of the national higher education sector, higher education was officially identified as a second level (or branch) discipline within the field of education. In 1984, the Institute of Higher Education in Xiamen University was authorised to be the first official master's degree-granting institute for the discipline of higher education. Professor Pan was also the convener for compiling the first higher education textbook for China in 1981, laying the theoretical foundation for this new discipline. He also participated in many aspects of Chinese higher education management and became one of the first research consultants in this field.

Xiamen University has also set up a database of higher education research, including an English version in 2009, to allow more experts to know about the higher education system in China. The database includes basic information on universities and colleges in China, including enrolments, graduates, curriculum, faculty, expenditure, environment and infrastructure. It aims to offer current and thorough information for research and decision making on higher education, making it more convenient for administrative planning, and to provide public access to learning more about higher education in China.

However, there is space for improvement at Xiamen. First, the outstanding development of higher education in the university has created a single dominant discipline, which means less work in and support from other areas of education. The lack of a strong education foundations element makes the disciplinary background weaker. Second, Xiamen is located in the south-eastern corner of China, far away from the major cities, creating a danger of isolation and making it harder to attract first-class scholars.

Shangai Institute of Human Research Development

Founded in February 1985, Shanghai Institute of Human Research Development (SIHRD) is now a part of the Shanghai Academy of Educational Sciences (one of its five research departments, the others being the General Education Institute, the Higher Education Research Institute, the Vocational Education and Adult Education Research Institute, and the Private Education Institute). The SIHRC is a research organisation that works on human resources development and educational development. It is also a member of the International Institute for Educational Planning (IIEP). Hundreds of experts, scholars and educational officials around the world have visited SIHRD. The researchers of the institute also visit overseas for academic exchanges each year.

Its main areas of research include: talent demand forecasting and education planning, human resources and educational development policy, educational management, educational evaluation and educational finance, and management information system development. In its work, SIHRD always insists that research on human resources development should be closely related to wider issues of economics, social science, technology culture and labour force structure changes. In terms of methodology, SIHRD has a preference for comprehensive methods including international comparisons and quantitative and qualitative analysis.

SIHRD consists of 19 researchers and professors at various ranks. It also invites and employs up to 20 important domestic and foreign scholars as advisers and guest researchers. Professor Guoliang Chen, president of the Shanghai Academy of Educational Sciences and the director of the basic education monitoring centre in the Department of Education, may be the most influential of these. He participated in the formulation of the National Education Reform Plan for Medium- and Long-term Development (2008–09), which is critical to the future development of education in China. Moreover, he participated in writing a series of research reports that have been adopted by relevant government departments (see Guoliang, 2007; Guoliang et al, 2003, 2005, 2006).

As an important base of China's education research, SIHRD emphasises the application of research to practical issues. This approach is reflected first in its research reports. These attach great importance to quantitative research and cite plenty of data, which tends to give them greater credibility. Second, SIHRD provides a wide range of research-related services, not only for the Ministry of Education, but also for the development of education in central and western provinces and non-governmental sectors in China. The consultancy SIHRD provides has two aspects: educational macro policy making and socioeconomic development. It has also strengthened international academic exchange activities. Despite (or perhaps because of) its relatively small size, SIHRD is very flexible, which enables it to make timely adjustments to its work. In this regard, it is quite difficult for Xiamen University and East China Normal University, which also have a large effect on China's educational development, to compete with SIHRD.

However, every coin has two sides, as mentioned in *The Book of Changes* – the Yin and Yang, which deeply affects the thinking habits of the Chinese people. As a public institution in China that provides consultation and service for education, SIHRD also needs to enhance and improve itself. For instance, in the use of research methods, SIHRD stresses quantitative research, which generally refers to researchers who investigate variables that are thought to have cause–effect relationships. Then certain tested tools are used to measure and analyse these variables to verify the researchers' hypothesis. Quantitative research has its advantages, but qualitative study in pedagogy also merits use. As a research paradigm, compared with quantitative research, qualitative researches still does not have a common definition. To put it simply, it is a research approach that involves detailed study of the research object in natural conditions. Quantitative research and qualitative research should be equally respected. One approach is to take the view that education research should use a regression approach of 'qualitative-quantitative-qualitative' (see Hua Yang, 2001; Qunhui, 2001).

As an important education research and consulting institutions in China, SIHRD aspires to become China's RAND, a famous policy research unit in USA. But it still lacks the ability to grasp the details of policies and programmes well, although it has many important research achievements. SIHRD needs ways to make its research achievements known by more Chinese people. There is no denying that producing important research results is very important, but knowing how to makes these results known and used by more people is also important.

Features of KM work in contemporary China

KM and educational decision making in contemporary China are inseparable from the political, economic and cultural development of China, as shown in **Figure 10.8**.

Figure 10.8: Characteristics of KM and educational decision making

Traditional decision-making model transformed to scientific one

In the knowledge era, the power of knowledge has become more and more significant. Consequently, China's administrative decision making has to depend more on scientific research. The previous phenomena known in Chinese slogans as 'babbling without thinking' and 'one person lays down the law' have been gradually devalued and discarded. Instead, scientific investigation and data-based decision making have been promoted. The quality of senior administrative officials is steadily improving, and a growing number of scholars are joining the decision-making process. Grounded in scientific research and experience, these scholar decision makers tend to make decisions from a more scientific perspective with more regard to research evidence. Examples mentioned earlier also show that the experts and scholars in China contribute greatly to educational decision making. Examples are still on the rise. Overall, academic decision making is gradually becoming embodied in KM in China. It is the pursuit or the ideal for China to make decision making more scientific in the long road of reform and development.

Chinese characteristics under formation

KM has a long history in China. It is not only part of the traditional heritage of the country, but also draws extensively on the fruits of civilisation and world excellence. In China, where respect for intellectual tradition remains a very powerful force, knowledge about the wisdom of the ancient sage kings in decision making is far reaching. The Qin Warring States period (475–221 BC) gave birth to the Confucian, Maoist, Taoism, Legalism and other important ideologies. Those scholars and their disciples could be considered as similar to today's think tanks. They influenced posterity and deeply affected policy makers then, and now they are still shining the light of wisdom on decisions.

While these traditions remain valuable and important, the introduction of foreign democratic decision-making models is improving China's educational decision-making mechanism and promoting better education in China. We believe the future of Chinese education policy will be more open to efficient, democratic and scientific ways of policy making from other parts of the world, leading to a new and different model of education policy making.

Faster development and wider influence of KM

The impact of KM on educational decision making is becoming deeper as shown in three respects. First of all, KM depends on the rapid development of the internet, which has become an indispensable part of daily work and life. The influence of the internet on educational decision making in China is growing steadily. The internet can, if used well, allow synthesis of the wisdom that runs through the whole process of human development via a global information network. Through the internet, decision makers at any level, including national education policy makers, can communicate with each other at any time or in any place. A short message or an e-mail can help us communicate instantly with our counterparts far across the ocean. All of this was unimaginable 30 or 40 years ago.

Second, the establishment and improvement of large databases has promoted KM. The development of information technology allows more ways to make good use of data. These databases enable decision makers to grasp more comprehensive and accurate information and extract useful decision-making information more quickly and easily, which can significantly reduce the distance between theoretical knowledge and practice.

Third, institutions that focus on policy inquiry and research are increasing in China, resulting in a stronger influence of research. When the national government attaches importance to a research field and sets up research institutions through its administrative power, those institutions are considered as authoritative in the relevant field. Decisions without the participation of the authoritative institution will not be accepted by society.

Current problems of KM in China

Although there is some progress for KM in China, there are also challenges. The main challenges could be described as follows.

Challenges related to knowledge producers

Research producers are a main factor in the efficient mobilisation of knowledge, including their motivation, research, communication practices and experience. Often, however, knowledge producers lack the low motivation to pay attention to this aspect of their work. How to motivate researchers to take this work more seriously remains a problem to be analysed and solved. Chinese scholars are good in their field of research, but, with some exceptions already noted, most of them lack experience in effective communication with policy makers. They may send their books to policy makers, but they do not know how to make their points clearly in a shortened version, even though good relations with policy makers are a foundation for KM. How to develop these relationships requires more experience. In our study, we found some scholars of the older generation have more confidence and skill in this area. How to help younger scholars develop this confidence is also an important issue.

Challenges related to policy makers

The main challenge for policy makers is how to mobilise the various producers or sources of knowledge. Research teams are scattered across different universities and even different countries. How to integrate these small teams into larger ones is an urgent issue. Government should invest more energy in creating larger research networks.

Another challenge is the imbalance of policy making across provinces, because they play a vital role in providing and governing education in China. Some provinces have more research institutes, others fewer. It is necessary for the national government to build some mechanism to provide the intelligence and support to those regions with less research capacity. The last point is the attitude of policy makers. In the past, few higher officials would have a large body of policy knowledge, but now they can improve themselves through information technology and personal connections. However, the result may be an increase in their confidence and also their arrogance. If arrogant, policy makers will devalue research findings and continue to use traditional ways of policy making. In China today, the case of executive-led final decisions still appears far more frequently than research-facilitated decision making, and sometimes education research still plays a ritual rather than a real role.

In China, executive-led decision making is manifested in various forms: for example, some educational studies involving the performance evaluation of schools or educational institutions, or having certain political orientations, will be subjected to administrative intervention. Moreover, many administrative leaders not only participate in, but also lead educational studies. The leading nucleus in the Ministry of Education has also served as team leaders of the National Education Science Planning Leading Group.

Since the time of the Sixth Five-year Plan a considerable number of important projects have been led by administration staff within the operational divisions or bureaus of the Ministry of Education. Sometimes this has resulted in excessive administrative control over the work of research institutions, which have become too cautious in publication of their products, while assessment of other educational institutions can remain superficial. An example of the latter was the first round of undergraduate education evaluation, assessing universities around the nation using uniform standards, which resulted in more than 95% being rated as 'excellent'. Lacking clear standards and quality control, education research institutions may be excessively influenced by the subjective judgment of higher agencies that do not have the requisite expertise. In particular, when their own research projects are involved, administrators who have authority tend to intervene in the research results and inevitably hinder the independence and objectivity of the research.

Challenges related to the process of the KM

The processes of KM in China are not yet sufficiently grounded. There are problems both in the amount and speed of the mobilisation of education knowledge. The efficiency of KM is a problem, and, as yet, governments have not built mechanisms and institutions to improve knowledge mobilisation. What is more, the national government has not established any formal reward system to attract scholars to translate their research into policy proposals.

There were already more than 700 research institutions of higher education in colleges and universities in China in 2002. But in 2004, further development of Chinese colleges and universities led the Ministry of Education to issue the document *Views on Further Strengthening the Building of Research Institutions of Higher Education* (Ministry of Education, 2004). This paper led to the creation of yet more education research institutes. Although the original intention is good, with so many institutes the quality of research is not always adequate, and there are too many separate organisations and research teams. The high number of institutes suggests the need for integration as a way to address a fragmented system of education research and development that is too politicised, too distant from practice and lacking an international perspective, and the situation has continued to deteriorate. Currently, there is no effective evaluation mechanism for the quality and efficiency of education research organisations. Moreover, the products of these research institutions are not widely spread and applied. The institutes do not ensure adequate matching of human resources even to maintain the system, not to mention achieving the goal to provide effective policy recommendations for improving educational practice.

The future of KM in China

Knowledge mobilisation in China will change even more quickly in future for four reasons: the merging of information technology and cognitive science; the integration of Chinese experience and international standards; the appearance of international think tanks in China; and the development of large-scale and intensive professional teams.

Marriage of information technology and cognitive science with KM

The development of information and communication technology (ICT) will facilitate education science by providing more convenient tools. Knowledge production and mobilisation will be speeded up with the help of the internet and databases, which are developing at a rapid pace, and these will in turn improve the power and impact of knowledge. On the other hand, ICT and its development will be facilitated by knowledge mobilisation. What is more, the development of KM will receive more attention from governments through the exchange of knowledge. ICT and knowledge application will be mutually conducive.

Integration of Chinese experience and international standards

No doubt the different parts of the globe will increase their integration and understanding in a peaceful environment. So far, the western policy model has been the international model and standard for research. However, the Chinese model is attracting attention, and more and more nations will study how the Chinese model of research and connection to policy could be applied to other contexts. In the near future, China could exert more impact in the field of education development for several reasons. First, it is widely known that China is one of the largest markets for international students. International student transfers will make China more open, while education knowledge and policies in China will also influence other countries. In 2009, there were about 230,000 Chinese students studying abroad, which is 27% more than in 2008. Now China has become the number one student exporter in the world (see Students studying abroad, available via www.moe. gove.cn). Second, China may offer more practical experience to other countries, especially the developing ones. As more nations admire the economic development of China, it is likely that they will look into the education behind the economy. Some aspects will catch the attention of both developing and developed countries, such as the excellent Programme for International Student Assessment (PISA) results achieved in Shanghai. In a word, China will try to build its own national education standards supported by international experiences.

The appearance of international think tanks in China and research-intensive teams

It is not known whether China now has its own education think tanks. It is likely that there are a few institutions in China that are more or less similar to think tanks, such as the faculty of education of BNU and the Centre of Education Development attached to the Ministry of Education. Whether they are independent, or government related, they are now providing consultancy to policy makers. We are confident that soon there will be some international education think tanks in China, focusing on Chinese issues and also on international problems. Already there are countless international cooperation projects such as the conference that gave rise to this book. What is more, because Chinese think tanks can help policy makers of other nations, it is highly possible that one or more international education consultant enterprises will come into being in Beijing.

As the requirement for policy-making knowledge increases, policy makers will depend more on professionals. Large-scale and intensified professional groups will appear. These groups will be flexible in organisation, cooperative in approach, and work in teams across subjects. Without these groups, it will be difficult to satisfy the demands from policy making. Scientific needs will push the development of professional groups. With the maturing of these groups, the application of education knowledge to policy making will improve. Policy making and knowledge mobilisation will be more interrelated.

References

BIS (Business, Innovation and Skills) (2009) *Higher ambitions: the future of universities in a knowledge economy*, research report, London: Department for Business, Innovation and Skills.

China Institute of Education Policy (2010) 'Main responsibilities for the institute' (available at http://ciep.bnu.edu.cn/html/9/s1/columnnews_222.html).

Government of Canada (2010) 'Canadian networks of centers of excellence program' (available at http://www.nce-rce.gc.ca/NCESecretariatPrograms-ProgrammesSecretariatRCE/NCE-RCE/Index_eng.asp).

Government of China (2009) 'Quantity and position of postgraduate advisors in Chinese universities from 2006 to 2009', *China Education Statistical Yearbook*, China (available at www.moe.edu.cn).

Government of China (2010) 'National education science planning from the "sixth five-year" to the "eleventh five-year Plan"', *China Education Statistical Yearbook*, China (available at www.moe.edu.cn).

Guoliang, C. (2007) *Human resources development and educational development strategy*, strategy research report, Shanghai: Shanghai People's Publishing House.

Guoliang C., Ruiwen, H., et al (2003) *From the population of big country towards human resources power*, China's education and human resources issues report, Shanghai: Higher Education Press.

Guoliang C., Ruiwen, H., et al (2006) *Chinese educational development in the new period (1983–2005)*, Shanghai: Shanghai Academy of Social Science Press.

Guoliang C., Ruiwen, H., et al. (2005) *Shanghai educational development in the new period (1983–2005)*, Shanghai: Shanghai Academy of Social Science Press.

Hayhoe, R., Jun, L., Jing, L. and Qiang, Z. (2011) *Portraits of 21st century Chinese universities: in the move to mass higher education*, Hong Kong: Hong Kong University Press and Springer, pp 192-220.

Hua Yang (2001) 'The philosophical thought of qualitative and quantitative research in the study of education', *Jiangxi Social Science*, vol 11, pp 219-20.

Japan Society for the Promotion of Science (2010) *FIRST program* (available at http://www.jsps.go.jp/english/e-first/index.html).

Manfredi, D., Vickers, L., Secker, J. and Montgomery, M. (2009) *The impact of the process to promote equality and diversity in the research assessment exercise 2008*, research report for the Equality Challenge Unit, London: Equality Challenge Unit.

Ministry of Education (2004) 'Views on further strengthening the building of research institutions of higher education', *China Higher Education Research*, no 10.

Ministry of Education (2010) *General statistics of all the universities and colleges,* National Institute for Education Assessment (available at http://niea.neea.edu.cn/show_sort.jsp?class_id=40_01&supclass_id=&isinfo=0).

Postiglione, G. (2010) *Education impact study: the global recession and the capacity of colleges and universities to serve vulnerable populations in Asia*, ADBI Working Paper no 208, Tokyo: Asian Development Bank Institute.

Qunhui, O. (2001) 'Toward a diverse educational research methods – qualitative research and quantitative research comparison', *Journal of Yunnan Normal University*, vol 2, no 5, pp 28-31.

Tianshan Z. and Gao. B. (2009) 'Analysis on the status quo of educational scientific research achievements and its influence in China', *Educational Researcher*, vol 8, pp 11-19.

ELEVEN

The federal challenge to university-based education research in the United States: turning research into policy and practice

Sarah A. Mason, Wisconsin Center for Education Research, School of Education, University of Wisconsin-Madison

Introduction

This chapter explores the current environment for education research in the United States (US) and the ways in which recent changes in the national policy framework, resources, infrastructure, and roles have introduced both new options and key challenges for university-based education researchers in developing, disseminating, and transferring research knowledge. The chapter begins by describing the federal government's recent role in defining the education research environment and framing the research agenda. This federal influence has been exercised through building and funding research capacity, infrastructure, and resources and federalising policy and national education priorities established under the No Child Left Behind legislation (NCLB, 2002). The main premise of this chapter is that current national policies and priorities for education research set a new course by prescribing what is to be researched and how that research is to be designed, conducted, and disseminated to education policy makers and practitioners.

The main body of the chapter explores new trends likely to shape university-based education research going forward. These include changes in federal funding priorities; research quality, design, and rigour; information technologies and data systems; publication, audience, and knowledge transfer; and research relevance and utilisation. The roles of public and private entities such as state governments and foundations are also considered. These factors have implications not only for university researchers, research scholarship, and the education research process itself, but also for schools of education and national and local policy and practice.

The chapter concludes by discussing the implications of these trends for how university-based education research is conducted and consumed. The current context presents university scholars and researchers with new opportunities, and resources, while also imposing limitations, trade-offs, and competition. The trends in federal policy, funding, and infrastructure development that began with the passage of NCLB continue to influence the process of education research and the roles of universities in that process. The extent to which the new federalism will shape the future direction of university-based education research and its transformation into education policy and practice depends on whether universities respond to these trends as opportunities or impediments.

National influence: framing the education research agenda and resources

The national institutions and policies that oversee and support public education in the US, including those that serve education research initiatives, have a long and complex organisational history (Rudalevige, 2008, pp 17-40).[1] The current federal infrastructure, the modern US Department of Education (ED), and the policy arena are an outgrowth of the politics, legislation, and debates about the federal role in public education that began well before the 1960s. The evolution of these institutions and the ongoing policy debates have major implications for the development of the education research branch of the federal education infrastructure and also for federal influence on the trajectory of education research nationwide. An understanding of this evolution – as well as the development of new ideas and resources since the beginning of the Obama administration in 2008 – is key to grasping the federal context for education research today and its implications for education researchers at post-secondary institutions. This section describes the most recent relevant changes in policies, priorities, institutional components, and resources at the federal level, and the future direction of education research and the roles of the university education research community.

Federal legislation and policy: setting priorities for education research

In 2001, the Elementary and Secondary Education Act (ESEA), reauthorised as the No Child Left Behind Act (NCLB) (US Department of Education, 2010a), was a watershed for public education in the US and for education research. Perhaps more than any other piece of recent legislation, NCLB asserts a federal presence in education and wrests control of public education from state and local entities by setting and regulating policies and priorities from the top down.[2] NCLB aims to increase accountability, performance, and achievement for schools, teachers, and students through standards-based reform, assessment, school choice, charter schools, and teacher quality, among other strategies and mechanisms. NCLB requires states to adopt test-based accountability systems to improve student performance and increase equity for traditionally underserved students. The law also emphasises new standards for measuring performance and producing evidence and puts pressure on states, school districts, and schools to make local policy decisions based on scientifically based research.

NCLB policies have had an impact on education research in three main areas over the last decade. First, the legislation sets forth and focuses the education reform agenda for the country, states, and school districts. By making state aid and grant funding conditional on compliance with NCLB Title I and Title II requirements, NCLB ties priorities to the funding and determines the primacy of each policy area to be developed and researched at each level of public education and by education researchers. In general, areas of emphasis in NCLB focus on measuring student education outcomes and achievement and teacher quality and performance. Second, NCLB seeks to increase the visibility, rigour, relevance, and use of education research by promoting 'scientifically based research', a term used throughout the legislation. Although education researchers largely agree on the concept, they have yet to reach consensus on its definition. They do, however, agree that emerging definitions 'directly shape the future of education research' (Eisenhart and Towne, 2003, p 32). Third, NCLB promotes the use of experimental and quasi-experimental research design – such as randomised controlled trials (RCTs), meta-analysis, and systematic statistical analysis – to demonstrate causal effects and successfully replicate and scale results (Slavin, 2002, pp 15-21; Eisenhart and Towne, 2003, pp 31-8).

In response to the 2008 recession, the US federal government passed the American Recovery and Reinvestment Act of 2009 (ARRA), investing US$97.4 billion in education-related appropriations by autumn 2010 (US Department of Education, 2010b). The goals of this large but short-term investment were to 'improve schools, raise achievement, drive reform and produce better results' (US Department of Education, 2010c) and thereby stimulate the economy. ARRA funds were dispersed mainly in the form of grants to states, school districts, and other education entities and intermediaries. Of those initiatives planned and awarded, three – Race to the Top (RttP), Investing in Innovation (i³), and the Teacher Incentive Fund (TIF) – are illustrated here as examples of how ARRA influenced education research. While the ARRA programmes were intended to jump-start state and local education reform initiatives and infrastructure, many of the funds were authorised for evaluation, research, and data system development.[3] A requirement of each of these ARRA programmes was to evaluate educational programmes and innovations, use data from state and district longitudinal data systems, monitor performance, and statistically analyse teacher and student outcomes.

Federal resources for education research: institutions and funding

The primary federal agency with responsibility for education research is the Institute of Education Sciences (IES), housed within ED. Established under the Education Sciences Reform Act of 2002,[4] IES has a mission to expand fundamental knowledge and understanding of education and document the nation's education condition and progress by advancing quality research and its dissemination to educators, practitioners, researchers, and the public. IES pursues its mission through four major centres: the National Center for Education Research (NCER), the National Center for Education Statistics (NCES), the National Center for Education Evaluation and Regional Assistance (NCEE), and the National Center for Special Education Research (NCSER).[5] Also managed by ED is the National Assessment of Educational Progress (NAEP). Commonly known as the Nation's Report Card, NAEP was created by Congress to assess students' knowledge in a variety of subjects and report on the condition and progress of US education since 1969. NAEP remains a valuable data source for the study of large-scale and longitudinal issues in student achievement.[6] The 15-member National Board for Education Sciences (NBES), appointed by the President and confirmed by the Senate, approves IES research priorities and gives the IES director advice on the institute's activities, collaboration with federal agencies and states, and strategies for strengthening education research, funding, scientific standards, and scientific review.[7]

The federal government invests a significant amount of funding in annual appropriations for ED, but only a fraction of those funds are available for education research. Budget appropriations for ED have declined from approximately US$72 billion in 2005 to US$68.5 billion in 2008 (US Department of Education, 2008). However, as a share of total outlays at ED, research and development (R&D) funds have increased from US$16.91 billion in 1997 to US$28.81 billion in 2005 (NSF, 2006, Table 7). In 2005, 67% of the R&D monies went to applied research, 30% went to development, and only 4% went to basic research (NSF, 2006, Table 7).[8] In 2009, IES received US$4.69 billion in discretionary funds for research, development, and dissemination; statistics; NAEP; and Statewide Data Systems, and the FY 2011 Budget Request calls for increases of 3.6%–30.2% in each category (US Department of Education, 2010d). In 2009–10, ARRA infused an additional US$98 billion into the education economy on top of the annual fiscal outlays (US Department of Education, 2009a). The IES portion of the ARRA discretionary funding totalled just over US$10 billion and was dispersed to further develop state-wide data systems and other programmes and activities, as already mentioned. These recent funding trends at the national level indicate that while funding for education in general remains tight, funding for education research is on the rise and is targeted towards applied research, development of national and state data systems, and research and evaluation that prioritises rigorous analysis of student outcomes.

The National Science Foundation (NSF) also contributes to the federal infrastructure that supports education R&D, particularly in the area of science, mathematics, engineering and technology (STEM) education. Most of the NSF funding that goes to universities and colleges is for basic and applied research in the sciences and engineering. Within NSF, the Directorate for Education and Human Resources (EHR) promotes excellence in STEM education for all levels of the educational system. EHR invests in rigorous research on learning, integrates research and education, and facilitates the transition of research to policy and practice through broad participation and partnership. With respect to education research, NSF is particularly noted for prioritising and funding research that involves interdisciplinary collaboration among STEM, education, and social science faculty members and research scientists and for investing in models of education reform that engage educators at all levels through networking, partnerships, alliances, and collaborations. Total NSF funding through EHR programmes and grants in 2009 exceeded US$945 million (including US$100 million in ARRA funds), which supported education research and evaluation at more than 1,900 colleges and universities across the US (NSF, 2009).[9]

Roles of states and local educational agencies (LEAs) in education eesearch

In the loosely distributed hierarchy of the US education system, states, school districts and schools each play a role in setting, prioritising and interpreting policy; directing finances; and producing and consuming education research, evaluation, and data. Local governance operates under varying degrees of what is known as local control, in which education entities have different amounts of autonomy, decision-making power, and accountability that varies across states and among levels of the education enterprise. States often act as brokers and intermediaries between ED, districts, and schools, and the universities and colleges seeking to produce and consume education research. The federal policy priorities and funding that influence education research efforts typically flow through state departments of education, and are selectively absorbed and interpreted at the local level, although districts, schools and independent charter schools vary greatly in how they operate within this environment. With the advent of NCLB, local education organisations are under pressure to be more accountable, to monitor student achievement and teacher performance, and to make policy decisions on scientifically based evidence and research. This has led to a growth in local demand for education research results and more local data system capacity and analytical sophistication. However, most of the local data and research capacity resides at the state and large district level, and district data capacity is being undermined by recent local budget cuts in education. As noted previously, the federal government has responded by funding the development of state-level data warehouse systems, made IES and ARRA evaluation and research grants and contracts available to local entities, and has encouraged partnerships with education researchers. These resources provide opportunities for university researchers to collaborate with local educators under federal sponsorship (see also Henig, 2008–09).

Foundations and other intermediaries

A growing number of non-profit, membership, partisan and advocacy organisations, as well as private foundations, have entered the education research arena to answer the demand for education research. Often these organisations have their own agendas, priorities, sources of funding, and quality standards for education research, and the majority of their education sponsorship tends to go to development, advocacy, or marketing research—not education research.[10] With regards to the limited amount of education research these organisations do fund, (some of which may be their own in-house research on specific topics), they also act as intermediaries by synthesising, and translating extant research and data for policy makers, educators and the public (Arbaugh et al, 2010). Often they are also consumers of education research themselves (Manna and Petrilli, 2008). Private foundations such as the Bill and Melinda Gates Foundation[11] often sponsor education research through academic institutions, but such funding does not come without compromise and limitations. Often private foundations tie research sponsorship to their own interests and agenda, establish their own standards for quality and integrity, and retain control of dissemination of results to their constituents and the public. Despite these limitations, foundations have become a significant source of research funding for some university education researchers.

The number of other intermediaries engaged in education research, such as policy groups, think tanks, and private technical assistance providers have increased in recent years, and as they have gained greater capacity themselves, and gained access to federal funding sources, they compete with university-based researchers for education research funding and audiences.

New directions for the university-based education research community

The university-based education research community in the US is large and diverse. Academic research in education is pursued by a wide variety of faculty members, research scientists, and graduate students from a broad range of disciplines (education, psychology, statistics, sociology, history, economics, philosophy, anthropology, and political science), at public and private four-year colleges, graduate degree-granting institutions, and large comprehensive, Research I and Research II universities. More than 4,400 universities and colleges offer degree-granting undergraduate and graduate programmes, and of those, more than 1,117 award graduate degrees in education programmes.[12] The American Education Research Association currently has approximately 25,000 members, including members from colleges and universities, federal and state educational agencies, school systems, foundations and the private sector. While many colleges and smaller university faculties conduct education research, the Research I and Research II universities receive the bulk of federal funding for education research. Of the US$72,089.6 (in millions of current dollars) distributed by ED in 2009, US$30,267.1 went to post-secondary institutions and of that, US$658.2 went towards education research and statistics (US Department of Education, 2009b).

The remainder of the chapter focuses on this university-based education research community and discusses the opportunities and challenges brought about by the recent federalism in education, in particular regarding changes in the research process – knowledge generation, dissemination and utilisation – and the implications for rigour and relevance, scholarship, and policy.

Changes in the university-based education research process

The traditional avenues of academic research in education are based in the norms and culture of scholarship, academic freedom, and autonomy that allow faculty members and research scientists to determine areas of interest and expertise. Standards and incentives in the academy are structured and enforced by discipline area and tenure requirements. The academy assures quality and validity of research and directs publication through peer-reviewed scholarly journals and dissemination to the field at large. For most faculty members research participation is a requirement of tenure and the ability to obtain external funding for research also factors into tenure and promotion decisions and contributes to scholarly reputation. Often departments and disciplines are isolated from one another and operate in silos, and the education faculties have historically been separate from the academic disciplines in the arts and sciences (Goldhaber and Brewer, 2008). The recent changes at the federal level described previously have already had an influence on the traditional modes of university research practice by determining the funding streams and research priorities, and by changing the way many faculty members and research scientists generate knowledge and transfer knowledge beyond academia. The current federally prescribed framework affects university-based education research by influencing what is researched, who produces research, the quality of research, how research is conducted and supported, and how and when research is disseminated and utilised.

Funding priorities

University faculty members and researchers are normally required to procure their own research funding and tend to follow the money, which for education researchers typically means entering the federal competitive grant process. Federal law, policies, agencies and programmes (for example NCLB, ARRA, IES, and RttP) that support education research have become increasingly prescriptive about what is to be researched (for example student outcomes, teacher performance, charter schools), and how research is to be designed and conducted (for example randomised controlled trials, impact evaluation, value-added analysis, and regression-discontinuity designs). Recent education debates and politics have extended the NCLB focus on accountability, performance, and market-driven education to encompass teacher performance and compensation, charter schools, and school reform innovations that provide evidence of reducing educational inequities and achievement gaps. Until recently, faculty members and researchers selected a research topic, a research design, and appropriate research methods based on their area of scholarship and expertise. But now, research topics and methods are frequently determined by the priorities of the funding source.

Another aspect of the new funding priorities is the increased competition for limited federal education research dollars. Federal funding for education research, despite recent increases, is still less abundant than for other social science research, is more 'tightly defined and controlled', and favours applied research over basic research.[13] Such grant competitions as the i³ development grants, TIF and the NSF and ED's Math and Science Partnerships,[14] have required collaboration among researchers and programme participants, and have opened research opportunities to think tanks, advocacy groups, and state and local educational agencies. These organisations have been building their own research capacity, and their increasing ability to meet the federal research requirements and respond to client and partner needs make them a viable alternative source for research support.

These funding priorities and constraints force a trade-off for university researchers – between scholarship autonomy and the limitations imposed by competitions for research funding prescribed by a federal research agenda. Henig (2008b) points out that given these constraints, some education researchers have been turning to foundations for funding, but foundation funding has its own set of limitations. Foundations tend to fund education research related to their own missions, such as in the area of vouchers, charters, and school choice and tend to control dissemination that typically by-passes the peer review process. The challenge to university education researchers is how to acquire funding without compromising control of their own research agenda and scholarship.

Research quality and rigour

The debate continues among education researchers as to how the federal drive towards scientifically based research and more statistically rigorous methodologies is changing the nature of education research itself. Debate also continues on how the new federalism influences education policy and practice. Meanwhile, the federal government has moved forward with defining expectations for high-quality research that is both rigorous and relevant. Beginning in 2002, Grover J. Whitehurst, the new director of IES, separated the grant review and contracting process and established more rigorous requirements in the grant application rules and in standards for grant reviewers (Hess, 2008a). At the same time, IES began to establish stricter methodological standards and review criteria for its four main centres (NCER, NCES, NCEE, and NCER) and any agency reports or research results disseminated by the new IES What Works Clearinghouse (WWC, 2008). These priorities have been extended under the Obama administration and the current IES director, John Q. Easton. An evaluation of the effectiveness of IES, conducted in 2008, concluded that IES had been mostly successful in increasing the rigour and number of efficacy and effectiveness studies, and ensuring the high standards for quality of research reporting through the efforts of the WWC (Baldwin et al, 2008).

The federal standards and expectations for scientifically based research have been redefined and raised, shifting the emphasis of education research towards applied research and evaluation and statistically sophisticated methodologies such as RCTs and use of large, longitudinal data sets. This poses challenges for academics whose research concentration is on developing the basic knowledge base of teaching and learning, or who rely heavily on non-experimental designs and qualitative methodologies. Moreover, the push to advance quantitative methodologies has challenged even those university researchers who are well versed in those methods. Applied research methods and analytical models require not only quantitative analytical sophistication, but the skill to develop and access large longitudinal databases. Experimental research designs such as RCTs are difficult to set up, and costly to run and maintain over time; not all academic researchers have the capacity and skills to meet these requirements. However, the new direction towards scientific methods, rigorous standards, and applied research is a boon for academics who can meet the priorities and requirements. This new direction has opened the door to more interdisciplinary engagement by social and political scientists and economists, who bring new perspectives and analytical tools to the research process.

For example, sociologists and economists who conduct research using national and state assessment databases (expanded under NCLB) and deploy analytical models such as value–added analysis are finding many opportunities to expand their work and scholarship in the current research environment.

Quality and rigour of education research have typically been vetted by scholars within the academic field and through peer-reviewed journals that enforce high standards of research, design, analysis and publication. University and discipline reward and recognition systems rely on these mechanisms to ensure both scholastic and research excellence. Despite the oversight of education scholars and researchers, education research has generally been criticised for a lack of quality, accuracy, and relevance (Hess, 2008a; see also Goldhaber and Brewer, 2008). The poor reputation of education research fuelled the NCLB emphasis on scientifically based research and the IES emphasis on establishing standards and mechanisms that promote rigour and quality in research supported by the federal government.[15] The federal policies that push for rigour and quality could be interpreted by academics as a government intrusion on their scholarship, and indeed, much criticism has been levelled at IES and the WWC for overstepping their role in specifying and judging the quality of education research, and restricting grant awards and publication.[16] Or, these priorities for rigour and quality could be embraced by university researchers as an opportunity to improve and repair the reputation of education research.

Technology and data: resources for generating knowledge

Over the last decade changes in technology resources and data infrastructure sponsored by the federal government have created new opportunities for education research, but have also been accompanied by changes in expectations for data, the research process, and knowledge generation. The federal and state governments have invested heavily in developing the capacity of instructional technologies, information systems, and data for educational accountability and research. NCLB spurred states and school districts to ramp up their test-based accountability systems, and required states to define and measure student proficiency annually in reading, mathematics and science for Grades 3–8 (and one year in high school), and comply with new school and district accountability standards. States were also required to collect more extensive data on student characteristics (for example ethnicity, economic, and disability status) to be used to determine equity and effectiveness of schooling for diverse student populations. Mounting pressure for local educators and policy makers to be competitive for state and federal development grants (most of which now require at least baseline data and evidence for application) has also led to an increase in consumption of data at the local level. To handle, process, and provide access to the massive increase in student data called for under NCLB, the federal government built up technical resources and infrastructure at the federal level and provided significant funding to states to develop state-wide longitudinal data systems, such as US$250 million for Statewide Data System development through 2009 ARRA funding (US Department of Education, not dated). The NAEP assessment, sponsored and managed by ED, has also been expanded over the years to include data and reports on national results, state-level samples, and long-term trends.[17] NCES[18] collects all forms of education data, ensures data quality, and analyses and advises on use of its databases under statistical and methodological standards. The number and quality of available data sets and analytical tools has grown significantly since NCLB was enacted, and the proliferation of the internet and universal computing.

This federal investment in local and national data infrastructure and resources reinforces the federal framework for scientifically based research and the use of more rigorous methodologies and at the same time provides an extensive set of data sources for university-based education researchers to mine. Technology innovations have also increased the capability for data to drive research, but education researchers still face several hurdles. While the large, longitudinal federal data sets are fully accessible and provide substantial opportunity for large-scale and longitudinal analysis, they do not provide individual school and student-level data for researchers interested in conducting more localised and time-sensitive research. Access to state, district, and school-level individual data can be difficult and time-consuming for researchers to obtain, and transfer of data is often complicated. Data collection is dependent on assessment cycles and structured reports from test vendors, and school-level data collection and submission – often leading to delays and data quality issues. Local data systems are typically out of sync with researcher needs, because local data systems are organised for accountability and administrative purposes, transactional systems are not easily linked to one another (for example linking student and teacher data), and databases are not designed to support research in general, let alone inferential or predictive research models.[19] For example, the emphasis on RCT research designs requires researchers to have access to high-quality individual-level data that are timely, longitudinal and easily organised for analysis. But, as many university researchers have found, there is often a mismatch between the long-term RCT and research requirements and the immediate needs of local practitioners for decision support and instructional improvement, around which the local data systems are typically designed.

While local educators have greatly expanded their data collection in the past decade, many still need the technical expertise that universities can provide in designing the data system architecture, dealing with data quality and security, and ensuring that the databases are designed for analysis. Local educators are aware that data per se will not meet their information and decision-support needs. They typically lack the capacity to manage and analyse their data to facilitate instructional improvement, performance measurement, programme evaluation and research, as well as administrative decision support and accountability reporting.[20] Increasingly, local entities are seeking outside expertise and partnering with external organisations for help generating knowledge from their data – to turn the data into relevant and meaningful information they can use. Already many universities are pursuing new relationships with local educators by taking steps to provide information technology technical assistance and analytical expertise, and by creating mutually beneficial partnerships with local educators to bridge this data–knowledge gap. The benefits are that researchers attain access to high-quality data for research, and local educators and decision makers receive assistance in transforming their data into relevant knowledge for policy and practice.

Knowledge dissemination and transfer

The ways in which scholarly education research is shared and distributed nationally have changed dramatically over the last 10 years. For university researchers, disseminating research results is no longer just about publishing research findings in peer-reviewed journals and books, or submitting grant reports to funding agencies. New technologies, practices, and expectations for knowledge dissemination and transfer oblige university researchers to reach more audiences, in new and timelier ways, with knowledge that is credible, concise, and easily consumed. The politics of vetting and reviewing research now extend beyond the academy, involving federal agencies and intermediaries as new gatekeepers in the review and dissemination process.

Innovations in technology have changed the patterns of communication as well as the quality and quantity of research dissemination. Online resources and universal access to the Internet have contributed to the growth of traditional scholarly education research outlets, such as increasing the number of peer-reviewed and specialised journals, enabling distribution of conference papers, increasing access to digital libraries, and encouraging a proliferation of small publishers. Innovations have also led to an explosion of online dissemination tools and networks: online publishers, digital libraries, blogs, websites, professional networks, specialised information clearing houses, newsletters, and online versions of traditional print media such as newspapers and magazines. Free online search options such as Google Scholar and Web of Science allow researchers and consumers alike to locate publications while also providing options for tracking scholarly output, its influence and impact.[21] Online communication incorporates technologies that are both push and pull, and asynchronous and synchronous;[22] these technologies support broad distribution, as well as collaboration, immediate feedback, and debate.

Publication and communication technologies deployed through the Internet have changed the publication, distribution, and consumption of scholarly education research. Many of the traditional academic and education research peer-reviewed journals and publishers have established online options for disseminating scholarly research that maintain established peer-review and publication criteria. The proliferation of other online dissemination options offers quick visibility and distribution of results, but these options often forego any scholarly review process, and the shorter research-to-distribution turnaround times can be at odds with the time needed to conduct and vet rigorous research, making these options less attractive for academic researchers. However, the sheer quantity of education research available online, much of it unsupported by quality review or standards, creates a complex array of resources for consumers to navigate. Academic and scholarly papers are often difficult for readers to understand, so they turn to online resources that summarise and explain research results in terms they can understand and use. Often, in translation, the research becomes oversimplified or misinterpreted as it enters the public domain through these channels.

The federal government has also built up its online presence for dissemination of education research. Two notable examples are the Educational Resources Information Center (ERIC), established in 1965 as a library to disseminate education research nationally, and the relatively new WWC. The WWC is a new breed of government-sponsored website, designed to promote informed educational decision making through review and dissemination of education research, innovations and products that meet the IES rigorous evidence standards.[23] More than just another internet repository, the WWC was intended to transform how the federal government manages education knowledge, and ensures its quality and accessibility. IES established the WWC in 2002 to identify valid and reliable research that meets stringent evidence standards, and to make research, evidence, and best practices accessible to the public online. The development and operation of the WWC and its guiding standards and products has not been without struggle and controversy (Henig, 2008a; US Government Accountability Office, 2010). Many researchers and academics criticised the quality, application and timeliness of the early WWC, voicing concerns about the standards and review process, and complaining that university research experts did not participate in the development of the standards (Chatterji, 2004; Schoenfeld, 2006; Slavin, 2008; US Government Accountability Office, 2010).

The early WWC vetting criteria qualified three types of research studies for publication: randomised experiments, quasi-experiments with equating, and regression discontinuity designs. Some researchers felt that the WWC criteria were too narrow and failed to consider other relevant research criteria. Schoenfeld (2006) raised concerns about the role and potential conflict of interest of federal organisations vetting and possibly suppressing research that casts doubts on its own policies. Few early postings on the WWC passed the review standards, and of those that did, the majority provided evidence of what 'doesn't work' rather than 'what works', offering little guidance for educators and prompting the WWC to be nicknamed the 'What doesn't Work Clearinghouse'. But it appears that the WWC was listening and has been hard at work to address these issues. By 2008, an evaluation of the effectiveness of IES noted that the WWC received more than 11 million internet hits in 2007. Of those accessing the WWC, the majority were teachers and administrators, who planned to use the information for curricular decisions and making local, state, and federal policy decisions (Baldwin et al, 2008). Also in 2008, Mathematic Policy Research Inc (which operates the WWC) reported that of the 100 reports posted on the WWC, more than 62% include at least one positive finding (Viadero, 2009). More recently, a US Government Accountability Office report on the WWC found that the WWC had met recommendations by an expert panel to improve the review and reporting process. WWC responded to researcher's concerns about screening criteria that excluded certain rigorous research designs by creating new standards that include two additional research designs, and increased the WWC use by creating practice guides (a new product that includes a broader range of research and information). The report also recommended that while the WWC had increased its output and scope, it still needed to attend to improving the dissemination and the timeliness of product releases to increase its usefulness and effectiveness (US Government Accountability Office, 2010). The WWC has successfully revised its reputation and has become a more trusted source of research evidence. It has established itself as a viable dissemination tool in the eyes of researchers and educators.

Other trends affecting the dissemination of education research and results are the privatisation and commercialisation of academic research products. As seen recently in the fields of science, medicine, and engineering, university research is becoming increasingly market driven, and product and service oriented. Government sponsors of research require universities to demonstrate their economic and social contributions by disseminating products, informing policy, and building public knowledge capacity (Mintrom, 2008; Stine, 2008). Also seen influencing university research practice is the concept of knowledge transfer, in which sharing of information and ideas between public and private domains becomes more useful and actionable through effective management and distribution. Universities in the US have long debated the proper balance between the primary missions of teaching and basic research, and the generation and transmission of knowledge for the public good. In Europe, the 'third sector' or mission at many universities is knowledge transfer through outreach, service, and technical assistance (Mintrom, 2008).[24] These trends are beginning to have an influence on education research at US universities as federal pressures mount for scientifically based research and for researchers to make their research relevant and viable for public consumption. Along with the introduction of privatisation and commercialisation comes the growing presence of intermediary organisations (for example policy and advocacy groups, technical assistance providers, private vendors, think tanks, etc) who mediate dissemination and translation of scholarly work, synthesise education research for consumption by policy makers, market research by-products, and serve as technical assistance providers to link policy and practice (Honig, 2004; see also Manna and Petrelli, 2008). Of concern to the university education research community is the varying capacity of these organisations to synthesise and communicate research that is accurate and unbiased, and does not solely advocate political agendas or commercial products or compromise scholarship.[25] Many researchers are still unsure about whether to engage at all in these trends, and if so, how best to interact and develop productive relationships with the public–private educational enterprise.

The positive implications for universities of this new world of education research dissemination and knowledge transfer are that the changes create access to scholarly research by new audiences in potentially more productive ways. Not only does the internet create countless opportunities for public access to research information and results, but it also creates new options for interaction and debate among researchers and policy makers and intermediaries. At the same time, university researchers are concerned that these new patterns of dissemination expose their research to new pressures and vulnerabilities. The new technologies have changed the timeline and expectations for research publication. By allowing for more immediate release of results, research enters the public domain often prior to review, fuelling public debates in the media, and exposing findings to immediate interpretation. The worry of academics is that these new modes of dissemination may circumvent the more rigorous, albeit time-consuming, process of scholarly peer review and come at the expense of quality research and scholarship. It is difficult for the academy and the disciplines that conduct education research to ensure scholarly and research publication excellence, and to control interpretation of research findings, in a medium such as the internet that is designed to be an open source of information.

Research relevance and utilisation

In its first five years IES was successful in promoting and advancing its main priority – rigour in education research – as demonstrated by the reorganisation of the institution, the improved structure of IES-sponsored programmes, increases in education research capacity of the field (for example postdoctoral fellows and training institutes), and the dissemination of results through the WWC. The aim was to establish higher standards for production of rigorous research design, quality, and reporting, and reinforce the call for consumption of scientifically based research in the NCLB legislation. The early IES priorities also included improving the relevance and utilisation of education research, but with these priorities, the newly established IES fared less well. An evaluation of IES in 2008 found mixed results coming from reviews of NCER, NCSER and NCES regarding attention to *relevance* (defined as the usefulness, alignment to goals, and timeliness of education research) from 2002 to 2007. Of particular concern was the need to improve the ability of the efficacy and scale-up studies in providing relevant findings to the field. Of concern too was the lack of emphasis on ensuring timeliness of findings related to rigorous research (although the evaluation showed a high level of satisfaction with the improved NCES databases, publications, and timeliness). The IES priority of *utilisation* (defined as translating the results of education research for use in evidence-based decision making in policy and practice) was not as much of an institutional focus in the first five years as rigour, and received the lowest marks in the evaluation. Evaluators noted they had difficulty in identifying and measuring utilisation, and recommended that the research base for knowledge utilisation be strengthened in order to learn what types of evidence practitioners and policy makers use and how they use it (Baldwin et al, 2008).

Beginning in 2009, under the direction of John Q. Easton, IES continued to build capacity for education research rigour but also became more serious about improving research relevance. In 2010, Easton set forth five 'big ideas' for IES to support education research 'that matters to schools and improves educational outcomes for children'. These involved IES in: (a) making research more useful and relevant; (b) shifting from a model of dissemination to a model of facilitation; (c) creating stronger links between research development and innovation; (d) building state and district capacity to use longitudinal data systems for research and evaluation; and (e) developing an understanding of schools as learning organisations (Easton, 2010a). The current IES call for increasing research relevance, use, and application was confirmed by the NBES in autumn 2010, when it approved 'relevant research' as one of three priorities for IES, recommending that 'effective research meets the needs of policy makers and practitioners through partnerships' (NBES, 2010).

Much of what is known about education research utilisation – how policy makers and educators interpret and apply research and evidence in their decision making – comes from a relatively small body of work developed over the last 30 years (Weiss, 1979, 1982, 1998, 1999; Fusarelli, 2008; Honig and Coburn, 2008). Recently, studies of research utilisation and data use have been revitalised under the demands of evidence-based decision making by NCLB policies.[26] Older and more recent studies tend to agree in their main findings regarding what influences evidence use in decision making. The studies generally agree that while policy makers and practitioners do consult scholarly journals and reports for research results, they are seldom influenced solely by scholarly research findings in making specific policy decisions. More often, they are influenced by a variety of sources, such as their own pre-existing knowledge and beliefs, local education politics, public and legal issues, economics, media pressure, and the welfare of individuals, rather than by research evidence. Findings also indicate that educators are most likely to use research evidence developed in a local context that they can trust, that meets their immediate needs, is timely, and is easily interpreted and summarised (Weiss, 1982; Honig and Coburn,

2008; Coburn et al, 2009; Nelson et al, 2009; Urban and Trochim, 2009). Common reasons as to why practitioners fail to make use of research results include a lack of time to search and read the extensive research available; the fact that few studies produce high-quality evidence that is transferrable to practitioners' needs and context; the fact that studies lack relevance and applicability to practitioners' work or for improving instructional practices; and the fact that rigorous longitudinal studies take too long to complete and publish, the results come too late, and the results are out of sync with the immediate needs of practitioners (Honig and Coburn, 2008; Nelson et al, 2009; Shankland, 2010). Both policy makers and practitioners indicate that to use scholarly research results effectively they need distilled information that is locally relevant and credible, provides examples from multiple studies, and considers long-term impact and sustainability for the entire local educational system (Nelson et al, 2009). Other studies have also found that educators and policy makers typically lack the ability and time to search for and interpret research evidence and data in their decision making (Arbaugh et al, 2010) – eliciting recommendations for more research training of educators in pre-service and in-service development, school learning communities, and University/K-12 partnerships (Honig and Coburn, 2008; Urban and Trochim, 2009; Easton, 2010b; Shankland, 2010; NCER, not dated).

The NCLB legislation places specific policy demands on practitioners, policy makers, and education researchers to utilise scientifically based research, and the recent IES emphasis on the three priorities of research rigour, relevance, and utilisation reinforces these demands. Practitioners are required to use scientifically based research, and to draw on the abundance of student achievement data for data-based decision making, to select curricula and programmes, to improve teaching and learning, and to inform school reform. Policy makers are under pressure to evaluate programmes and demonstrate effective allocation of resources. Now, education researchers are also feeling pressure to make their research more useful in order to identify remedies and inform improvements in policy and practice at both the national and local level. But producers and consumers of education research define 'what is relevant' based on different sets of needs, purposes, and incentives. As described earlier, federal education officials maintain that relevance comes from rigorous research that is tied to education priorities and policies; identifies solutions and 'what works'; is timely; and has sufficient internal and external validity to be replicated and scaled-up by local practitioners. Yet local practitioners define research as relevant if it considers their own local data and context, consists of examples from multiple studies, and aligns with local needs, experiences and policies. To make defining relevance even more complicated, university researchers tend to think of relevant research as that which is more question driven rather than solution driven, contributes to the education knowledge base, meets discipline norms for scholarship and rigour, and establishes credibility and authoritative expertise. There is a clear disconnect between what policy makers, practitioners and researchers value when it comes to relevance in education research, and this disconnect contributes to the gaps between research, policy, and practice in education today.[27]

As many have observed, there is discontinuity in the research process between production and consumption, and a mismatch between the federal priorities for research rigour, academic emphasis on scholarship, and reliance on local relevance for policy and practice. The gaps that exist between research, policy, and practice lead to less utilisation of research, unmet local needs, and missed opportunities to reform schools and improve student achievement.[28] In June 2010, Secretary of Education, Arne Duncan advocated the need to build a bridge between research, policy and practice and implored university researchers to lead the way by moving 'out of the Ivory Tower and into the schoolhouse' (Duncan, 2010). While much has changed already under the first eight years of NCLB implementation, changes in the education research process at universities that reinforce policy and practice, relevance and utilisation, are slow to emerge and have yet to become institutionalised. Education research and policy analysts suggest that in order to make education research more central to education policy and to integrate research into practice, university researchers must change their research processes and create a connection between knowledge generation and application (Urban and Trochim, 2009). These types of changes will require many universities to revisit their primary mission and their discipline norms to give serious consideration to what they value, and how they promote and reward knowledge transfer, outreach, service, and technical assistance. To successfully take on this challenge and bridge the research–practice gap, universities may also need to reorganise and restructure the roles of education faculty members and researchers.

New roles for education researchers

University faculty members and research scientists have already begun to respond to the calls for new modes of research collaboration and communication, and new roles and relationships both within academia and externally with policy makers, intermediaries and practitioners.

Traditionally, education faculty members and research scientists have worked and produced research autonomously, often in isolation from their peers or departments, and on a single project-by-project basis. If they did work collaboratively, it was typically done so on an ad hoc basis, without developing sustained relationships with fellow researchers or local educators, and without the intention or organisation to integrate, synthesise, and develop capacity at the local level. The Consortium on Chicago School Research (CCSR) has identified four traditional roles university education researchers have pursued in the past to influence educational practice.[29] CCSR acknowledges that over time each of these roles has met success in various ways, but what each of these traditional roles lack are sustained connections between education researchers and local policy makers and practitioners, which results in research output that fails to contribute to the local capacity for reform.[30] These shortcomings of the traditional roles of education researchers and the shifts in national education policy inspired the development and organisation of new models of collaboration between universities and the K-12 education system.

As early as 1965, the federal government began to facilitate a shift in the role of universities in education research. Federally sponsored education researchers were asked to take their research beyond academia and produce research results that would serve local and national education policies, and provide local educators with technical support. By 1965 the federal government had established two sets of national education research institutions affiliated with major universities – the research and development centres (to conduct long-term and large-scale research) and the regional education labs (to support development and technical assistance to practitioners stemming from research).[31] For decades, these centres and labs managed and conducted the majority of federally sponsored education research and technical assistance. Today, there are fewer labs and centres, and those that remain receive less direct federal funding, which has forced the regional labs to become partially privatised and the centres to rely more heavily on competitive government grants and foundation funding. In the last 10 years, the federal support of university-based education research has altered the way universities organise and manage their research. ED and NSF have both instigated competitive grant programmes that require interdisciplinary involvement of researchers and faculty members, partnerships with local educators, cooperation in collecting and analysing student outcome data, technical assistance, and scaling and sustaining of reform efforts. The result is that universities have organised new ways of partnering with school districts and collaborating with think tanks, non-profit bodies and foundations.

These trends are illustrated by three models of collaboration among higher education, public K-12 education and private organisation collaboration in education research. The first example is of a model that directly pairs a major research university with a specific school district. CCSR, formed as a result of the Chicago School Reform Act of 1988, is an independent organisation and partnership between the University of Chicago and Chicago Public Schools (CPS) aimed at conducting rigorous research and evaluation to build local capacity for improvement of CPS's school reform efforts.[32] Researchers at the University of Chicago conduct technical, policy-relevant research in Chicago schools that is designed to build the district's capacity for reform by being accessible to local practitioners and administrators and by increasing the district's use of data, effective strategies and evaluation. The CCSR model engages researchers and practitioners in research within a local context or lab setting that allows for long-term relationships, research collaboration, data access, coherence across research studies, and rigorous research design and implementation, thereby producing evidence that is both locally relevant and more broadly instructive to the field of education reform (Roderick et al, 2009).

A second model is the technical assistance centre model, exemplified by the Center for Educator Compensation Reform (CECR). CCER is a federally funded technical assistance centre that is comprised of researchers from the University of Wisconsin[33] and Vanderbilt University who work in conjunction with Westat and Learning Point Associates (a private education research organisation and former regional lab that is now privatised). As part of ED's Teacher Incentive Fund (TIF) programme, CECR was established to provide research-based expertise, ongoing research support, and technical assistance to state and school district TIF grantees in developing new teacher compensation systems based on rigorous evaluation methods and analytical models such as value-added analysis. This model is unique in that it brings together university researchers, private organisations, local practitioners, and federal sponsorship to generate and test new teacher compensation systems based on existing research, and on development of new analytical models and evaluation approaches, within a framework of ongoing programme support and technical assistance. The CECR model demonstrates a new role for universities in generating and transferring knowledge directly to policy and practice.

A third model is the partnership model, advocated by both the NSF and ED in their Math and Science Partnership (MSP) initiatives.

These MSP partnerships take a variety of forms, but each has in common participation by both higher education and K-12 partners, interdisciplinary faculty engagement at the leadership level, and a required research and evaluation component that yields evidence of progress and sustainability.[34] The partnership model connects faculty members and educators, researchers, and practitioners in ongoing relationships that are designed to integrate and bridge research, policy, and practice.

Within the universities, the federal opportunities for education research funding and application of scientific methods to education research have drawn faculty members and staff from other disciplines, such as economics and sociology, resulting in interdisciplinary teams and collaborations. Universities have also created expanded roles for education researchers and faculty members who conduct evaluation studies, who handle impact analysis, and who connect research and practice through formative studies and technical assistance (Urban and Trochim, 2009). These new roles and relationships help university-based education research bridge the research–practice gap by meeting federal standards for rigorous analytical models for evaluating teacher and student performance, by supporting development of district and state data system capacity and shared knowledge management, and by meeting local decision making and technical assistance needs, while at the same time maintaining university interests in scholarship and research credibility and integrity. These are just a few examples of the ways universities and education researchers have already adapted their roles and reorganised in response to the federal prerogative to bridge the gap between research, policy, and practice.

Implications for university-based education research

The trends in federal policy that began with the passage of NCLB and continue to evolve today have already had an undeniable influence on the process of education research and on the roles of universities in that process. In 2002, NCLB established the current education research framework, by (a) legislating education and research priorities, (b) mandating methodological design, (c) controlling research funding streams, (d) investing in national data and technology resources and infrastructure, and (e) by setting standards for everything from student and teacher performance to research quality and dissemination. Since 2008, the federal government has extended these parameters through (a) increasing the education research funding budget and stimulus monies, (b) reorganising ED and IES, (c) expanding the competitive grant and contract process to intermediaries, practitioners, and partnerships, and (d) prioritising research relevance and utilisation along with rigour. The extent to which the new federalism will continue to change how the university education research community conducts, shares, and integrates research with education policy and practice depends on whether universities consider and respond to these factors as opportunities or as impediments.

The federal influence on education research affords universities: (a) more federal funding options; (b) improved access to improved national and state education data systems; (c) support for large-scale, long-term, experimental research studies; (d) additional online resources for dissemination of research; (e) new research partners and collaborators; and (f) expanded audiences for consumption of research results, products and services. Research trends such as privatisation, commercialisation, and knowledge transfer are also influencing university research and becoming significant factors that education researchers must consider. Increasingly, university research is market driven, and researchers are moving away from developing the knowledge base of their field to conducting applied research and developing related products and services. Together these trends and the federal influence have the potential to revitalise the education research process and its reputation, create more productive relationships and roles, improve communication, and transform research into policy and practice.

However, the new direction for education research does not come without serious considerations for the university research community. To accommodate the new federalism, university education researchers face a tall order – they will need to come 'down from the Ivory tower' (Duncan, 2010), change their discourse and relationships with government and the public, and learn to navigate between research and advocacy, and between knowledge and politics, while at the same time maintaining the academy's standards for research quality and relevance.

Universities may need to revisit their incentive and reward systems, and reconsider which aspects of education research are valued for tenure and promotion. The university community will need to consider how a stronger emphasis on research-related products, services and knowledge transfer will affect the institutions' knowledge development imperative, and its service and outreach missions. Education researchers will need to decide how dependent they are on federal funding, and if they are willing to diversify and work collaboratively with researchers from other disciplines, with intermediaries, and with local practitioners. To remain competitive for federal funding, individual faculty members and research scientists will need to consider if they want their research to be more applied than basic, to become more policy and practice relevant, and to be vetted and debated in the public domain. Should university researchers accept these challenges, an optimal balance between traditional academia and the new federalism could fundamentally change the education research process and the relationships between universities, government and the public.

Notes

[1] For a detailed history of the US education research infrastructure until 2007, see Rudalevige (2008).

[2] More information on how the NCLB has influenced US federal education policy can be found in Henig (2008a) and Manna and Petrilli (2008).

[3] The RttP was designed to support and accelerate state education reform efforts by funding competitive proposals to adopt internationally benchmarked standards, prepare students for college and careers, build data system capacity for measuring student achievement and educator performance, and increase teacher quality and distribution. The i3 programme, run through ED's Office of Innovation and Improvement, awarded grants to local educational entities or partnerships to expand on proven achievement and attainment to demonstrate impacts on student achievement, student growth, achievement gaps, drop-out rates, high school graduation rates, and college enrolment and completion rates. The i3 awards had significant and graduated research and evaluation requirements, designed to develop promising evidence, test causal linkages and validate impact, and demonstrate outcomes at scale. TIF was designed to develop and implement performance-based educator compensation, targeting high-needs districts and schools (for more about RttP, see http://www2.ed.gov/programs/racetothetop/index.html; for more about i3, see http://www2.ed.gov/programs/innovation/index.html; for more about TIF, see http://www2.ed.gov/programs/teacherincentive/index.html).

[4] For more information about ESEA, see http://www2.ed.gov/policy/elsec/leg/esea02/index.html; for more about IES, see http://www.ies.ed.gov/.

[5] NCER supports research and development on the quality of education and student outcomes by awarding grants and contracts to researchers across the country. NCES is charged by Congressional mandate with the primary collection, analysis, and reporting of US education data. NCEE was established to promote evidence-based education, evaluate programme effectiveness, and disseminate research. It is within NCEE that the Regional Educational Laboratory Programme, the What Works Clearinghouse (WWC), the Education Resources Information Center (ERIC), and the National Library of Education, are housed. NCSER sponsors research to understand the needs, improve services, and evaluate effectiveness of education for children under the Individuals with Disabilities Education Act (IDEA).

[6] For more on NAEP, see http://nces.ed.gov/nationsreportcard/. The NAEP assessment is not mandated, but to receive federal aid under NCLB all states are required to participate in the NAEP assessments in reading and mathematics in fourth and eighth grade every two years.

[7] On 1 November 2010, NBES approved the most recent set of IES priorities. Expanding on the mission of IES to 'provide rigorous evidence on which to ground education practice and policy', the priorities emphasise (a) *quality research* (rigorous studies that support causal inferences), (b) *relevant research* (effective research that meets the needs of policymakers and practitioners through partnerships), and (c) a broad range of *student outcomes* (including outcomes for students with disabilities). IES is also to (a) promote research to improve educational outcomes of all students and generate knowledge to support educators and policy makers in improving the education system and (b) support the 'synthesis and dissemination of ongoing research to construct coherent bodies of scientific knowledge about education'. For details, see NBES (2010).

[8] Percentages do not add up to 100% because of rounding.

[9] For more information on NSF and EHR funding, awards, and programmes, see http://www.nsf.gov/dir/index.jsp?org=EHR and *FY 2009 Performance and Financial Highlights* at http://www.nsf.gov/pubs/2010/nsf10002/nsf10002.pdf.

[10] For a discussion of intermediaries see Henig (2008a).

[11] For more information on the Bill and Melinda Gates Foundation see Topics, Education and Information at http://www.gatesfoundation.org/Pages/home.aspx.

[12] For more information on education graduate programmes in the US see Graduate Guide (2011).

[13] Applied research is 'referred to as the "four Ds": development, dissemination, data, and direct services' in Henig (2008b, p 359).

[14] For more on the NSF's Math and Science Partnership Program see: http://www.nsf.gov/ehr/MSP/.

[15] For a discussion of the phrase 'scientifically based research' and how it came to be featured in the NCLB legislation, its interpretations, and implications for research, see, for example, Manna and Petrilli (2008).

[16] See Schoenfeld (2006) and Viadero (2009).

[17] For more details on the National Assessment of Educational Progress, see the NAEP website (http://nces.ed.gov/nationsreportcard).

[18] The National Center for Education Statistics (NCES) is charged with gathering and analysing national education-related data, and providing access to these data to the research and education communities and the public. For more information on NCES, see their website (http://nces.ed.gov/).

[19] For a description of educational information systems and knowledge management issues, see Petrides and Nodine (2003) and Thorn (2001).

[20] The IES Practice Guide *Using Student Achievement Data to Support Instructional Decision Making* provides an overview of the current research and literature on local data barriers and use. See Hamilton et al (2009).

[21] For more information on online scholarly publication search engines, see Van Aalst (2010).

[22] 'Pull' technologies involve the user in seeking out and selecting static on-line information (for example websites, streaming video and audio). 'Push' technologies involve the producer of the information sending targeted users specific content and information (for example e-mail, RSS). 'Synchronous' communication technologies support direct communication at the same time between producers and users of information (for example videoconferencing, chat). 'Asynchronous' communication technologies support sharing of information any time and consuming information at times convenient to users (for example e-mail, discussion boards.)

[23] For more information on the What Works Clearinghouse (WWC) and to view its resources, see the website (http://ies.ed.gov/ncee/wwc/).

[24] For more information on universities and knowledge transfer, and the 'third sector' of higher education activity, see Ozga and Jones (2006) and Cain et al (2008).

[25] For a discussion of these issues, see Fusillari (2008).

[26] See the William T. Grant Foundation (2010), whose current education funding priority is supporting research on what effects policy makers' and practitioners' acquisition, interpretation and use of research evidence.

[27] For more on the debate about the role of relevance in education research, see Bulterman-Bos (2008) and rebuttal articles by Labaree (2008), Lagemann (2008) and Noffke (2008).

[28] For a discussion of these issues see Hess (2008a, 2008b), Henig (2008a) and Urban and Trochim (2009) .

[29] For more on the four traditional roles of university researchers identified by CCSR, see Roderick et al (2009).

[30] Hess (2008a, 2008–09) also describes a mismatch between local leaders and researchers, citing a disconnect between incentives for researchers to conduct scientifically based research and the incentives, needs and capacity of local leaders to consume the results.

[31] For more on the Regional Education Laboratory Program, see http://ies.ed.gov/ncee/edlabs/about/.

[32] See Roderick et al (2009). John Q. Easton, the former Director of CCSR and co-author of this publication, became the Director of the Institute for Education Sciences in 2008 and has been a proponent for linking education research to local practice.

³³ CECR research is housed at the Wisconsin Center for Education Research (WCER), at the University of Wisconsin-Madison. WCER is one of the 13 original research and development centres started in 1965 by the US Department of Education.

³⁴ For more on the NSF's Math and Science Partnership Program see http://www.nsf.gov/ehr/MSP/.

References

Arbaugh, F., Herbel-Eisenmann, B., Ramirez, N., Knuth, E., Kranendonk, H. and Quander, J.R. (2010) *Linking research and practice*, The NCTM Research Agenda Conference Report, Reston, VA: The National Council of Teachers of Mathematics.

Baldwin, S.E., Muller, P.A., Akey, T.M., McManus, J., Phillips, M., Plucker, J. and Sharp. S. (2008) *An evaluation of the effectiveness of the Institute of Education Sciences in carrying out its priorities and mission: final report*, Washington DC: US Department of Education, Institute of Education Sciences.

Bulterman-Bos, J.A. (2008) 'Will a clinical approach make education research more relevant for practice?', *Educational Researcher*, vol 37, no 7, pp 412-20.

Cain, T.J., Brainin, J.J. and Sherman, W.M. (2008) 'Knowledge management and the academy', *EDUCAUSE Quarterly*, vol, 4, pp 26-33.

Chatterji, M. (2004) 'Evidence on "what works": an argument for extended-term mixed-method (ETMM) evaluation designs', *Educational Researcher*, vol 33, no 9, pp 3-13.

Coburn, C.E., Toure, J. and Yamashita, M. (2009) 'Evidence, interpretation, and persuasion: instructional decision making at the district central office', *Teachers College Record*, vol 3, no 4, pp 1115-61.

Duncan, A. (2010) *Education research: charting the course for reform*, remarks given at The Institute of Education Sciences Annual Research Conference, June, National Harbor, MD (retrieved from http://www.ed.gov/news/speeches/education-research-charting-course-reform).

Easton, J. (2010a) *Five big ideas for IES*, speech presented at the American Association of Colleges for Teacher Education (AACTE) Conference, Atlanta, GA (retrieved from http://ies.ed.gov/director/pdf/easton022010.pdf).

Easton, J. (2010b) *Director's final proposed priorities for the Institute of Education Sciences, November 1, 2010*, Washington, DC: Institute of Education Sciences (retrieved from http://ies.ed.gov/director/board/priorities.asp).

Eisenhart, M. and Towne, L. (2003) 'Contestation and change in national policy on "scientifically based" education research', *Educational Researcher*, vol 32, no 7, pp 31-8.

Fusarelli, L.D. (2008) 'Flying (partially) blind: school leaders' use of research in decisionmaking', in F.M. Hess (ed) *When research matters: how scholarship influences education policy*, Cambridge, MA: Harvard Education Press, pp 177-96.

Goldhaber, D.D. and Brewer. D.J. (2008) 'What gets studied and why: examining the incentives that drive education research', in F. M. Hess (ed) *When research matters: how scholarship influences education policy*, Cambridge, MA: Harvard Education Press, pp 197-217.

Graduate Guide (2011) *Graduate school search: education*, (retrieved from http://www.graduateguide.com/search/Education).

Hamilton, L., Halverson, R., Jackson, S., Mandinach, E., Supovitz, J. and Wayman, J. (2009) *Using student achievement data to support instructional decision making* (NCEE 2009-4067), Washington DC: National Center for Education Evaluation and Regional Assistance, Institute of Education Sciences, US Department of Education.

Henig, J.R. (2008a) 'The evolving relationship between researchers and public policy', in F.M. Hess (ed) *When research matters: how scholarship influences education policy*, Cambridge, MA: Harvard Education Press, pp 41-62.

Henig, J.R. (2008b) 'The evolving relationship between researchers and public policy', *Phi Delta Kappan*, vol 89, no 5, pp 357-60.

Henig, J. R. (2008–09) 'The spectrum of education research', *Educational Leadership*, vol 66, no 4, pp 6-11.

Hess, F.M. (ed) (2008a) *When research matters: how scholarship influences education policy*, Cambridge, MA: Harvard Education Press.

Hess, F.M. (2008b) 'The politics of knowledge', *Phi Delta Kappan*, vol 89, no 5, pp 354-6.

Hess, F.M. (2008-209) 'Data: now what?: the new stupid', *Educational Leadership*, vol 66, no 4, pp 12-17.

Honig, M.I. (2004) 'The new middle management: intermediary organizations in education policy implementation', *Educational Evaluation and Policy Analysis*, vol 26, no 1, pp 65-87.

Honig, M.I. and Coburn, C. (2008) 'Evidence-based decision making in school district central offices: toward a policy and research agenda', *Educational Policy*, vol 22, no 4, pp 578-608.

Labaree, D.F. (2008) 'The dysfunctional pursuit of relevance in education research', *Educational Researcher*, vol 37, no 7, pp 421-3.

Lagemann, E.C. (2008) 'Education research as a distributed activity across universities', *Educational Researcher*, vol 37, no 7, pp 424-8.

Manna, P. and Petrilli, M.J. (2008) 'Double standard? "Scientifically based research" and the No Child Left Behind Act', in F.M. Hess (ed) *When research matters: how scholarship influences education policy*, Cambridge, MA: Harvard Education Press, pp 63-88.

Mintrom, M. (2008) 'Managing the research function of the university: pressures and dilemmas', *Journal of Higher Education Policy and Management*, vol 30, no 3, pp 231-44.

NBES (National Board for Education Sciences) (2010) *Director's final proposed priorities for the Institute of Education Sciences, November 1, 2010* (retrieved from http://ies.ed.gov/director/board/priorities.asp).

NCEERA (National Center for Education Evaluation and Regional Assistance) (not dated) 'Building evidence based education', Washington DC: US Department of Education, Institute of Education Sciences (retrieved from http://ies.ed.gov/ncee/pdf/ncee_brochure.pdf).

NCER (National Center for Education Research) (not dated) 'Building evidence-based education', Washington DC: US Department of Education, Institute of Education Sciences (retrieved from http://ies.ed.gov/ncer/pdf/ncer_brochure.pdf).

NCLB (2002) No Child Left Behind Act of 2001, Pub L, No 107-10, 115 Stat 1425 (2002) (20 USC §6301 et seq).

Nelson, S.R., Leffler, J.C. and Hansen, B.A. (2009) *Toward a research agenda for understanding and improving the use of research evidence*. Portland, OR: Northwest Regional Educational Laboratory (Retrieved from www.nwrel.org/researchuse/report.pdf).

Noffke, S.E. (2008) 'Research relevancy or research for change?', *Educational Researcher*, vol 37, no 7, pp 429-31.

NSF (National Science Foundation) (2006) 'Federal funds for research and development: fiscal years 2003-2005', Arlington, VA: NSF Division of Science Resources Statistics, Table 4 (retrieved from http://nsf.gov/statistics/nsf06313/pdf/tab4.pdf) and Table 7 (retrieved from http://nsf.gov/statistics/nsf06313/pdf/tab7.pdf).

NSF (National Science Foundation) (2009) 'FY 2009 performance and financial highlights' (retrieved from http://www.nsf.gov/pubs/2010/nsf10002/nsf10002.pdf).

NSF (National Science Foundation) Math and Science Partnership Program (not dated) (retrieved from http://www.nsf.gov/ehr/MSP/).

Ozga, J. and Jones, R. (2006) 'Traveling and embedded policy: the case of knowledge transfer', *Journal of Education Policy*, vol 21, no 1, pp 1-17.

Petrides, L.A. and Nodine, T.R. (2003) *Knowledge management in education: defining the landscape*, Half Moon Bay, CA: The Institute for the Study of Knowledge Management in Education.

Regional Education Laboratory Program (not dated) *About us homepage*, Washington DC: US Department of Education, Institute of Education Sciences (retrieved from http://ies.ed.gov/ncee/edlabs/about/).

Roderick, M., Easton, J.Q. and Sebring, P.B. (2009) *The Consortium on Chicago School Research: a new model for the role of research in supporting urban school reform*, Chicago, IL: Consortium on Chicago School Research at the University of Chicago.

Rudalevige, A. (2008) 'Structure and science in federal education research', in F.M. Hess (ed) *When research matters: how scholarship influences education policy*, Cambridge, MA: Harvard Education Press, pp 17-40.

Schoenfeld, A.H. (2006) 'What doesn't work: the challenge and failure of the What Works Clearinghouse to conduct meaningful reviews of studies of mathematics curricula', *Educational Researcher*, vol 35, no 2, pp 13-21.

Shankland, L. (2010) 'Research update: the current state of research use in education', *SEDL Letter*, vol 22, no 2, pp 3-5.

Slavin, R.E. (2002) 'Evidence-based education policies: transforming educational practice and research', *Educational Researcher*, vol 31, no 7, pp 15-21.

Slavin, R.E. (2008) 'What works? Issues in synthesizing educational program evaluations', *Educational Researcher*, vol 37, no 1, pp 5-14.

Stine, D.D. (2008) *Science and technology policymaking: a primer*, CRS Report for Congress, Order Code RL34454, Washington DC: Congressional Research Service.

Thorn, C.A. (2001) 'Knowledge management for educational information systems: what is the state of the field?', *Education Policy Analysis Archives*, vol 9, no 47 (retrieved from http://epaa.asu.edu/epaa/v9n47/).

Urban, J.B. and Trochim, W. (2009) 'The role of evaluation in research-practice integration: working toward the "golden spike"', *American Journal of Evaluation*, vol 30, no 4, pp 538-53.

US Department of Education (2008) *Budget history table, education department budget by major program*, 29 February (retrieved from http://www2.ed.gov/about/overview/budget/history/edhistory.pdf).

US Department of Education (2009a) *Department of Education American Recovery and Investment Act (ARRA)* (retrieved from http://www2.ed.gov/about/overview/budget/budget09/09recovery.pdf).

US Department of Education (2009b) *US Office of Management and Budget, budget of the US government, fiscal years 1982 through 2010,* Table 377 (retrieved from http://nces.ed.gov/programs/digest/d09/tables/dt09_377.asp/).

US Department of Education (2010a) *NCLB* (retrieved on 29 November 2010 from http://www2.ed.gov/nclb/landing.jhtml).

US Department of Education (2010b) *Recovery Act* (retrieved from http://www.ed.gov/recovery).

US Department of Education (2010c) *Department of Education Recovery Plan* (retrieved from http://www2.ed.gov/policy/gen/leg/recovery/recovery-plans-2010.pdf).

US Department of Education (2010d) *Summary of discretionary funds, FY 2011 request* (retrieved from http://www2.ed.gov/about/overview/budget/budget11/summary/appendix1.pdf).

US Department of Education (not dated) *National assessment of educational progress* (retrieved from http://nces.ed.gov/nationsreportcard).

US Department of Education, National Center for Education Statistics (NCES) (not dated) (retrieved from http://nces.ed.gov/).

US Government Accountability Office (2010) *Improved dissemination and timely product release would enhance the usefulness of the What Works Clearinghouse,* GAO-10-644 Department of Education), Washington, DC: US Government Accountability Office.

Van Aalst, J. (2010) 'Using Google Scholar to estimate the impact of journal articles in education', *Educational Researcher,* vol 39, no 5, pp 387-400.

Viadero, D. (2009) 'STAT of the Week: is "What Works" living up to its name?', *Education Week*'s blog post, 27 March (retrieved from http://blogs.edweek.org/edweek/inside-school-research/2009/03/stat_of_the_week_is_what_works.html).

Weiss, C.H. (1979) 'The many meanings of research utilization', *Public Administration Review,* vol 39, no 5, pp 426-31.

Weiss, C.H. (1982) 'Policy research in the context of diffuse decision making', *Journal of Higher Education,* vol 53, no 6, pp 619-39.

Weiss, C.H. (1998) 'Have we learned anything new about the use of evaluation?', *American Journal of Evaluation,* vol 19, no 1, pp 21-33.

Weiss, C.H. (1999) 'The interface between evaluation and public policy', *Evaluation,* vol 5, no 4, pp 468-86.

What Works Clearinghouse. (2008) *Evidence standards for reviewing studies, version 1.0.* Princeton, NJ: IES What Works Clearinghouse (retrieved from http://ies.ed.gov/ncee/wwc/pdf/wwc_version1_standards.pdf).

William T. Grant Foundation (2010) *Request for research proposals: understanding the acquisition, interpretation, and use of research evidence in policy and practice*, New York, NY: William T. Grant Foundation.

TWELVE

Reflections on the mobilisation of education research

Sandra Nutley, School of Management, University of St Andrews

Introduction

National governments around the world are concerned about the effectiveness and efficiency of their education systems and this inevitably leads them to question how they can improve or at least maintain their comparative performance, particularly as measured by international studies of student performance such as PIRLS, TIMSS and PISA.[1] Delivering high-quality education requires knowledge about the scale, source and structuring of educational problems and what might work in addressing these. Education research can provide some of the knowledge needed to tackle these issues, so it is not surprising that there is a growing demand for education research that is useful and for efforts to ensure that this research is used in developing education policies and practices.

However, as is well illustrated by earlier chapters in this book, the promise of research-informed policy and practice is often not matched by the reality. The reasons for this are rooted in the multiple influences that shape whether and how research gets used. These include: the nature of the research itself – particularly the extent to which it is relevant, credible and meets users' needs; the characteristics of those actually using the research – particularly their willingness and ability to use research; and the degree of linkage between researchers and relevant policy and practice communities. In addition, the context for research use is key to understanding when research knowledge is likely to be used, and in what ways (Nutley et al, 2007).

Chapters One and Two introduced knowledge mobilisation (KM) as the broad term used in this book to refer to the dynamic relationship between all these factors because it is 'essentially about building stronger connections between research, policy and practice' (see Qi and Levin, this volume). Those chapters also emphasised that the purpose of this book is to capture similarities and differences in the way in which education research is organised and shared around the world, with particular emphasis on the role played by universities in mobilising research knowledge.

This final chapter reflects on the key issues to emerge from earlier chapters. These reflections were prompted by reading those chapters, but they also draw on the work undertaken by the Research Unit for Research Utilisation (RURU; based at the University of St Andrews), which is a unique cross-sector resource devoted to documenting and synthesising the many diverse strands of conceptual, empirical and practical knowledge about the use of research in policy and practice settings. The staff team at RURU have engaged with a wide range of stakeholders from academic, policy and practitioner communities, as well as others interested in research use, such as research funders, research brokers and charitable organisations. RURU's review work draws on and contributes to studies of research use in four settings: health care, social welfare, education and criminal justice. Much of this work has been distilled in our latest book, *Using Evidence* (Nutley et al, 2007), and further details about many of the issues raised in this chapter can be found in that resource. Details of other RURU reports and papers are available on the unit's website (www.ruru.ac.uk).

The reflections that follow are structured as responses to four main questions:

- What are some of the most interesting differences across the countries represented in this book?
- What ideas, practices and issues in the country-specific chapters merit wider consideration and what factors might make these more or less feasible in other places?
- Which aspects of knowledge mobilisation deserve more amplification because they have not been given much coverage thus far?
- What lines of future research and development emerge both from the country accounts and from wider work on knowledge mobilisation as a field of practice and as an emerging discipline in its own right?

Differences across countries

The country-specific chapters offer a fascinating insight into some of intricacies of education systems around the world, and the difficulties and complexities associated with mobilising research knowledge. The accounts suggest that in many instances similar questions are being addressed, such as how can we increase the quantity and quality of education research, what incentives are needed to encourage knowledge mobilisation (particularly by researchers), and how can we scale up from promising resource-intensive pilot initiatives to knowledge mobilisation strategies and activities that work on a much wider scale. However, there are some marked differences in the responses to such questions. Of course, as pointed out in Chapter One, some of the contrasts in the country accounts will reflect not only differences on the ground in these countries, but also the differing viewpoints of the authors of these accounts. Nonetheless, this section focuses on three apparent areas of difference: the relative emphasis on top-down versus bottom-up approaches to knowledge mobilisation; the extent of institutional supports for knowledge mobilisation (including the prevalence of intermediary organisations); and the extent to which knowledge mobilisation strategies are product and/or service focused.

Top-down versus bottom-up approaches to knowledge mobilisation

The US case account stands out as an example of a top-down approach to knowledge mobilisation. In that account, Mason underscores the role of the federal government in setting the course of education policy over the last decade. She clearly articulates how decisions made at federal level have had a profound effect on the demand for particular forms of education research and the ways in which this research is supplied. By contrast, north of the border in Canada there have been no significant KM initiatives for education at federal level, while within provinces the approach has been primarily bottom up and facilitative rather than top down and orchestrated. The UK falls somewhere between these two extremes. As Gough (focusing mainly on the situation in England) points out, there have been many centrally funded initiatives aimed at improving the supply of education research and its use in policy and practice, but these initiatives have not been tightly planned or coordinated, and the approach has at times had the appearance of scattering many seeds in the hope that at least some will take root, thrive and have the desired effect.

In Singapore, the overall direction for mobilising knowledge in education has been set nationally and in some ways the approach could be described as top down and orchestrated. However, because the approach (especially in recent years) has been to facilitate local autonomy at school and school cluster levels, the 'top-down' label is rather misleading. Singapore is a relatively small country and, as Teh et al point out, even though the national government is concerned to maintain the excellent reputation of its education system, the long-standing, tightly coupled relationships between the National Institute for Education, the Ministry of Education and the school system mean that it is possible steer the overall system without recourse to a high level of central direction.

The scale of the education system in Singapore clearly enables the tightly coupled relationships reported in that chapter, but Denmark, which is similar in population size, does not exhibit the same close relationships. Indeed, Holm's chapter describing the Danish context highlights the fractured nature of relationships in the research, policy and practice nexus. So, scale does not seem to be a factor that determines the nature of knowledge mobilisation in education systems.

The contrast between top-down and bottom-up approaches is also reflected in the extent to which different countries view the mobilisation task as the translation and implementation of research knowledge or whether the emphasis is on the co-production of knowledge at a local level. The emphasis in the US, for example, has been on the former, while in Singapore it seems to be increasingly on the latter. The Singapore chapter talks about shifting the locus of knowledge production to schools so that in effect they co-produce the research agenda and collaborate with university researchers in knowledge creation and learning. In such a scenario, the mobilisation challenge is less concerned with the vertical dissemination of research knowledge, from the centre to the periphery, but instead needs to ensure that there is horizontal knowledge exchange and learning between schools and school districts.

The extent of institutional supports for knowledge mobilisation

The chapter on Canada comments that the mobilisation of education research in that country relies heavily on individual efforts, particularly the efforts of individual researchers. The broader literature on research-informed policy and practice also focuses on individuals and tends to assume that it is primarily the responsibility of individual policy makers and practitioners to ensure that their decisions and practice are informed by research (Nutley et al, 2007). While individuals in many settings play an important role in mobilising research knowledge, individual efforts on their own are unlikely to bring about a step change in KM – that requires more in the way of institutional supports.

As the country chapters are mainly concerned with the knowledge mobilisation role of universities, they inevitably focus on the institutional supports available within universities. In relation to university human resource policies and systems, most country accounts report a rather patchy provision of incentives for researchers to engage in mobilisation activities, and the extent of these incentives seems to vary as much between universities in the same country as it does between countries. The same is also the case for the extent to which different universities provide an infrastructure that supports mobilisation activities (such as event organisation, specialist support in writing for policy makers and practitioners, and KM-related ICT support). In general, as discussed in Chapter Two, knowledge mobilisation in faculties of education tends to be under-institutionalised and the supporting infrastructure is largely piecemeal.

A key difference between the countries seems to be the extent to which there are institutional supports for knowledge mobilisation outwith universities. The US chapter comments on the growing presence of intermediary organisations that seek to distil research knowledge and translate it for a range of policy and practice audiences. Some of these organisations are linked to universities, but others are based in the wider for-profit and not-for-profit sectors. In the UK, there is also a plethora of intermediary organisations, although very few of these are in the for-profit sector. In Canada, many of the intermediary organisations concerned with mobilising education research are based in universities and they are concentrated in one province – Ontario (Cooper, 2012). There is a growing range of intermediary organisations in South Africa, and in developing countries in general international foundations and aid agencies often play an important intermediary role. In China there do not appear to be any independent intermediaries; everything is connected into the state structure, but the state does seem to be creating quite a few new intermediary bodies.

Product and/or service-focused knowledge mobilisation strategies

The approach to knowledge mobilisation reported in the country accounts tends to be product focused – concerned with the dissemination of research findings. Several chapters hint at the need for a greater service focus. Indeed, Mason comments that in the US university research is already becoming 'increasingly market driven, and product and service oriented' (see Mason, this volume). The authors of the Singapore account talk about the need for a radical rethink of the relationship between research and practice, and their comments are very much in line with a greater service orientation for researchers and universities.

Such a shift in thinking and practice is far from straightforward. Most universities are set up as research production systems, and moving significantly towards more of a service orientation, where research influence and impact are placed centre stage, would indeed require a radical rethink of current practices (Walshe and Davies, 2010). There is a substantial literature on service management, and some of the headline messages from this literature provide an insight into what this might mean for the role of universities in knowledge mobilisation: successful service management lies in both governing and responding to the service expectations of consumers and in training and motivating staff to interact positively with consumers; service marketing is not about packaging products but about building trust and enduring relationships with consumers; and co-production is not something in the gift of service providers – it is fundamental to any service encounter (Osborne, 2010).

There are drawbacks in going too far in the direction of a service orientation for university research, and most of the country accounts comment on the dangers of a policy-driven research agenda and the threat this poses to the independence of education research (see, for example, the discussion of the relationship between research and policy in Muller and Hoadley's chapter on South Africa). This point is worth re-emphasising here. As Rein (1976) points out, it is possible to identify at least three stances that researchers can adopt in relation to public policy:

- *a consensual approach* – where researchers work within and contribute to existing policy paradigms by providing policy makers and practitioners with knowledge about how to improve service delivery and service outcomes within these frameworks;
- *a contentious approach* – where researchers place themselves on the sidelines of public policy and act as a 'moral critic' in order to keep the system honest;
- *a paradigm challenging approach* – where researchers problematise existing ways of thinking and propose alternative principles for action.

All three stances are important, and there are dangers that too great an emphasis on a service-oriented consensual approach undermines the other two.

Ideas, practices and issues that merit wider consideration

The country accounts offer much food for thought, and it is only possible in this chapter to highlight a few of these morsels. Three things that merit wider consideration are discussed along with some of the factors that might make specific country practices more or less feasible in other places. These are: moving from one-way knowledge transfer to multi-way knowledge exchange, incentives for knowledge mobilisation, and the promise of information and communication technologies (ICT).

Moving from one-way knowledge transfer to multi-way knowledge exchange

The broader literature on knowledge mobilisation suggests that we may need to extend our thinking beyond a movement from one-way knowledge transfer to multi-way knowledge exchange. Reflecting on knowledge to action in the health field, Best and Holmes (2010) argue that there are three generations of knowledge-to-action thinking: knowledge transfer – where knowledge is a product and the degree of use is a function of effective packaging; knowledge exchange – where knowledge is the result of social and political processes and the degree of use is a function of effective relationships and interaction; and knowledge integration – where knowledge is embedded in systems and cultures and the degree of use is a function of effective integration with organisations and systems.

Research use is rarely a simple linear process or a one-off event whereby packages of knowledge (isolatable 'facts') are passed from researchers to research users and used in a rational decision-making process. Studies suggest that research use is a more social, interactive and iterative process than this. It involves people – individually and collectively – engaging with research over time, bringing their own and their organisation's beliefs, values, narratives and experience with them (Nutley et al, 2007).

There is a substantial body of empirical work that has highlighted the multiple routes and channels through which research may enter policy and practice (see Nutley et al, 2007, especially chapter 3). Formal dissemination of research reports and research summaries plays a part in this, but more often research spreads through other routes by word of mouth and through informal as well as formal networks. The links and interactions among researchers and research users are important, but equally important are the various roles of actors and communities beyond research, policy and practice, such as research funders, interest groups and other intermediaries.

As pointed out in the first two chapters of this book, interactive models provide a relevant frame for understanding the messy, dynamic and contingent process of research use. They emphasise that research use involves multiple connections and two-way flows of empirical, theoretical and experiential knowledge. Research use emerges as a social and collective process that takes place through iterative dialogue and debate. The meaning of research is negotiated and reconstructed in the process of its use.

Given this understanding of the process of research use, it is important to reflect on how the mobilisation ideas and practices outlined in the country accounts tap into the need for multi-way knowledge exchange and iterative dialogue. While most accounts focus on the largely one-way dissemination activities of universities, they also comment on a recognised a need to shift the balance from dissemination to dialogue and facilitation. There are many intriguing references to enabling practices that merit further investigation. These include:

- *fluidity of people movement between research, policy and practice roles* – this is evident in the accounts of both Korea and Singapore, and is discussed further in the next sub-section on incentives for knowledge mobilisation;
- *collaborative practices that enhance the interactions between universities, schools and school districts* – these include the three models of collaborations described in the US chapter, the experimental school projects and agreements with local education authorities outlined in the China chapter, and the facilitation of practice-based research that is mentioned in several of the chapters;
- *specific funding initiatives that support knowledge sharing and network building across research, policy and practice communities* – these include the KNAER initiative, which is discussed briefly in the Canada chapter, and the knowledge exchange grants provided by the Economic and Social Research Council (ESRC) in the UK;
- *enabling research-informed public debate of educational issues and choices* – this is mentioned briefly in the Korean account and seems to be underpinned not only by disseminating research findings to a wide audience but also by long-standing policies and values that have generated a highly educated population that cares about the future of the education system.

The problem with some of these practices and initiatives is that they tend to be short term, particularly if they are reliant on one-off funding grants (for example the knowledge exchange grants provided by the UK ESRC typically have a duration of only 12 months). Many collaborative practices also tend to be small scale and resource intensive, and there are significant challenges in scaling them up to operate at regional or national levels. As discussed in Chapter One, this challenge is particularly marked in education because the size of the education research community is so small in comparison with the scale of the education sector, which means that a resource-intensive approach that involves researchers working closely with schools is never going to reach most schools.

Incentives for engagement

As mentioned earlier in the chapter, the country accounts reveal a rather patchy provision of university-based incentives to engage in knowledge mobilisation. A promising practice example is provided in the Australian account. The University of Melbourne accords mobilisation activities and impacts the status of being a key indicator of performance in the staff development system. Mobilisation activities are also considered a legitimate inclusion in staff workload models, and they feature as one of four criteria used in staff promotion decisions.

Promotion criteria for university researchers have a significant impact on the shape of university careers. The fluidity of staff movement between the research, policy and practice worlds reported in the accounts of both Singapore and Korea would seem to be an important enabler of knowledge mobilisation, but such fluidity of movement is much more difficult to achieve in countries that either formally or informally have inhibiting expectations about the career trajectories of successful researchers, policy makers or practitioners. For example, in the UK these expectations have meant that regular staff interchange is not the norm. Where it does happen, staff may experience one such movement in their career, and this will tend to be either an early or late career experience. The same seems to be true in Canada.

The promise of ICT

Several of the country accounts talk about the promise of ICT in enabling and facilitating knowledge mobilisation. The authors of the China account emphasise the importance of ICT in such a large country and the US chapter refers to an explosion of on-line dissemination tools, which merit further consideration. Further investigation of ICT strategies and activities may reveal some promising practices but, as noted in Chapter One, existing studies by OISE (Canada) suggest that universities have so far made only limited use of ICT capabilities. The emphasis seems to be on making research products available for download online, and to date social media are rarely exploited as a means of sharing and discussing university research. Nor do we know very much about the impact of these practices. While the potential seems great, whether more active use of ICT will in fact lead to greater knowledge and use of research findings remains to be seen.

Factors that might make specific country practices more or less feasible in other places

The policy transfer literature is replete with examples of countries seeking to copy promising or successful policies and practices from other jurisdictions, although in the event they usually end up adapting these policies and practices rather than merely copying them (Dolowitz and Marsh, 2000; Rose, 2004). In developing their mobilisation strategies for education research it is likely that policy makers and researchers will seek to draw on and learn from promising practices in other jurisdiction. While this is understandable, there is a need to consider the extent to which KM practices can be readily transferred, which requires a better understanding than we currently have of what works, for whom, under what circumstances, and why.

There are a range of political, cultural and administrative factors that are likely to limit the transferability of country-specific practices. These include:

- *governance structures and processes* – such as constitutional arrangements, the machinery of government and how education services are organised and delivered;
- *cultural values* – such as attitudes towards large-scale policy experimentation and the level of deference to technical expertise;
- *the history of cross-organisation and cross-sector relationships* – particularly the extent to which these relationships have tended to be adversarial or consensual;
- *the goals, capacities and routines of key organisations* – for example the extent to which universities are concerned primarily with their ranking in global league tables or the extent to which university goals and capacities relate to local economic and social development.

An OECD/Centre for Educational Research and Innovation (CERI) discussion paper on the interaction of governance and knowledge offers a framework for thinking about the ways in which the learning modes of policy makers and practitioners might vary with the form of governance (Fazekas and Burns, 2011). However, we have very little systematic evidence on the precise effect of such factors (Nutley et al, 2010), and, as is discussed at the end of this chapter, one line of inquiry for future research is to develop a better understanding of how various contextual factors help or hinder research use. This need is illustrated here by reference to just one factor – population size.

Earlier in the chapter, when contrasting the accounts provided for Denmark and Singapore, the reflection was that population size does not seem to be a simple determinant of the nature of KM in educational systems, but size nevertheless seems to matter. This issue is considered in *Using Evidence* (Nutley et al, 2007). and there we comment that smaller countries (that is, those with populations of say three to six million people) may have some advantages with regards to researchers' relative ease of access to ministers and civil servants, and the level of knowledge possible about what key people are working in various policy areas. This being the case, we might expect that interactions between these groups, and consequently greater research/policy engagement, would be more possible in smaller countries than larger ones. However, smaller countries can also suffer from a lack of capacity in both research and policy terms, and they may be less able to support the array of research production and research brokering activities that are possible in larger states.

Thus, population size may be important, but quite how is difficult to discern because size and governance structures are inextricably bound up. Indeed, size may be a poor proxy for interconnectivity, with geography and the extent of political integration perhaps having a greater influence. For example, densely populated countries may find it easier to develop linkages than countries with far-flung populations, though the availability of a variety of ICTs may be an important confounder to any such relationship.

Issues that deserve more amplification

Many knowledge mobilisation issues are touched upon in the country accounts but inevitably the word limit and focus of these chapters mean that some issues get only a passing reference. The aim of this section is to amplify three of these: the interaction between research and other forms of knowledge, the KM roles and activities of non-university actors, and the need to identify and assess the effectiveness of KM activities.

Interaction between research and other forms of knowledge

Research differs from other ways of knowing by being more careful and deliberative in how observations and inferences are made, by acknowledging the need for a degree of robustness and replicability, and by opening itself up to peer scrutiny and appraisal. It is these characteristics that, for many, make research-based knowledge worthy of special attention (Davies and Nutley, 2008). However, in order to understand the use of research findings we need to understand the interaction between three different ways of knowing (Brechin and Siddell, 2000):

- *empirical knowing* – the most explicit form of knowing, which is often based on quantitative or qualitative research study;
- *theoretical knowing* – which uses different frameworks for thinking about a problem, sometimes informed by research, but often derived in intuitive and informal ways;
- *experiential knowing* – craft or tacit knowledge built up over a number of years of practice experience.

It is relatively rare for research findings to provide clear-cut messages that can simply be adopted by policy makers and practitioners and implemented across a range of contexts. More often, research findings suggest a direction of travel but specific actions are negotiated locally. In this process, research knowledge interacts with other forms and sources of knowledge (including organisational knowledge, practitioner knowledge, user knowledge, and policy community knowledge – Pawson et al, 2003).

This means that mobilisation frameworks that advocate that research should be disseminated and adopted through the development and faithful replication of research-based programmes are only likely to be helpful in fairly limited circumstances. This can be a contentious point, particularly for readers in the US, where pursuit of the 'what works' agenda appears to have centred on the identification and faithful replication of research-based programmes. In practice, research use is likely to mean finding a balance between strict forms of replication, and the need to adapt research-based knowledge and programmes to particular contexts. In this process, research knowledge is combined with local knowledge to develop effective interventions adapted to meet local needs.

Several of the chapters comment on what such thinking might mean for the design of research projects and broader mobilisation practices. For example, the Singapore account emphasises the importance of action research in schools and it also introduces the concept of 'design research', where emphasis is placed on designing and testing solutions as well as analysing problems (Stoker and John, 2009). The UK chapter discusses briefly the implications of these ideas for the ways in which different bodies of evidence are drawn together via systematic review techniques.

Knowledge mobilisation roles and activities of non-university actors

Mobilisation strategies aimed at improving the use of research may be developed by discrete groups or organisations operating in policy, research or service provider roles. They can also be developed at sector level through discussions involving people in all of these roles. This book concentrates on the role of universities in mobilising research knowledge, and this focus inevitably overshadows the extent to which other actors and institutions are involved in KM.

The country accounts provide some glimpses into the knowledge mobilisation roles and activities of other actors. For example, the Singapore account mentions that knowledge mobilisation is part of the job description of some 200 Ministry of Education officials and specialists. The references in the Canadian, South African, US and UK accounts to the growing presence of a range of intermediary organisations with KM roles also highlight the importance of non-university actors and organisations. We need to know more about the activities of these actors and organisations. And universities need to be more aware of and connected with these other actors, especially in settings where those links are not already strong, or even existing.

Identifying and assessing the effectiveness of knowledge mobilisation activities

Several of the country accounts comment on the difficulty in identifying mobilisation practices, let alone assessing their effectiveness. Knowledge mobilisation is a developing field of practice and an emerging discipline in its own right, but it is still an immature field. There are many conceptual models that can be used to shape activities on the ground (a review by Ward et al, 2009 uncovered 63 such models), but the field as a whole is under-theorised and there is only limited empirical evidence on the effectiveness of different strategies and activities. Furthermore, there is no agreed terminology or taxonomy for describing and analysing mobilisation practices.

In Chapter One, Qi and Levin refer to work in OISE that has found that the most common mobilisation strategies used by faculties of education include: traditional academic knowledge dissemination channels (particularly publications and conferences); establishing connections between researchers and potential users; and providing institutional supports and incentives (Sá et al, 2010). They also comment that, based on the country chapters, research mobilisation capacity seems to require strong leadership, appropriate infrastructure, sufficient funding, effective communication facilities, and the ability to network among researchers, policy makers and other research users.

Although empirical evidence is limited, a cross-sector review of what makes for effective research use has revealed some remarkably consistent messages about the key features associated with success (Walter et al, 2005). The following key features have been derived by RURU from a range of studies covering different contexts (in education, health, social care and criminal justice) and encompassing different approaches to implementing research-informed practice. Whether the task is the establishment of a research–practice collaboration or the implementation of a research-based tool, the principles for success seem to be very similar. They are:

1. *Provide opportunities for translation.* To be used, research needs to be adapted for, or reconstructed within, local practice contexts. Simply providing the findings is not enough. Adaptation can take multiple forms, including tailoring research results to a target group, enabling debate about their implications, 'tinkering' with research in practice, or developing research-based programmes or tools.
2. *Develop local ownership.* Ownership, whether of the research itself, of research-based programmes or tools, or of projects to implement research, is vital to uptake. Exceptions can, however, occur where implementation is received or perceived as a coercive process.
3. *Encourage local enthusiasts.* Individual enthusiasts or 'product champions' can help carry the process of getting research used. They are crucial to selling new ideas and practices. Personal contact is most effective here.
4. *Conduct a contextual analysis.* Successful initiatives are those that analyse the context for research implementation and target specific barriers to, and enablers of, change.

5. *Ensure credibility.* Research take-up and use is enhanced where there is: credible evidence, endorsement from opinion leaders – both expert and peer, and a demonstrable high-level commitment to the process.
6. *Provide leadership.* Strong and visible leadership, at both management and project levels, can help provide motivation, authority and organisational integration.
7. *Give adequate support.* Ongoing support for those implementing change increases the chance of success. Financial, technical, organisational and emotional support are all important. Dedicated project coordinators have been core to the success of many initiatives.
8. *Develop integration.* To assist and sustain research use, activities need to be integrated within existing organisational systems and practices. All key stakeholders need to be involved. Alignment with local and national policy demands also supports research use.

Lines for future research and development

This chapter has already highlighted the relatively weak theoretical and empirical underpinning of much mobilisation activity. In order to build knowledge mobilisation both as a discipline and as a field of practice there is a need to get to grips with a substantial research and development agenda. Thus far the chapter has highlighted the need for further investigation of the role of intermediaries, and the nature and effectiveness of different mobilisation practices.

In 2008, RURU was asked by the William T. Grant Foundation (US) to comment on the research agenda associated with improving our understanding of how research knowledge is used in policy and practice settings and how this can be improved. In response, we highlighted three major areas for further study: knowledge source, presentation, and integration; context and connections; and strategies and processes (Davies and Nutley, 2008). The key research themes under each of these headings are summarised in Table 12.1. As we comment in the 2008 paper, not all of the research themes outlined in Table 12.1 relate to untilled ground, but existing work in the field has been uneven.

Because of the cross-national nature of this book, it is worth saying a little more about one aspect of this research agenda – the need to understand more about context. While context is generally recognised as a key factor influencing whether and how research knowledge is used, it has not been well conceptualised or incorporated in empirical study.

Much of the research and debate around the role played by policy contexts in the uptake of research has focused on macro-level

Table 12.1: An emerging research agenda

Knowledge source, presentation, and integration
- What models of research supply and synthesis might better support knowledge integration by potential research users?
- How do different kinds of messaging and messengers affect the use of research knowledge?
- What is the role of the web in providing access to existing research?
- To what extent are policy makers and service managers conducting their own in-house research through the examination of administrative and other sources of local data?
- How is new knowledge integrated into current ways of thinking and modes of practice?

Context and connections
- What are the important policy communities in the setting of interest? How are these communities connected, how are they linked to practice-based, researcher, and research intermediary communities?
- How, where, and under what circumstances do practitioners source new knowledge?
- To what extent are policy and practice communities becoming better networked and facilitating freer flows of research-based information across these networks?
- What models of research brokerage or intermediary activities have the best potential for fostering research use?
- How can lay people, service users, and others (non-policy, non-professional) contribute more fully to evidence-informed discussions?
- How are education and continuing professional development connected to and supportive of knowledge accumulation and integration?

Strategies and processes
- To what extent do different models of research use co-exist in different practice settings (for example the balance between research-based practitioner approaches, embedded research, and organisational excellence models? (See Nutley et al, 2009)
- What knowledge management strategies are in use across the sector?
- What models of push, pull, and linkage-exchange are in place? How are these evolving and connecting? What are the challenges of sustainability?
- Emerging from a consideration of all of the above, what strategies aimed at increasing research use and impact have the best suggestive evidence in support of them, and how might such strategies be tested as a means of consolidating the evidence base on supporting research use?
- How can new knowledge of the research-action process be encouraged to impact the future actions of researchers, funders, intermediaries, policy/decision makers, and practitioners/end users within the setting of interest?

Source: Abstracted from Davies and Nutley (2008)

policy making. Less attention has been paid specifically to the influence of context at the meso- or organisational policy level. Of course, the kinds of issues that will shape research use among policy makers and system managers at local levels will often be similar to those among national level policy makers. Issues of interests, ideologies, information and institutions (Weiss, 1999) still apply, albeit these will operate around local issues and with local stakeholder groups. One of the central issues at the meso-level of making policy, however, is the potential for tension between national policies and legislation, and local needs, priorities and agendas. Research uptake is likely to be shaped by the interplay between these local and national concerns. And tensions between national and local policy concerns may feed through to tensions within universities with regards to the focus of research mobilisation activities, perhaps leading to conflict or competition among individuals or organisational units.

The highly politicised environment in which policy making takes place means that political context is particularly pertinent in shaping policy uses of research. However, many of the barriers to using research that practitioners report are related to the local and organisational contexts in which they work. For example, practitioners often describe contexts characterised by heavy workloads and competing pressures, and research-use takes a low priority in these kinds of circumstances or else is seen more as a burden than a benefit (for example Sheldon and Chilvers, 2000; Wilson et al, 2003). Moreover, limited budgets may restrict projects to apply research, and parent and pupil expectations or preferences may also be prioritised over the findings from research. We need to understand more about how such contextual factors help or hinder research use.

Finally, while on the subject of context, one of the questions raised at the 2011 meeting of the International Alliance of Leading Educational Institutions (IALEI), where the country accounts presented in this book were first discussed, was 'Is knowledge mobilisation a westernised concept?'. While the term 'knowledge mobilisation' certainly does not have global recognition, the issues with which it is concerned certainly seem to be of importance to the nine countries represented in this book. That is not to say that they are tackling these issues in similar ways or that it would be appropriate to do so, but it does suggest that there is a basis for cross-country learning, especially when a consideration of context features strongly in this learning process.

Conclusion

There are multiple routes and pathways by which research knowledge impacts on education policy and practice. Knowledge mobilisation strategies and practices need to be based on an understanding of these pathways, and they should not only seek to strengthen known pathways but also experiment with forging of new routes. As knowledge mobilisation tends to be a non-linear process – whereby evidence, expertise, information and opinions are exchanged – mobilisation practices need to provide opportunities for multi-way knowledge flows, dialogue and debate. They should also encompass more facilitative practices that enable system change and programme redesign. Ultimately, the aim should be to enable the effective integration of research knowledge with other ways of knowing, to the betterment of education service delivery and educational outcomes. We are beginning to understand more about these processes, and the chapters in this book contribute to that knowledge. This is a base on which we now need to build in order to refine both the theory and the practice of knowledge mobilisation.

Note
[1] The main international studies of student performance are PIRLS – Progress in International Reading Literacy Study, TIMSS – Trends in International Mathematics and Science Study, and PISA – Programme for International Student Assessment.

References

Best, A. and Holmes, B. (2010) 'Systems thinking, knowledge and action: towards better models and methods', *Evidence and Policy*, vol 6, no 2, pp 145-59.

Brechin, A. and Siddell, M. (2000) 'Ways of knowing', in R. Gomm and C. Davies, (eds) *Using evidence in health care,* Buckingham: Open University Press.

Cooper A. (2012) *Knowledge mobilization intermediaries in education across Canada,* unpublished PhD thesis, Ontario Institute for Studies in Education, University of Toronto.

Davies, H.T. O. and Nutley S.M. (2008) *Learning more about how research-based knowledge gets used: guidance in the development of new empirical research*, New York, NY: William T. Grant Foundation.

Dolowitz, D. and Marsh, D. (2000) 'Learning from abroad: the role of policy transfer in contemporary policy making', *Governance*, vol 13, no 1, pp 5-24.

Fazekas, M. and Burns, T. (2011) 'Exploring the complex interaction between governance and knowledge', unpublished draft paper, Paris: OECD, Centre for Educational Research and Innovation

Nutley, S.M., Walter, I. and Davies, H. (2007) *Using evidence: how research can inform public services*, Bristol: The Policy Press.

Nutley, S., Walter, I., and Davies, H.T. (2009) 'Promoting evidence-based practice models and mechanisms from cross-sector review', *Research on Social Work Practice*, vol 19, no 5, pp 552-9.

Nutley, S., Morton, S., Jung, T. and Boaz, A. (2010) 'Evidence and policy in six European countries: diverse approaches and common challenges', *Evidence and Policy*, vol 6, no 2, pp 131-44.

Osborne, S.P. (2010) 'Editorial essay – Delivering public services: time for a new theory?', *Public Management Review*, vol 12, no 1, pp 1-10.

Pawson. R., Boaz, A., Grayson, L., Long, A. and Barnes, C. (2003) *Types and quality of knowledge in social care*, London: Social Care Institute for Excellence.

Rein, L. (1976) *Social science and public policy*, Harmondsworth: Penguin Education.

Rose, R. (2004) *Learning from comparative public policy: a practical guide*, London: Routledge.

Sá, C., Li, S. and Faubert, B. (2010) 'Faculties of education and institutional strategies for knowledge mobilization: an exploratory study', unpublished discussion paper, University of Toronto.

Sheldon, B. and Chilvers, R. (2000) *Evidence-based social care: a study of prospects and problems,* Lyme Regis: Russell House.

Stoker, G. and John, P. (2009) 'Design experiments: engaging policy makers in the search for evidence about what works', *Political Studies*, vol 57, pp 356-73

Walshe, K. and Davies, H.T.O. (2010) 'Research, influence and impact: deconstructing the norms of health services research commissioning', *Policy and Society*, vol 29, pp 103-11.

Walter, I., Nutley, S.M. and Davies, H.T.O. (2005) 'What works to promote evidence-based practice? A cross-sector review', *Evidence and Policy,* vol 1, no 3, pp 335-64.

Ward, V., House, A. and Hamer, S. (2009) 'Developing a framework for transferring knowledge into action: a thematic analysis of the literature', *Journal of Health Services Research and Policy*, vol 14, pp 156-64.

Weiss, C.H. (1999) 'The interface between evaluation and public policy', *Evaluation,* vol 5, no 4, pp 468-86.

Wilson, R., Hemsley-Brown, J., Easton, C. and Sharp, C. (2003) *Using research for school improvement: the LEA's role*, Local Government Association Research Report 42, Slough: National Foundation for Educational Research (NFER).

Index

Note: 'KM' = 'knowledge mobilisation'.